GABRIEL MARCEL'S PERSPECTIVES ON THE BROKEN WORLD

GABRIEL MARCEL'S PERSPECTIVES ON THE BROKEN WORLD

THE BROKEN WORLD,
A FOUR-ACT PLAY

followed by

CONCRETE APPROACHES TO INVESTIGATING THE ONTOLOGICAL MYSTERY

Translated by Katharine Rose Hanley

Introduction by Ralph McInerny

MARQUETTE
UNIVERSITY
PRESS

Marquette Studies in Philosophy No. 18
Andrew Tallon, Series Editor

All translations (the play, the essay, the commentaries,
and the appendices) are by Katharine Rose Hanley.

Library of Congress Cataloging-in-Publication Data

Marcel, Gabriel, 1889-1973.
   [Monde cassé. English.]
   Gabriel Marcel's perspectives on the broken world / translated
by Katharine Rose Hanley ; introduction by Ralph McInerny.
   p. cm. — (Marquette studies in philosophy ; no. 18)
   Includes bibliographical references (p.) and index.
   ISBN 0-87462-617-X
   1. Existentialism. 2. Ontology. I. Marcel, Gabriel, 1889-1973.
Positions et approches du mystère ontologique. English. II. Hanley,
Katharine Rose. III. Title. IV. Series: Marquette studies in philosophy ; #18.
   B2430.M253 M613 1998
   111—ddc21

                                                    98-8998

© 1998 Katharine Rose Hanley
Second printing, 1999

MARQUETTE UNIVERSITY PRESS
MILWAUKEE

The Association of Jesuit University Presses

Contents

Acknowledgements

I wish to thank Monsieur and Madame Jean-Marie and Anne Marcel for their kind permission to publish English translations of Gabriel Marcel's play *Le Monde Cassé* and his essay "Approches concrète du mystère ontologique." I also wish to express my deep gratitude for their generous and cherished friendship and the constant encouragement it provides.

I wish to express my gratitude to Madame Michèle Sacquin, Director of the Gabriel Marcel Archives at the National Library in Paris, for her kind care in assuring me access to these richly significant documents.

I am also especially grateful to Madame Jeanne Parain-Vial, friend and disciple of Gabriel Marcel, and most helpful patron to me and many who would study his work, for her loyal friendship and her enlightening clarifications of some textual references in "Approches concrètes du mystère ontologique."

Special thanks are due to Madame Henri Gouhier, who graciously allowed the printing of my translation of the essay of her late husband, Henri Gouhier, member of the French Academy and of the Academy of Political and Moral Sciences, and to Monsieur l'Abbé Marcel Belay, who generously allowed me to print my translation of his essay, thus providing opportunity for readers to reflect in dialogue with two outstanding drama critics' commentaries on *The Broken World*.

My gratitude extends to Roland Reed, Professor of Drama at Catholic University of America, for his careful reading of this and other Marcel plays, and his generous suggestions of adaptations of format and phrasing more comfortable for those familiar with the style of American theater.

I thank the officers of the Gabriel Marcel Society, Professors Thomas Anderson, Patrick Bourgeois, Thomas Flynn, Bernard Gendreau, Robert Lechner, James Marsh, Thomas Michaud, Denis P. Moran, S.J., and others for including dramatic readings of Gabriel Marcel plays by various university players in the cities where our annual meetings were held.

I gratefully acknowledge the support of the many professional colleagues and friends who have applauded this work of publishing Gabriel Marcel's theater in English, and highlighting its importance for a correct appreciation of his philosophy, especially Professors Kenneth T. Gallagher, Gerard Kreyche, Francis J. Lescoe, Ralph McInerny, Paul Ricoeur, and Gerard Verbeke.

I also wish to acknowledge the help of generations of students who by the enthusiasm of their response and the depth and clarity of their insights have proved, in its most important way, that Marcel's theater offers a privileged and easy access for entering into a wisdom he illuminates.

I thank Mr. Stephen Healy for his artful illustrations, which highlight the dramatic significance of some of the play's most poignant moments; Mr. Alan Clark for his excellent editorial skills; and Mrs. Andrea Adams-McKnight for her personal energy, professional resourcefulness, and wordprocessing skills, all of which have contributed significantly to the quality of this book.

I gratefully acknowledge several Faculty Research and Development Grants from Le Moyne College that were significantly helpful over the years.

I am most grateful to Professor Ralph McInerny, Grace Professor of Philosophy at the University of Notre Dame, for his personal and professional inspiration, his wonderful wit and wisdom, and his kind gift of the introduction for this volume.

Introduction

The French are different from you and me. They are also different from one another. You might imagine a line on which Jacques Maritain occupies a point to the right, Paul Claudel one to the left, and in the middle, smiling like a somewhat enigmatic Cheshire cat, sits Gabriel Marcel. Marcel refers to both men in "Concrete Approaches to Investigating the Ontological Mystery." Claudel his senior—Marcel's father would have been a contemporary of Claudel's in the French diplomatic corps—was both dramatist and poet, and his Catholicism influenced his imaginative work in a fairly overt way. Early on, in *Le partage du midi,* Claudel dealt with dramatic problems like those that occupy *The Broken World.* He also reflected on his art, but his reflections are themselves a species of poetry.

Maritain for a time exercised a literary influence in Paris that aspired to rival that of André Gide. He never quite brought this off and there are those who feel that his influence on writers, when he intruded into the creative process—as with Bernanos in his first novel—was anything but happy. Marcel finally resisted the lure of the Maritain salon at Meudon which drew Cocteau, Sachs, Julian Green, and many other artists. Maritain was not himself an artist (the doodles in his diaries do not count). Furthermore, the book that most influenced artists at a distance was *Art and Scholasticism,* an extremely didactic and, well, scholastic book. But it can be argued that it is Maritain's best work in aesthetics, better even than his Mellon lectures, *Creative Intuition in Art and Poetry.*

Compared with Claudel and Maritain, Gabriel Marcel strikes us as what the other two never succeeded in being. He is at once creative artist and genuine philosopher. One experiences an initial incredulity in going from the play to the essay in the work before us. It is as if Evelyn Waugh made an appearance in *Mind* or *The New Scholasticism.* Of course one can imagine an artist mimicking a philosophical style, but not writing a complete study that is as different from a play as one can imagine. Katharine Rose Hanley suggests that we read the philosophical essay as if it were a piece of music, and what she says apropos of Marcel is always to be heeded. Still, I would never have thought of that without her suggestion. Untutored by my betters, I would have said that, while Marcel was right to see his mode of philosophizing as out of what considered itself to be the mainstream of the time, his affinities with phenomenology and existentialism make it clear that his philosophical credentials are in good order. Marcel both represents for us, and treats thematically, the question as to whether there is an artistic and philosophical approach to the same issue.

Maritain's view of poetic knowledge—the mode of union of poet and reality—as connatural, a knowledge through inclination, an experiential knowledge that differs from conceptual knowledge, is, after all, a theory. While not for a moment imagining that what he has to say as a philosopher could replace the poet, Maritain must assume that he is attaining the same thing in a different way. But how could he know that? It is not a sufficient answer to say that his wife Raissa was a poet and mystic.

Claudel did not try and fail to be a philosopher, but his reflections on art simply do not give us the kind of conceptual clarity we find in Marcel. For a change we feel we are in good hands—here is a poet who philosophizes and a philosopher who is an artist. And not at the same time. Santayana's *Three Philosophical Poets*, while fruitful to read as one ponders the achievement of Marcel, does not really have room for Marcel. Lucretius, Dante, and Goethe will not be in the same circle of the Paradiso as Marcel and Kierkegaard (and Sartre too, if the story of his deathbed conversion is true).

Marcel's achievement, as Katharine Rose Hanley indicates, creates its own problem for us, however. We are the third point at which Marcel's drama and his philosophy converge. Nothing he says about his artistic work is a substitute for it; the plays do not reveal insights in the way the philosophical works do. The putting together of the two is something we must do. Furthermore, it is not something anyone else can do for us, not even Gabriel Marcel. In that lies his almost unique position in twentieth-century French philosophy.

The common target of the play and the essay is mystery—*not* mystery in the full religious sense, but the sense of mystery that Marcel distinguished from the problem. We may be tempted to say that philosophy deals with problems and art with mysteries, but this is not at all what Gabriel Marcel holds. It is the sense of mystery and its unique revelatory role that he seeks to restore to philosophy. If he had done nothing else, his success in this matter would constitute a major contribution to philosophy.

Gabriel Marcel was a Catholic, and this mattered in both his artistic and his philosophical work—more important, it mattered in his life. Marcel alludes to the essay Maritain delivered at Louvain on Christian Philosophy. During the year *The Broken World* was published—1933— there was a meeting at Juvisy of the *Société Thomiste*, its second *Journée des études*, the topic Christian Philosophy. Marcel was not there in person, but he is referred to again and again by the participants. He will continue to haunt anyone who devotes time to that perennial topic whose interest can never be exhausted.

You and I might be reminded a bit of Graham Greene's theatrical work when we read *The Broken World* in the excellent translation put before us here. Of course any influence would have gone in the other direction. Greene signals the role that Péguy and Mauriac played in his artistic development as a Catholic writer. I do not remember similar allusions to Marcel. Perhaps there are some. I hope so. We will also think of T.S. Eliot's theatrical works. Eliot and Greene provide the kind of surprise Marcel provides in the final act of the play before us.

I have said the translation is excellent. It is. It reads easily and with almost no sense that the very idiomatic English is replacing a very idiomatic French. No one but Katharine Rose Hanley could have provided such a translation. I turn you over now to it and to her with the assurance that you are in for a very powerful aesthetic and then philosophical experience.

Ralph McInerny
University of Notre Dame

Translator's Preface

Gabriel Marcel and *The Broken World*

Gabriel Marcel (1889-1973) was a distinguished existential thinker of international renown. He authored some 30 plays and an equal number of philosophic writings. He won numerous literary prizes and even some peace prizes and was elected to the Institute of France—the highest honor his country can bestow upon an intellectual. In the 1950s and 1960s, he lectured throughout Europe and North and South America and along the Pacific Rim.

Marcel is probably best known to English-speaking audiences for his philosophic writings, since most of these have been translated into English, whereas only ten of his plays are thus far available in English. In Marcel's 1961 William James Lectures at Harvard University, he expressed the hope that American audiences would someday be familiar with his theater.[1]

It is a joy to see *The Broken World* available again to readers of English, for it is one of Marcel's finest and most important plays and marks a capital moment in the evolution of his thought. He chose to include it in the 1973 Plon edition of *Cinq Pièces Majeures* (Five Major Plays). It is a powerful, touching, and deeply moving piece, full of intrigue and surprising turns, including a stunning ending that takes readers into the realm of mystery.

Written in the winter of 1932-33, the play represents an amusing picture of the Paris of the time and displays Marcel's gift for social satire. It also, however, gives expression to an awareness of our human condition that is perhaps more poignantly relevant to today's reader than it was 60 years ago, as Louis Chaigne and Joseph Chenu have observed.[2]

Presentation of the Play

The heroine of *The Broken World* is Christiane Chesnay, a brilliant, gifted, and very attractive woman who is married to Lawrence, a high government official but an individual who is so lacking in personality that people often fail to even notice him. Christiane, by contrast, is the center of a constant whirl of activity—travel, social engagements, artistic projects. Her many friends vie for her attention, and most of them would like her to be in love with them, but she keeps her distance in that respect, and does not really give herself to anyone.

The play portrays what critics confirm was the Parisian atmosphere of the 1930s, when a society of the elite had lost the sense of life yet tried frantically to enjoy life and live it with abandon. The recent war years had left an atmosphere of disorientation wherein people merely created a life-style according to their individual taste and preference. There was no question of morality, only a question of the individual's free choice. The scene allowed people to discover and lose themselves in café bars, touring cars, and the pleasures and intoxicating rhythms of jazz from Harlem and tangos from Argentina. The circles in which Christiane moved took pride in the free-spiritedness they expressed by ridiculing anything conventional or traditional.

Christiane busies herself by writing a novel in the form of letters. Her naive young friend, Gilbert, writes the woman's letters and Christiane writes the man's. She is also working on a ballet with Henry, a somewhat older and worldly man. She arranges for Antonov, a Russian composer, and his companion, Natalia, to use an upstairs apartment while he completes his compositions for concerts he's been preparing. She's been invited to play the lead in a film to be produced by Démétriopoulous, a friend of Gilbert's mother. Other friends and acquaintances from Biarritz appear very liberated. Denise Furstlin, a childhood friend of Christiane's, flaunts her lover, Bertrand, for her husband, Max, to see. The latter can't say much by way of objection, given his preference for young boys. Denise is willing to support her lover's drug habit and also his cure if necessary. Then there's Dolores de Solveredo, a lesbian who wants Christiane's company and attention.

Christiane, in conversation with Denise, confides her feelings about this life that attracts, but does not satisfy, her. She describes the uneasiness she feels at living in what she calls a "broken world."

> Christiane: (solemnly) Don't you have the impression that we are living…if we can call that living…in a broken world? Yes, broken like a watch that has stopped. Its mainspring no longer works. To all appearances nothing has changed. Everything is in place. But if you put the watch to your ear…you hear nothing. Remember, the world, or what we call the world, the human world…used to have a heart. But it seems that heart has stopped beating. Lawrence codifies regulations, Daddy has season tickets at the Symphony and keeps a mistress on the cheap, Henry is preparing a trip around the world…
>
> Denise: Oh! I didn't know.
>
> Christiane: Antonov conducts rehearsals of his symphonic poem. Everyone has their own little niche, their own little thing, their own petty interests. People meet, or more accurately, bump into each other. That makes quite a racket.

Denise: How else could it be?

Christiane: (Following her thought) But there's no center, no life, any-where.

Denise: And where are you in all this?

Christiane: Me...let's say, I listen.

Denise: In a vacuum?

Christiane: You said it, in a vacuum.

Denise: And the rest of the time?

Christiane: I suppose...I exist. I am what you might call a "busy woman."

Denise: (Bitterly) I can't stand such talk. Actually all that means...

Christiane: Don't start again, Denise.

Denise: If you would at least recognize...

Christiane: Sorry, but I won't give you that satisfaction. (Act I, pp. 46-47)

This image of the "broken world" refers not only to a world that appears fractured and fragmented, one that no longer has coherent unity. It refers also to Christiane's growing sense of dissatisfaction with her own being, her increasing uneasiness with the emptiness of her personal life—shallow relations, hollow gestures, artificial posturing above a void.

How is it that Christiane, whose life to all appearances goes from one success to another, has this sense of living in a broken world? We have only to look at her marriage to Lawrence Chesnay.

Marcel affirmed that at the origin of this play, as with most of his dramas, was his observation of a concrete situation, more exactly a specific interpersonal relationship that sparked his dramatic imagination. He noticed a friend's sister, a charming, gifted, and very attractive woman who was married to a gentleman so colorless in personality that outside the office people most often didn't even notice him or acknowledge his presence. This situation took hold of his imagination, and he wondered, "Why would a young woman so intelligent, sensitive, and attractive marry a man so lackluster and boring?" Then he wondered whether the husband would not take offense at seeing his wife receive so much adulation when all the while he was simply ignored. And would he not be wounded more in his pride than in his love?[3]

These two questions: Why did these two ill-matched people agree to marry? and Would Lawrence not suffer from wounded pride, being over-shadowed as he was by his wife's brilliant personality and social success? focus the play's conflict and suggest the direction in which dramatic in-trigue will develop.

There are other subplots and conflicts: Denise and Max Furstlin and their shifting to Bertrand and Mademoiselle de Brucourt as their new respective partners, the adventures of Henry and of Dolores, and the changing fortunes of young Gilbert. There are also the wonderfully amus-ing interludes with Antonov and Natalia—the Russian composer and his companion—and the somewhat rough comic relief of Augsburger, Christiane's widowed father. But the main focus of the drama remains on the question "What will become of Christiane and Lawrence's relation-ship?"

Eventually we learn the circumstances in which Christiane agreed to marry Lawrence. As a young girl, she had fallen wonderfully, ecstatically in love with a childhood friend, Jacques Decroy. Just as she was about to tell him of her love for him, he announced that he was leaving to join a monastery. That moment traumatized Christiane's life. It was as if that deception destroyed her ability to love. In the rejection she suffered, her soul went out of her. She no longer had any life to her; she no longer knew who she really was.

She told no one of this painful secret, but repressed and tried to deny its reality. Outwardly she denies any possibility of such a love. However, from her hidden, still tender wound, she over-reacts when there is any mention of the music of Solesmes, the Benedictine monastery Jacques Decroy had entered.

On one level, Christiane's soul had died, and she married Lawrence as a kind of spiritual suicide. On another level, having experienced so much suffering around her, she thought, "Why add to it? Why not give Lawrence the pleasure of accepting his marriage proposal?" Later, she realized that this decision was a mistake.

While she never did tell Lawrence or anyone else of her tragic romance, she did tell Lawrence when she agreed to marry him that she did not love him. Again, on another level, she did hope that "love" might come with time as it had for others. But such was not to be the case.

Christiane even hoped that some action of determination by Lawrence would quicken her affection or bring some meaning and purpose to her love, but this did not occur. For Lawrence, realizing that Christiane had married him without love, was too much the gentleman to ask anything or make any demands of her. He merely left her "free" to be herself and to do as she chose.

On both Christiane's and Lawrence's parts, there is a certain "bad faith." There is, at least to some degree, self-deception and deception of others. Some of this is certainly both unconscious and unintentional, but it clouds their relationship nonetheless.

Christiane longed for a true friend and genuine communication, yet her relationships were shallow and were not transparent and her activities, even her conversations, were mere diversions to distract her from the pain and loneliness within.

In her marriage, she merely went through the motions. She was a dutiful wife and mother and, as a basically loyal person, she was faithful to her husband. But she longed for something more.

One day, while talking with Henry about everyone else's problems, Christiane realizes that while technically she had been faithful to Lawrence, she had in effect treated him badly. She also realizes that Lawrence's pride is wounded and his self-esteem threatened by the fact that she receives such adulation and attention while he receives none.

So she devises a scheme to bring Lawrence out of himself and to win his affection. He knows that to love is to give, but he cannot give unless he is made to feel superior by this giving. So Christiane plans to tell him that she has become infatuated with someone who has rebuffed her. She pretends to be humiliated and helpless and begs Lawrence's help lest she be tempted to disgrace herself further.

Christiane's devious plan to win Lawrence's attentions and to bring life to their relationship succeeds. But she is repulsed by his prideful pity, a poor substitute for the compassion and love she desires. She despises his meanness of spirit, and she is disgusted with the deception she used to manipulate him.

Her scheme backfires. One cannot build a life on lies. (This was also clear to Abel and Jacques at the climax of *The Iconoclast*.)[4] Christiane is dismayed. She tries everything she can think of to help solve her problem with Lawrence, but her efforts are to no avail. Her broken world is crumbling.

Meanwhile, the dramas in the lives of the other characters also evolve. Augsburger, Christiane's father, finds himself alone and lonely after his mistress, Lucy, whom he supported cheaply, leaves him. He settles into self-pity and his own lamentations. Antonov, the Russian composer who leaves his natural-law wife, Natalia, to marry the rich widow Morgenthaler is deceived when he finds that she will not give him his own checkbook and access to her money. The acquaintances Dolores, a lesbian, and Max, who is gay, drift off to their own ways.

Other dramas touch Christiane and Lawrence's more closely, particularly Denise Furstlin's. The two women's lives seem interconnected, although in some respects they are very different. It is with Denise that Christiane voices her sense of living in a broken world. Denise, more enmeshed than Christiane in the ways of that world, does not like hearing Christiane speak of it. Later on, Denise challenges Christiane's right to speak so, she who never experienced its full impact. Christiane has avowed that, although she seemed to be like the others, at times she detests their life and hates herself for those moments when she participates in and enjoys their pleasures. She protests that there is another part of herself, not like them, a part of herself she hardly knows but which is not one of them.

Denise blames Christiane's talk for influencing Bertrand, Denise's lover, to break off with her so as to marry the wealthy young Mademoiselle de Brucourt. Denise sees the cold, cruel logic of the "broken world" of which Christiane speaks; its consequences are either suicide or conversion. Bertrand too has seen that logic and decided to end his life of decadence and save himself by a marriage to a woman who was willing to accept him. Denise has sensed the painful truth. With no hopes, no exit from her ruined life, she quietly goes off and commits suicide. Henry asks, "Did she kill herself because she thought no one cared? Or did she do it because she hoped someone would care?" "Probably for both reasons," is Christiane's response. (Act IV, pp. 129-30)

Christiane is bitterly disappointed in Lawrence's response to her pretended plight. Knowing her humiliation seems to have energized his life. He is so pleased with himself that he even lets it slip to Gilbert what Christiane's problem really is. Deeply saddened, Christiane practically despairs of ever having real love in her life. Then, as she is conversing with Gilbert, Lawrence brings in a formal obituary notice for a Dom Maurice. Lawrence doesn't recognize the name. Christiane murmurs, a friend from her youth, perhaps someone she knew before he took vows. Then, alone with Gil and hearing abruptly of the death of the one real friend she'd had, Christiane suddenly feels totally abandoned. She falls into his embrace, crying in desperation, "Gilbert dearest, don't abandon me." (Act III, p. 127) She gives herself to Gil, "not out of love, but out of longing for love." (Act IV, p. 151)

The Broken World is well structured and artfully composed in many respects. It is certainly a drama full of intrigue. And as the play moves into its final act, we note that there is a sense of mystery—both in the popular and in the spiritual sense.

By now, the prospects for Christiane and Lawrence's marriage seem almost nil. Christiane's deception to win her husband's attention succeeds as a scheme but fails utterly as an attempt to move them from a shallow, superficial relationship toward any deeper or more genuine bond. As a matter of fact, seeing Christiane's romantic involvement with young Gilbert, Lawrence is prepared to give her her freedom. The center of suspense is Christiane. What will become of her? What path will she choose?

As the fourth act begins, Henry has just returned from his trip around the world. Having only recently learned of Denise's suicide and of Christiane's affair with Gilbert, he wants to discuss it all with Christiane.

As Christiane talks of Denise's suicide, she seems to entertain the idea herself. "They say one doesn't suffer." (Act IV, p. 130) But she is held back by fear of what happens afterwards. She also seems on the verge of going off with her new-found paramour, Gilbert. But will she leave Lawrence and their son, Claude? She is torn. But perhaps once she's with Gilbert completely, passionately all his, she'll be happy. But would a life with Gilbert and all the banality that this would eventually bring, just like the life with Lawrence and all its boredom, be enough to hold Christiane back from the temptation of suicide?

As the fourth act progresses, Christiane's prospects appear very bleak. Yet in the final scenes, her life takes an unexpected turn, and the play's ending occurs as a stunning surprise.

Surprise Ending

Marcel wrote that his plays often have a surprise ending, one that is unexpected and that leaves audiences with questions requiring that they reflect on the play and reconstruct it retrospectively in the light of the final scenes.

As a drama critic, a profession he exercised for 40 years, Marcel affirmed that it is the last act of a play, in particular its final scenes, that gives the entire work its unity, meaning, and power. *The Broken World*'s ending is powerful indeed, and even though it is in a sense prepared from the beginning, it occurs totally unexpectedly. It is an ending of the form Ibsen used—as in *Rosmersholm* (one of Marcel's favorite Ibsen plays), where the action deals with a past situation that suddenly encroaches upon the present.[5]

This translator's preface is not going to give away the ending. Readers deserve the opportunity to enjoy the entire play and to see for themselves what the surprise is. In this manner, the integrity of the medium is also respected. Drama invites audiences to enter into the life-world of the characters whose situation is being portrayed on stage; so spectators should be allowed to experience the development of the drama to its culminating moment. This dramatic experience is richer and far more meaningful than a flat, one-dimensional statement of a narrative's end.

However, to assure that those who wish to reflect on the drama or to discuss the significance of the play in its entirety, surprise ending and all, have that opportunity, two essays of commentary are included at the end of this book. One of these, dating from 1934, is by Henri Gouhier, an outstanding drama critic, member of the French Academy and of the

Academy of Political and Moral Sciences; the other, published in 1980, is by Marcel Belay, a critic whose work Marcel respected to the point of including Belay's commentaries on *L'Iconoclaste* (The Iconoclast) and *L'Horizon* (The Horizon) in a 1973 reedition of these two plays. These commentaries should prove interesting to many readers and scholars, because they appeared originally in publications that are not easily obtainable. They are published here for the first time in English translations.[6]

Gabriel Marcel as Dramaturge

A few words about Gabriel Marcel as dramaturge are in order. Marcel's love for theater dated from his early childhood, when he enjoyed reading plays with his father and creating imaginary characters to people the otherwise inner loneliness of an only child.[7]

As we have noted, Marcel stated that the concrete situations explored by his plays were often suggested to him by people he observed or met, as in the case of Major Percy, whose strange story was at the origin of the play *The Iconoclast*.[8] Marcel's plays show an extraordinary sense of the workings of the human psyche, and he allows that his dramas are drawn from his own being. The characters all have their source in the dramaturge, coming from either the light or the dark side of himself.

Marcel went even further and pointed out that his play writing enabled him to bring to the light of the theater his deepest searching and also his constant struggling with some of the fundamental conflicts and antinomies that were part of his life situation. In this way, he was able to forge a path for his own freedom.

Marcel's mother died suddenly when Gabriel was four years old. Questions of what becomes of loved ones after death and the possibility of communication from beyond death are part of a searching inquiry present in many of Marcel's early plays. Preoccupation with the prison of isolation and the sufferings of loneliness fueled Marcel's longing for genuine communication and communion through interpersonal relations. The quest for this dimension of life and love animated Marcel's own life and the searching inquiry present in many of his plays. For example, there is Rose's plaintive cry in *The Rebellious Heart*, "There is but one suffering, and that is to be alone."[9]

Suffering from the desert universe that surrounded him in a household where agnosticism reigned, and wherein music was the only spiritual presence that witnessed the sacredness of human dignity, Marcel, from his earliest works, searched longingly and lucidly to discover how one could accede to transcendence or access the spiritual dimension of human life without which our existences would be severely diminished. Witness his preface to *Le Seuil Invisible* (The Invisible Threshold, p. 8).[10] All of this longing impels his ongoing quest, which he first explored dramatically, his search for a life that would have meaning and value. Aspects of this quest are evidenced in *The Broken World.*

Another part of Marcel's lived experience from his early years was a keen awareness of conflicts arising from fundamentally opposite attitudes on basic life questions and most other issues. Acceptance of fundamental conflict among people of divergent views was brought home to Marcel early and in a particularly striking way by his extended family's division over the Dreyfus Affair. Recognition of the opposition stemming from different attitudes toward the case may well have influenced Marcel's portrayals of family situations in *The Just One* and *The Unfathomable.*

Marcel's awareness of conflict, but, more important, of what he calls "fundamental antinomies," or the opposition of divergent stances that spring from deep-set attitudes and basic presuppositions underlying tension or argument, influences not only his choice of subjects for particular plays but also accounts for the way Marcel explores any dramatic issue.

Theater enabled Marcel to sort out the different attitudes and ideas people formed about some of the fundamental issues that engaged their passions, minds, and lives. In this manner he was better able to perceive clearly what animated and informed various stances, and thus more lucidly and freely to adopt his own.[11]

Three Concentric Rings of Experience and Communication

Much of Marcel's theater arises out of the center and depth of his own world. He explained that his experience and communication had, as it were, three concentric rings or levels.[12] The first, the deepest and innermost, was music. In and through music certain deep and inward themes find expression on a level of consciousness that is beyond "eris" or argumentation. Marcel was a gifted musician, having improvised piano compositions, and during the years 1945-47 composed music for almost 50 of his favorite poems, thus "bringing them to full expression as song."

For Marcel the second level of experience and communication—both with oneself and with others—is theater. Theater gives incarnate and dialogical expression to the deepest longings and the concrete tensions that surround our lives. Dramatic characters—very real people—enflesh and speak their dawning awareness, their tragic consciousness, of the conflicts and antinomies that affect their lives. The concrete interaction of persons engaged in the same life situation enables the sensitive and intelligent characters among them to sense the roots of the tragic in people's stances and attitudes and in this respect be able to transcend it. Through the magic of the theater, actors and actresses are able to incarnate their dawning consciousness of the roots of the conflict and the possibility or impossibility of transcending it. In this manner spectators too can participate in this growing awareness and be moved to a place of understanding that blends intelligence and love.

In his essay "Théâtre et Mystère" (Theater and Mystery), Gaston Fessard wrote, à propos of Marcel's theater, that the actor or actress can enflesh, i.e., make incarnately present, the dawning awareness of tragic consciousness in the life of a sensitive, intelligent character, for example Rose in *The Rebellious Heart* or Christiane in *The Broken World.* This presentation of a dawning consciousness enables members of the audience to enter into the mystery that has become part of that character's life.[13]

Confirming this idea, Marcel wrote in *Le Secret est dans les Iles* (The Secret is in the Isles), in a preface to three of his later plays, that each play is like an island. To enter into the play one must jump with both feet into its life-world. Entering completely into the life-world of what the characters of the play are living facilitates spectators' actually experiencing and even participating in the mystery their lives reveal.

Because of the importance of experiencing the mysterious dimension of the life that the *dramatis personae* present for the audience's participation, Marcel wrote in his preface to K. T. Gallagher's book *The Philosophy of Gabriel Marcel* that in the future, people who wish to engage his philosophic thought must access it by way of his theater, and that those who have an affinity for music will have a privileged disposition.[14]

The third and outermost of Marcel's concentric rings or levels is philosophy. The deep inward experience and then the playing out of the longings and tensions dialogically through concrete people's interactions in their shared life situation are propedeutic to Marcel's philosophic reflections. His philosophic reflection investigates questions, views alternative interpretations, and seeks to clarify in general terms some key insights into life's crucial issues. Philosophic reflection presupposes depth in a person's experience and a sensitive, lucid awareness of alternative attitudes and interpretations on any capital issue, which music and drama can provide.

Marcel's approach to philosophy was always through concrete, lived experience. It was a ground rule for discussion among the groups who gathered at his home that any issue raised had to be considered concretely in terms of the experience of someone living that situation.

As for Marcel's philosophic method, Paul Ricoeur observed that if phenomenology had not existed Gabriel Marcel would have had to invent it. For, as Marcel De Corte put it, Marcel is one of the great and original thinkers who influenced the twentieth century.[15]

For Marcel, lived experience remains central to the philosophic enterprise. It is through recollection of the givenness of experience that critical reflection accesses the data it patiently and probatively clarifies. Reflection aims through critical clarification to bring to light the essential characteristics of a phenomenon. Reflection also aims to identify the subjective attitude requisite for the occurrence of a particular phenomenon.[16]

For example, Marcel identifies an I-Thou encounter, which can properly belong to the realm of intersubjectivity and not to the realm of control and manipulation of objects, as constituted by a dialogue of freedoms. This dialogue moves through one subject's appeal to the other person, the second subject's response (yes, no, maybe later, never, perhaps) and, if the response is affirmative, then those two persons are present with and for one another in a reciprocal and gratuitous self-gift. Furthermore, reflection critically clarifies the requisite subjective attitudes for phenomena's occurence. The conditions of possibility for the occurence of an I-Thou encounter that can create a relation or even a *co-esse* of intersubjectivity are revealed to include the following. There need to be two persons who enjoy an assurance of what they love and what they want to live for, i.e., individuals who have sufficient self-possession so as to be capable of self-disposition. For an I-Thou encounter to develop into a long and lasting interpersonal relationship, one that allows for commitment and that can also eventually provide for creative fidelity, there must be two individuals whose personalities are characterized by disponibility, i.e., that openness and availability whereby persons are able to live with and for the other or are simply capable of self-gift in love. Such persons are maturely capable of saying, "With all my heart what I want is to love you, to be with and for you, and together to create a fullness of life for us." Such subjective dispositions, summarized in the word "disponibility," constitute the requisite conditions of possibility for an encounter that can leave a deep and lasting trace upon one's life, an I-Thou encounter and intersubjectivity of being that can be lived out as creative fidelity.[17]

Dual Vocation as Philosopher-Dramatist

Marcel felt that he was in a unique and somewhat paradoxical position in that he exercised two distinct and autonomous vocations. During an interview for the Alliance Française, he mused about the paradox of his dual vocation, that of philosopher-dramatist. He pursued each discipline according to its own proper method and intrinsic purpose. Yet, given the integrity of the man and the highly personal character of his work, it was inevitable that there should be a complementarity between his theater and his philosophy.

Marcel knew that it was important that this complementarity be understood correctly, and so he commented on it in many of his writings.[18]

First, he always stressed that his theater played a prospective role in relation to his philosophy. The theater works were chronologically first, in that the plays that explored a given theme were composed often 5 to 15 years prior to the essays that take up a philosophic investigation of that theme.[19] Then too, as Marcel affirmed, dramatic imagination was the first way a situation of conflict and challenge came to mind for him. So this first moment of dramatic imagination always preceded a subsequent moment of philosophic reflection. In fact, Marcel judged that his theater was for him an indispensable prelude enabling him to recognize certain questions that preoccupied him and then also to discover perspectives of light that would enable him to explore these issues further.

Theater often anticipated Marcel's philosophic thought not only in the chronology of composition and originating awareness of questions and insights, but also in that theater, with its concrete existential approach, allowed him to explore deeply personal questions about life's meaning and value. Only when dramatic inquiry had brought these questions to the light of the theater could Marcel begin to formulate the questions and insights in philosophic language. It was also only as a result of his existential dramatic inquiries that Marcel was able to forge a fresh methodology, one adequate for processing the data and the kinds of inquiry that nineteenth-century British and German Idealism were inadequate to conceive or analyze philosophically.[20]

Marcel also emphasized the concretizing role of his theater. His plays not only stage concrete situations presenting time, place, and events in their particular details; they also present a concrete approach in the more important respect that they make present on stage the living relations among real people, who communicate their growing consciousness of the hopes, longings, and/or tragic situations that constitute their lives. This dramatic communication of individuals' dawning awareness of the spiritual and transcendent dimension of their lives is what gives Marcel's theater its "existential" character. "Existential" refers to a person's lived experience wherein questions arise about life's meaning and value, which questions are reflectively investigated in order to bring to light an authentically human way of living one's response to the appeal raised by these issues.

The concrete approach of Marcel's theater, focusing as it does on interpersonal relations, allows the author and the audience—through participation in the interaction and communication of the characters in the play—to encounter the realities revealing themselves in the dramatic interaction, realities that can subsequently come under investigation through both personal reflection and existential philosophic analysis. We believe that it was to stress this remarkable truth, that it is in and through the concrete individual that we encounter the infinite, that Gabriel Marcel placed a quote from E. M. Forster at the head of the chapter "Creative Fidelity" in the book of the same title. "It is private life that holds out the mirror to infinity; personal intercourse, and that alone, that ever hints at a personality beyond our daily vision."[21] It is the theatrical focus on interpersonal relations that allows author and audience alike to encounter the spiritual dimension present in human lives.

If one reads Marcel's plays after having studied his philosophy one will find that the plays do concretize and thus serve to illustrate some of his philosophic themes. But in no way is Marcel's theater composed as an illustration or argument of philosophic ideas or theses; nor is it a forum for puppets to propagandize ideologies. These are violations of the purpose of art and would compromise the integrity of the discipline. Marcel once observed that he could not dictate to his characters nor force any of them to act in one way or another; he had to wait for them to reveal how they chose to respond to new situations and challenges.

Theater always plays a prospective role in the development of his thought. The work of the dramatist comes first, that of the philosopher follows after it. The task of the dramatist is like that of the adventurer or prospector who first explores a given region. The work of the philosopher may then be likened to that of the cartographer who comes later and maps out that territory.

In Marcel's early works the prospective character of his theater was evident from the successive moments of inquiry in the chronology of composition of, first, plays and then philosophic essays addressing topics raised by the drama of the plays. There was also a clear difference of depth and level of exploration. Theater anticipated what was to become accessible to Marcel's thought in the philosophic register only much later. But with *The Broken World* the situation changes. A significant event in Marcel's own life enabled him to experience a spiritual dimension of his being that was not previously familiar to him. Earlier theatrical explorations had opened up paths of inquiry. His critical struggles with British and German Idealism's inability to deal with spiritual and interpersonal realities had brought him to a point where he developed his own fresh existential approach. And a breakthrough in his own personal experience of the depth and the fullness life can include prepared the capital explosion that *The Broken World* and the Meditation on the Ontological Mystery released onto the intellectual and cultural scene of the twentieth century.[22]

The Broken World and
"Concrete Approaches to Investigating the Ontological Mystery"

The Broken World was indeed a capital work in Gabriel Marcel's career. It gave dramatic expression to a fresh discovery of a spiritual dimension of life. It also showed how spiritual realities can be accessed or communicated between people. With this play, Marcel developed a fresh philosophic approach, one capable of dealing with interpersonal realities like despair and hope, love and fidelity or infidelity, and trust or betrayal. From that point on, Marcel saw his theater and philosophy interrelated "like two slopes of the same height," or "like the landscape on either side of one road traveled."

Marcel noted that with *The Broken World* and his Meditation on the Ontological Mystery the situation was no longer one of philosophy not being able to follow and chart the journey an explorer had made through previously uncharted territory. In his own foreword to the original 1933 edition, Marcel explained that by publishing two works of very different genres together in the same volume he wanted to demonstrate with startling emphasis that both of these arts of inquiry were capable of exploring and charting a whole new territory now open to those who would want to see that landscape for themselves and experience its vistas on their own.[23]

Marcel admitted that it was a great effort to stretch his creative faculties, on the one hand, to explore through dramatic imagination Christiane's plumbing the very depths of her being, and, on the other hand, to sustain a reflective clarification through rigorously reasoned analysis that forged a path that leads not just to logical conclusions from abstract or theoretical argumentation but rather to an existential assurance rooted, we might even say anchored and reflectively clarified, in the light of reasoned exploration of what was given within one's own and others' lived experiences.

The fresh originality of Marcel's methodology, and the significant richness of the immense realms that his new approach had opened up for philosophic investigation was proclaimed enthusiastically by Marcel De Corte in his preface to a second edition of "Position et approches concrètes du mystère ontologique."[24]

We cannot insist strongly enough on the pleasurable advantages of reading Marcel's dramatic and philosophic works in concert. They should be read in the order in which they were composed, the order in which Marcel intended them to be experienced. It's best to get into *The Broken World* first, and to follow this experience with a reading of "Concrete Approaches to Investigating the Ontological Mystery." For this essay lets us bring our own personal and philosophical reflections into dialogue with those of Marcel himself as he reflectively clarifies some of the issues brought to our awareness by the power of his theater.

Marcel always stressed the importance of his theater in relation to his philosophy. For theater plays a prospective and concretizing role, assuring an existential access to mysteries brought to light through dramatic inquiry, mysteries that can then be further clarified through subsequent personal reflection and philosophic investigation. Theater always provided Marcel with fresh inspiration in terms of the questions and insights it raises. And toward the end of his life he wrote that after his death some people, depending on their predilection, would prefer either his theater or his philosophy. Yet as he aged he was increasingly aware that he preferred his theater, for he hoped that audiences would continue to hear in it the sound of fraternity, the assurance of compassion that says, "You are understood."[25] Marcel also warned that study of his philosophy apart from his theater can account for failure to appreciate the balance that exists in his attitude and his world view. He gave as an example a doctoral dissertation that completely misunderstood and therefore misrepresented Marcel's understanding of hope because the writer failed to recognize that genuine hope arises in its purity and intensity in those situations wherein despair is a real temptation.[26]

It is entirely appropriate and especially gratifying that this English translation of *The Broken World* should appear in a single volume with the essay "Concrete Approaches to Investigating the Ontological Mystery." The original French publication included both works, and Marcel felt that such publication would show how dramatic inquiry and philosophic reflection complement one another appropriately. However, all editions since the 1933 original have published either only the play or only the philosophic essay. So we are especially grateful that for this edition it is again possible to present these interrelated works together in one book, for together they form the keystone of Marcel's life, work, and thought.

Since that 1933 edition, *Le Monde cassé piece en quatre actes suivi de "Position et approches concrètes du mystère ontologique,"* published by Desclée de Brouwer et Cie., Paris, there have been three subsequent publications of the essay "Position et approches concrètes du mystère ontologique." In 1949, B. Nauwelaerts, Louvain and Vrin, Paris, published the essay with an important 43-page introduction by Marcel De Corte. In 1977, the essay was reprinted as an appendix to Pierre Boutang's publication of his interviews in *Gabriel Marcel interrogé par Pierre Boutang*, (Archives du XXe siècle), published by Jean-Michel Place, Editeur, Paris. And as recently as 1995, Marcel Belay edited *"Existence et Objectivité" et "Positions et approches concrètes du mystère ontologique,"* Editions Paraître, Lyon.

There were two reeditions of *Le Monde Cassé*. An edition with the third act revised by Marcel in view of a stage production was published in *Paris Theatre*, No. 56, Janvier 1952. And in 1973 that revised edition reappeared in *Cinq Pièces Majeures* published by Plon, Paris.

In 1974 *The Broken World* appeared in an English version by Sr. J. Marita Paul Colla, R.S.M., published by McAuley Press, West Hartford, CT in a volume edited by Francis J. Lescoe entitled *The Existentialist Drama of Gabriel Marcel*. This English version included a third act that was part of the earlier version published in 1933, but which Marcel chose to revise in 1950 for subsequent publications and in hopes of a Paris stage production that did not occur. St. Joseph's College produced this English version of the 1933 text with Marcel's permission for adaptation to theater-in-the-round. We have chosen to translate for publication in English the version the author revised in 1950 and reissued in 1973 both because it was Gabriel Marcel's preferred version and also because it offers greater strength and unity to the development of the play.

The essay "On the Ontological Mystery," as translated into English by Manya Harari appeared in *The Philosophy of Existentialism*, first published in 1949 by Harvill Press, London, and The Philosophical Library, Freeport, NY. Fortunately this fine translation is still in print.

We have chosen to offer a fresh translation, not only to facilitate the presentation of both the dramatic and philosophic works in the same volume—as Marcel did originally and as was his wont—but also to provide philosophers and other readers interested in Marcel's thought with a carefully phrased translation that renders as faithfully and accurately as possible the progressive articulation of various ideas and themes that are highly significant for an exact understanding of his thought.

Notes to the Translator's Preface

1. *The Existential Background of Human Dignity*, Cambridge, MA: Harvard University Press, 1963. Cf. lists of Marcel's theater and philosophy given in the appendices to this book, pp. 222–25.

2. Louis Chaigne, *Vie et Oeuvres d'Ecrivains*, Paris: Fernand Lanore, 1954, pp. 181-259, esp. p. 224; Joseph Chenu, *Le Théâtre de Gabriel Marcel et sa signification métaphysique*, Paris: Aubier, (Editions Montaigne,) 1948, Ch. VI, "Le Monde Cassé et le Mystère Ontologique," pp. 127-68, esp. 128.

3. "Pour le Radio Belge, *Le Monde Cassé*," p. 2, Paris: Bibliothèque Nationale, Gabriel Marcel Archives Fonds 8708, Carton 89; "The Drama of the Soul in Exile," in *Gabriel Marcel: Three Plays*, London: Secker and Warburg, 1952; New York: Hill and Wang, 1958, 1965.

4. *The Existential Background of Human Dignity*, pp. 48, 50-53, 138.

5. "My Dramatic Works as Viewed by the Philosopher," in *Searchings*, New York: Newman Press, 1967, pp. 103-104. Conference given at the University of Freiburg in Bresgau, Germany, 1959, published in *Auf der Suche nach Wahrheit und Gerichtigkeit*, Freiburg im Bresgau, Germany: Verlag Knecht, 1964.

6. *Percées vers un Ailleurs* (Breakthrough Toward a Beyond), including a Preface (Preface); *L'Iconoclaste* (The Iconoclast), pp. 3-55; Commentaire de Marcel Belay (Commentary by Marcel Belay), pp. 169-97, *L'Horizon* (The Horizon), pp. 201-365; Postface de Gabriel Marcel (Postface by Gabriel Marcel), pp. 336-78; Commentaire de Marcel Belay (Commentary by Marcel Belay), pp. 379-404; "De L'Audace en Metaphysique" (Daring in Metaphysics), by Gabriel Marcel, pp. 405-21. Paris: Fayard, 1973. Cf. Henri Gouhier, "Le monde cassé de M. Gabriel Marcel," pp. 154–58 and Marcel Belay, excerpt from *La Mort dans le théâtre de Gabriel Marcel*, pp. 159–64 in this book.

7. "My Dramatic Works as Viewed by the Philosopher," pp. 96-97.

8. *The Existential Background of Human Dignity*, p. 48.

9. *The Rebellious Heart*, Act III, Scene 3, in *The Existentialist Drama of Gabriel Marcel*, West Hartford, CT: McAuley Press, 1974, p. 205.

10. *Le Seuil Invisible* (The Invisible Threshold), Preface, p. viii; "My Dramatic Works as Viewed by the Philosopher," p. 117; "An Essay in Autobiography," in *The Philosophy of Existentialism*, Secaucus, NJ: Citadel Press, 1956, pp. 109-15.

11. "My Dramatic Works as Viewed by the Philosopher," p. 99.

12. *Gabriel Marcel: Le Paradoxe du Philosophe-Dramaturge*, Réalisation Sonore: Hughes De Salle, Collection Française de Notre Temps Nous Confie. Sous le patronage de l'Alliance Française, présentation écrite sur la pochette de Marc Blancpain, no date.

13. Gaston Fessard, "Théâtre et mystère," Introduction to *La Soif* by Gabriel Marcel, Paris: Desclée de Brouwer, 1938.

14. Kenneth T. Gallagher, *The Philosophy of Gabriel Marcel*, Foreword by Gabriel Marcel, New York: Fordham University Press, 1962 and 1975, p. viii.

15. Paul Ricoeur, "Gabriel Marcel et la phénoménologie," pp. 53-74, discussion pp. 75-94, in *Entretiens autour de Gabriel Marcel*, Neuchâtel: à la Baconnière, 1976; Marcel De Corte, "Avant-Propos," *Position et approches concrètes du mystère ontologique*, Paris: Vrin, and Louvain: Nauwelaerts, 1949, pp. 5-6.

16. "Concrete Approaches to Investigating the Ontological Mystery," in this volume, pp. 172–96.

17. "Concrete Approaches to Investigating the Ontological Mystery" in this volume, pp. 172-96; *Creative Fidelity*, New York: Farrar, Straus & Company, Inc., 1964, reprinted by The Crossroads Publishing Co., 575 Lexington Ave., New York. Ch. II, Belonging and Disponibility (spiritual availability), pp. 38-57; Ch. VIII, Creative Fidelity, pp. 147-75. Translated from the original French *Du Refus à l'Invocation*, Paris: Gallimard, 1940.

18. *Gabriel Marcel: Le Paradoxe du Philosophe-Dramaturge; The Existential Background of Human Dignity*; "Avant Propos," *Le Monde Cassé suivi de Position et approches concrètes du mystère ontologique*, Paris: Desclée de Brouwer, 1933, pp. 7-9; *Paix sur la Terre*, deux discours et une tragédie, Paris: Aubier, 1968, p. 8; *En Chemin vers Quel Eveil*, Paris: Gallimard, 1971, p. 155.

19. Katharine Rose Hanley, *Dramatic Approaches to Creative Fidelity: A Study in the Theater and Philosophy of Gabriel Marcel (1889-1973)*, Lanham, MD: University Press of America, Ch. II-IX, pp. 50-162. Cf. Appendix V, pp. 226–27.

20. "Introduction by Gabriel Marcel," *The Existentialist Drama of Gabriel Marcel*, West Hartford, CT: McAuley Press, 1974, p. 12.

21. E.M. Forster, *Howard's End*, London: Edward Arnold & Co., 1910, p. 78, cited in *Creative Fidelity*, Ch. VIII, "Creative Fidelity," p. 147.

22. The title of the 1933 edition of Gabriel Marcel's book is *The Broken World a Four-Act Play followed by Concrete Approaches to Investigating the Ontological Mystery* (*Le Monde cassé pièce en quatre actes suivi de Position et approches concrètes du mystère ontologique*). Yet in the author's Foreword (Avant-Propos) he refers to the essay as the Meditation on the Ontological Mystery (la Meditation sur

le Mystère Ontologique). This translator's preface follows the same practice of designating the essay as the Meditation on the Ontological Mystery, the abbreviated form used by Gabriel Marcel, except when the reference specifically designates the precise and full title of the essay, i.e., "Concrete Approaches to Investigating the Ontological Mystery" ("Position et approches concrètes du mystère ontologique").

23. "Avant-Propos," *Le Monde Cassé suivi de Position et approches concrètes du mystère ontologique,* pp. 7-9; "Concrete Approaches to Investigating the Ontological Mystery," in this volume, pp. 172-96; "An Essay in Autobiography," in *The Philosophy of Existentialism,* pp. 115-17, 128.

24. Marcel De Corte, Préface, *Position et approches concrètes du mystère ontologique,* pp. 5-6.

25. "My Dramatic Works as Viewed by the Philosopher," pp. 115-16; Introduction to *The Existentialist Drama of Gabriel Marcel,* pp. 17-18.

26. "My Dramatic Works as Viewed by the Philosopher," p. 108-109.

Katharine Rose Hanley
Le Moyne College

The Broken World
A Four-Act Play

by

Gabriel Marcel

Translated by Katharine Rose Hanley

Cast of Characters

Christiane Chesnay .... 33 years old. Wife of Lawrence Chesnay.

Lawrence Chesnay .... 36-38 years old. Husband of Christiane.

Denise Furstlin .... 35 years old. Childhood friend of Christiane.

Augsburger .... 60 years old. Christiane's father, retired banker.

Henry Braunfels.............. 35 years old. Childhood friend of Christiane.

Julie .... The maid.

Gilbert Desclaux .... 28 years old. Young admirer of Christiane.

Antonov.. 40 years old. Russian musician.

Natalia .... Antonov's wife, no age.

Genevieve Forgue .... 38 years old.
  Childhood friend of Christiane's; sister of Jacques Decroy,
who became a Benedictine monk.

Tha action takes place in Paris in 1932.

ACT ONE

A small living room. Very modern furniture. A grand piano at the right
end of the room. It is 2:00 p.m.

(Lawrence smokes a cigarette in his chair. Christiane talks on the phone.)

Christiane: Don't forget, Mademoiselle, if you have any prob-
                   lem, Claude is not…you have to know how to deal
                   with him…just drop us a note…And if he is
                   homesick…of course I know life at the chalet is ev-
                   erything these children could dream of. But all the
                   same…And please make sure he writes to us regu-
                   larly.

Lawrence: His last letters were a mess.

Christiane: What? I beg your pardon; my husband was talking
                   to me.

Lawrence: Disgraceful!

Christiane: My husband reminded me that Claude's latest let-
                   ters were very poorly written. And the spelling was
                   atrocious! You don't want to read the children's mail.
                   Well, as long as he is happy and healthy…Good-
                   bye, Mademoiselle. What? He could come to the
                   phone?

Lawrence: More overtime.

Christiane: (Glances at Lawrence.) It's not necessary. Thank you.
                   He has a cold? Well, give him a big hug for us, will
                   you?

(She hangs up. A silence.)

Lawrence: So what was the problem?

Christiane: A slight cold and upset stomach.

Lawrence: I'm sure they feed them too much.

Christiane:	The mountain air always gives you a good appetite. I considered that when I took him there.
Lawrence:	What about his school work?
Christiane:	He's been sick.
Lawrence:	I am not talking about this past week. The question is, will he be promoted to the sixth grade in the fall? They still treat him like a sickly child.

(The telephone rings. Christiane answers.)

Christiane:	Hello, Henry? Yes, I got back this morning. A fine trip, thank you. Yes, on the whole quite pleasant. No, not many people. Well, the small hotel where I stayed was full. I recommend it. On the beach. A little expensive but it has a private bath. No, it wasn't cheap, but I was very comfortable. Who? Mademoiselle de Brucourt? Yes, she was there. She's very nice....No, not a good dancer. Yes, two or three times, with Gilbert, with Bertrand....No, not with Amadeo. The Hungarian? He's Rumanian...As if that were my style! You are silly. (In a different tone.) Yes indeed, he was kind of sick, the poor dear...No, nothing serious. Very well, thank you. He is with me...That's right, stop by for a while. I'm sort of tired so I'll stay home all day. Bye. (She hangs up. A silence. She looks at her husband.) You don't look well. A lot of work these days?
Lawrence:	That same tedious case to finish.
Christiane:	(Politely.) Oh! Do you think you get enough exercise?

(Lawrence laughs sarcastically.)

Christiane:	What's wrong with that?
Lawrence:	Nothing.
Christiane:	Did Pauline feed you well while I was away?

Lawrence:	Well, it only took ten minutes to eat her meals.
Christiane:	Oh!…Are you worried about something…?
Lawrence:	Not a bit!
Christiane:	Something at the office?
Lawrence:	We expect to learn of the President's death, any day now.

(The phone rings.)

Christiane:	Would you answer that please?
Lawrence:	(Taking the phone.) Hello, who is calling please? Monsieur who? Are you sure you dialed the right number? (To Christiane.) Here, take this. It's for you. A foreign name I can't understand at all.
Christiane:	(Taking the phone.) Hello, Monsieur, how have you been? No, not yet. I just got back this morning. Please understand, I must talk with my husband about it first. He might know of a problem that I hadn't thought of. Yes, yes of course, I'll write you immediately…Just a minute, let me get a pencil and paper. (She writes.) Hotel Bristol…Yes, I know it. What? Of course I'd be delighted to see you, but I promise, you'll get a note from me tomorrow, or the next day at the latest. What did you say? (Hesitation.) No, he's not here now, he just went out…Yes, I'm fine, but just be patient for another twenty-four to forty-eight hours. Please. That's right. And is the first performance of "Thunder" at Pleyel Hall still scheduled for the twenty-seventh? I'm delighted. Of course our conductors…You yourself should conduct…I hope so…That's right. See you soon. (She hangs up.)
Lawrence:	Who was that?
Christiane:	Antonov; I wrote you about him.

Lawrence:	Yes, he was at the same hotel with you, and Amadeo, and the Romanian singer, not to mention Gilbert, Bertrand, Lucien, and all the other gigolos. And what does this one want?
Christiane:	I had this idea. Maybe it's a good one, maybe not. You'll have to tell me. Antonov and his wife are at a hotel. They're not comfortable and it must be quite expensive. Of course a grand piano can't fit in their tiny room. I thought we might offer them the small apartment upstairs since no one's living there at the moment.
Lawrence:	Would they pay rent?
Christiane:	Don't know. It'll have to be gratis for a while. But their financial situation may change.
Lawrence:	Then how come they were at Biarritz?
Christiane:	They were guests of the Goldbergs.
Lawrence:	But I thought this man was famous?
Christiane:	Fame doesn't pay well.
Lawrence:	Is he a Bolshevist?
Christiane:	I don't think he's interested in politics.
Lawrence:	That may be…But didn't he give some concerts in Moscow last summer?
Christiane:	What does that prove?
Lawrence:	Naive question…Sadistic music is what those people like.
Christiane:	What do you mean sadistic? I think it's healthy, vigorous music.
Lawrence:	If noise means strength.
Christiane:	His music announces something.

Lawrence: Doubtless, the destruction of everything we've held
                    dear.

Christiane: We, who is this "we"?

Lawrence: Myself and somebody I used to think was you.

Christiane: I don't think that was me.

Lawrence: Someone who hadn't yet fallen in love with Biarritz
                    and jazz.

Christiane: But don't you understand…

Lawrence: (Sharply.) No. But anyway…

(He gets up and walks around with a vacant stare.)

Christiane: You know that if Lévy Kauffmann hadn't insisted so
                    strongly I wouldn't have gone to Biarritz.

Lawrence: Of course. There are also health reasons.

Christiane: Why "also"?…

Lawrence: I know how Paris intoxicates you.

Christiane: Why "also," Lawrence?

Lawrence: Biarritz wasn't forced on you. You chose to go.

Christiane: For once I had the chance to go somewhere with
                    Denise. Besides, you didn't object then. So why com-
                    plain now?

Lawrence: I'm not complaining.

Christiane: You're not being fair.

Lawrence: You know very well what my feelings are…

Christiane: What feelings?

Lawrence: To begin with, how I feel about the woman you went with.

Christiane: She's the only childhood friend I have.

Lawrence: What an innocent view of someone who flaunts her lover, right under her husband's nose…

Christiane: Would you prefer she lie to him?

Lawrence: It's you I'm concerned about. If they hid their affair, people wouldn't know you were aware of it.

Christiane: Honestly!

Lawrence: It offends me that you pretend not to mind their behavior, when in fact it disgusts you.

Christiane: You're wrong. I don't judge Denise.

Lawrence: She's your childhood friend. I've heard that one before.

Christiane: Her husband has wronged her terribly. She now admits she made a mistake marrying him, but she won't divorce him because they have a child whom Max adores. What can she do?

Lawrence: How admirable. And, what would you do in her place?

Christiane: No one can ever know. That's precisely why we should never judge.

Lawrence: But, what about morality?

Christiane: It is just a question of lifestyle. Each of us has to invent our own. Some people understand this…then there are others…I don't think her lifestyle would be good for me.

Lawrence: That's reassuring.

Christiane:	Do you need reassurance? (Lawrence does not answer. In a different tone.) So then, what'll we tell Antonov?
Lawrence:	What!
Christiane:	What do you mean?
Lawrence:	I don't see the connection.
Christiane:	I'm not sure I could tell you myself.

(Enter Denise)

Denise:	Hello my dear…How are you? Hello Lawrence. (To Christiane.) I met your dad on the stairs.

(Enter Augsburger)

Augsburger:	(German Jewish accent.) I'm out of breath…Your elevator is out of order again. Happens all the time.
Christiane:	(To her father.) I was going to call you.
Augsburger:	I didn't have lunch at home. Nowadays I rarely do.
Lawrence:	You are going to ruin your stomach.
Augsburger:	How so? I don't go to restaurants. Tell me now, did you enjoy Biarritz? You are still much too skinny.
Denise:	Not at all, she's just fine, aren't you, Christiane?
Augsburger:	As for me, I wouldn't go there if you paid me. Too many memories.
Lawrence:	Painful?
Augsburger:	Too pleasant. The Palace Hotel around 1908, 1909. High society, the upper crust…you just can't imagine. It's nothing like that anymore.
Christiane:	Mother was very bored there while you played golf.

Augsburger: You're sadly mistaken. She was delighted. She loved the luxury.

Christiane: So she told me.

Augsburger: What she said, her last years, doesn't really count. And St. Moritz and Cannes…well, all that. (He gestures that's all over, let's not think about it anymore. To Denise, indicating Christiane.) And this one, did she break any hearts at Biarritz?

Denise: You better believe it. I counted at least…three…four…four and one half.

Augsburger: The half intrigues me.

Denise: A young Brazilian girl at the Casino… she was ravishing. (Christiane protests, laughingly.)

Lawrence: (Getting up brusquely.) Excuse me…I have to mail a letter.

Christiane: But we could…

Lawrence: No, no. I want to do it myself. Good-bye, Father. (He bows to Denise and leaves.)

Christiane: (To Denise, reproachfully.) You know how he is.

Denise: What do you mean? What's wrong?

Christiane: That allusion to Dolores's morals…(Sharply.) Besides, we're not even sure…

Augsburger: I too am a bit old fashioned about that sort of thing. Those women are peculiar specimens.

Denise: They are just as normal as you and I.

Christiane: I'm not so sure of that.

Denise: Besides, who's to say what's normal?

Augsburger:	Well, in my day, people kept such things under wraps. (To Christiane.) I'm sure your dear mother died without knowing such things ever existed. (To Denise.) Such a simple soul. I'm not talking about her last years…
Denise:	She suffered so much. Actually her illness came soon after Christiane's marriage, didn't it?
Augsburger:	I'll say! Up to the last minute she was afraid Christiane might marry someone of the same faith. Moreover, I didn't want it either. For the children mixed marriages are preferable. But for Mathilda it was an obsession. Her maiden name was Coblentz, but over the years she became anti-Semitic. (Laughing.) Perhaps that came from living with me…
Christiane:	Daddy…
Denise:	After all, she called you Christiane…
Augsburger:	Ach! Not so, I chose that name.
Christiane:	(Dryly.) What difference does it make?

(A silence.)

Denise:	While we were away, Max bought stacks of records, some really great ones, especially some blues that are out of this world.
Augsburger:	(Disapprovingly.) Oh! la la….
Denise:	A Mozart concerto performed by Menuhin. And then all the recordings made at Solesmes.

(Christiane cringes.)

Augsburger:	(Laughing.) Quite a salad, you must admit!
Denise:	You must come and listen to the music from Solesmes Abbey on our new electric phonograph.
Christiane:	(Sharply.) No.

Denise:	You always liked church music…
Christiane:	In church, not sandwiched between a blues and a tango.
Augsburger:	Records, you know…I think too much is made of them. If I can just go Saturdays to a rehearsal at the Conservatory and Sundays to a concert hall.
Christiane:	How is it that they allowed a recording session at Solesmes, a monastery?
Denise:	Maybe they thought it was good publicity.
Augsburger:	And after all, it pays. (He makes a common gesture with his right hand.) It's like Benedictine cordial.
Denise:	That has to be a real money-maker for those monks.
Christiane:	(In an ambiguous tone.) You believe that? Really?
Augsburger:	(To Christiane.) I wanted to ask your advice. (To Denise.) You might help too, dear friend. A lady friend of mine wants a consultation with Lévy Kauffmann. Are you still pleased with him?
Christiane:	He seems very thorough.
Augsburger:	And his fees…not exorbitant?
Christiane:	Fifty francs a visit. One hundred francs for a house call.
Augsburger:	That's not cheap. But if there is a follow-up treatment, I suppose there is a reduction.
Christiane:	I don't know.
Augsburger:	Couldn't you inquire?
Christiane:	That would be a little awkward.
Augsburger:	Well, we'll talk about it another time…And Claude, how is he? Have you heard from him? (Getting up.)

| | Don't move darling, you're tired; and you really are too thin. (To Denise.) Good-bye Madame. |

(He goes out.)

| Denise: | A lady friend of mine…Tell me, is she still the same one? |

| Christiane: | I believe so. It's three years now. |

| Denise: | They'll end up marrying, won't they? |

| Christiane: | I doubt it, they seem quite content with things as they are… |

| Denise: | The way you say that! |

| Christiane: | With Daddy, what can you expect…(She is on the verge of tears.) Oh! No, let's talk about something else. |

| Denise: | Your father is having a pleasant retirement despite his financial losses. |

| Christiane: | Certainly. |

| Denise: | He's not a bad man. |

| Christiane: | Of course not. |

| Denise: | Well then? |

| Christiane: | I don't know what came over me. |

| Denise: | It's just since I mentioned the music records from Solesmes. |

| Christiane: | (Nervous.) Don't be ridiculous! |

| Denise: | Anyway, I don't see…You know what? I think Max has a girlfriend. Yesterday he received a perfumed letter, and today a post card. He wanted me to ask to see them, but I was discretion itself. Actually, it's |

the best thing that could happen. Those houses he used to go to, I knew that they didn't satisfy him. He needs something regular. Besides, even in our relationship...I sometimes had to... But, now... (Sensing a protest, she adds.) Yes, I realize, it's all very disgraceful. But what can I do? Because as long as Bertrand tolerates...

Christiane: Yes.

Denise: Didn't you think he had changed?

Christiane: In what way?

Denise: Well, in his attitude toward me. You talked with him several times at Biarritz. Very...Oh! That's by no means a reproach.

Christiane: (Touchy.) I should hope not...

Denise: Well, you might have let something slip, who knows?

Christiane: Nothing, I swear.

Denise: Are you sure? For a moment it seemed to me that young Mademoiselle de Brucourt caught his eye.

Christiane: She seemed ready to throw herself at him.

Denise: Oh?

Christiane: She's very bold.

Denise: That's strange, because Bertrand can't stand that type.

Christiane: So what...

Denise: Well, I suppose there is nothing to worry about there. Besides, what can we do? We have to adjust. Every one of us. That's true for you too, only in another way.

Christiane: No, I'm different. First of all, I don't love anyone.

Denise: Are you sure of that?

Christiane: As certain as one can be of anything.

Denise: That's not saying much. The night before we left, when you came back so late from the Esplanade with that young Gilbert Desclaux, I swear I wondered…

Christiane: (Good naturedly.) That poor boy, he was really counting on it. He planned those flat tires. We had several blowouts that evening. What an adolescent trick!

Denise: Just the same…he is charming…isn't he?

Christiane: I don't deny that.

Denise: You're not being honest with yourself; you won't face the truth.

Christiane: Well, I think I am.

Denise: He's a young man I just couldn't resist. He's so light-hearted, so simple…

Christiane: No one is simple.

Denise: Everyone is simple. Complexity is a facade we put on to deceive ourselves and others.

Christiane: (Solemnly.) Don't you have the impression that we are living…if we can call that living…in a broken world? Yes, broken like a watch that has stopped. Its mainspring no longer works. To all appearances nothing has changed. Everything is in place. But if you put the watch to your ear…you hear nothing. Remember, the world, or what we call the world, the human world…used to have a heart. But it seems that heart has stopped beating. Lawrence codifies regulations, Daddy has season tickets at the Symphony and keeps a mistress on the cheap, Henry is preparing a trip around the world…

Denise:	Oh! I didn't know.
Christiane:	Antonov conducts rehearsals of his symphonic poem. Everyone has their own little niche, their own little thing, their own petty interests. People meet, or more accurately, bump into each other. That makes quite a racket.
Denise:	How else could it be?
Christiane:	(Following her thought.) But there's no center, no life, anywhere.
Denise:	And where are you in all this?
Christiane:	Me...let's say, I listen.
Denise:	In a vacuum?
Christiane:	You said it, in a vacuum.
Denise:	And the rest of the time?
Christiane:	I suppose...I exist. I am what you might call a "busy woman."
Denise:	(Bitterly.) I can't stand such talk. Actually all that means...
Christiane:	Don't start again, Denise.
Denise:	If you would at least recognize...
Christiane:	Sorry, but I won't give you that satisfaction.

(Henry enters carrying a bouquet of roses in his hand.)

Henry:	Hello, Christiane.
Christiane:	Hello...Those tea roses are beautiful; you are too kind.

(Henry shakes Denise's hand.)

Henry: So what's new?

Christiane: What story could I tell you?

Henry: Don Alonzo?

Christiane: His name is Pepe.

Henry: How awful. Is he still conspiring?

Denise: Against?…

Henry: Against the security of our friend Lawrence.

Christiane: To have a conspiracy there must be at least two.

Henry: So! It seems there were more than enough there.

Denise: Four and one half.

Henry: Counting the young Brazilian I suppose…

Christiane: That's enough! No inventory please. That's so te-
                    dious. Let's not discuss that holiday anymore. Now
                    that it's over I find the memories it leaves rather
                    unpleasant.

Henry: How ungrateful!

Christiane: When I recollect that party crowd from a distance…

Denise: She's polite, isn't she?

Christiane: I'm not proud of myself that I enjoyed being with
                    such an odd bunch…

Henry: Nevertheless, it was fun…

Christiane: Gilbert felt the same as I did. We plan to get to-
                    gether next autumn on a quiet little beach near
                    Cantabre. Somewhere secluded, yes, very secluded.

Henry: Can't you just see it now!

Denise:	The two of you by the water's edge.
Christiane:	With one or two nice friends.
Henry:	Aha!
Denise:	Whose name might be…Antonov?
Henry:	Why Antonov?
Christiane:	She just picked that name at random.
Henry:	Was he one of the…conspirators?
Denise:	Actually that big bear doesn't endanger her reputation. The word is that he only goes for older women who live in ritzy neighborhoods. He's a very practical person, this gentleman. Besides, he has heavy financial responsibilities. Four children in college at l'Institut Jean-Jacques Rousseau.
Henry:	What do you mean by that? Is it a euphemism for saying he's put his children on welfare?
Denise:	That's blasphemy, my dear…L'Institut Jean-Jacques Rousseau is the sanctuary of the new pedagogy.
Henry:	And Madame Natalia Antonov…will she be welcome at this secluded beach?
Christiane:	She's a good woman.
Henry:	Dirty as a comb, probably.
Denise:	(She stands up. To Christiane.) What do you say, let's go to the Fragonard exhibit together at Charpentier's. Call me. Tomorrow at Bertrand's around 3:00 p.m.
Christiane:	All right.
Denise:	Bye.

(She goes out.)

Henry: Come to think of it…it makes no sense at all. Max's indulgence, Bertrand's resignation, Denise's accommodation, don't you think it's a little too much? It makes me want to break something. Anything. All these people adjust too easily.

Christiane: Name someone who doesn't! All those people who are yelling for a revolution, do you think by any chance they'll make one?

Henry: But you, Christiane, you're the only one who interests me.

Christiane: I wonder why? By now you should have no illusions! No, don't make those eyes at me, you look cross-eyed.

Henry: What a fun homecoming for you this morning, Lawrence and his cup of coffee!

Christiane: (Calmly.) You're wrong, he drinks tea.

Henry: This house reeks of boredom, you can smell it all the way to the sidewalk.

Christiane: You think too much with your nose. It's unpleasant.

Henry: (Without listening.) Why? Why? Why? Don't you realize it's absurd, it's wrong. No one can make heads or tails of it. You were not born to please a civil servant who has no charm, who is narrow-minded, who, in a word, is a bore. You're always bored with him. Just one look at you when you are with him at a concert or at the theater and I see your artificial smile is a mask.

Christiane: What's the matter with you? What set off that explosion?

Henry: Your situation is so bad that if someone were to tell me you're Gilbert's mistress I'd actually feel relieved.

Christiane: Stop it, please.

(A silence.)

Julie:	(Knocking at the door.) Monsieur Gilbert Desclaux is here to see you, Madame.
Christiane:	(To Henry in a low voice.) You've just made his visit extremely distasteful to me. (To Julie.) Yes, show him in.
Henry:	(Melancholically.) Maybe, but your door is still open to him.

(Gilbert comes in quickly, a bouquet of carnations in his hand. He bows to kiss Christiane's hand. He is much more courteous than Henry and less familiar.)

Christiane:	How beautiful!
Gilbert:	I'm glad you like them.

(He shakes hands with Henry.)

Christiane:	How nice of you to come and visit the very day I come home. But tell me, don't either of you have anything else to do?
Gilbert:	First of all, it's Sunday. And then, I'm unemployed. My publisher had to cut back his staff...so I'm between jobs.
Christiane:	What a shame.
Gilbert:	Not really. Since I was able to speak to him about...
Christiane:	Who did you talk to?
Gilbert:	My publisher, of course, Monsieur Plantier.
Christiane:	What did you talk about? I don't understand.
Gilbert:	Well...about our child.
Henry:	Good heavens!

Christiane:	That's ridiculous.
Gilbert:	(To Henry.) Madame Chesnay and I are collaborating, sir.
Henry:	(With uneasiness.) Congratulations.
Gilbert:	A novel written in letters. But what's really racy about it is that I write the woman's letters and she writes the man's.
Henry:	Oh! I hate role reversals.
Gilbert:	Too bad for you.
Christiane:	I must tell you that on the train I tore up all the letters I'd written at Biarritz.
Gilbert:	That's murder! You still have your notes, don't you?
Christiane:	Ah! No! You don't know me.
Henry:	In whatever she does, Christiane's hallmark is improvisation.
Christiane:	(Suddenly serious.) Please don't make fun of me.
Gilbert:	You'll just have to write them again, that's all there is to it.
Christiane:	Don't count on it. When I reread them, I saw how stupid they were. And your letters…Don't worry…I wouldn't have thought of destroying them…but they're not brilliant either.
Gilbert:	Fine. So let's start all over again, and we'll switch roles. I'll be the man and you be the woman.
Christiane:	Thanks, but no thanks. I don't want you writing love letters to me, not even in fun.
Henry:	Don't you think a novel written in letters is kind of out of date? You're about a hundred and fifty years late.

Gilbert: People always say that about artists who are ahead of their times.

Henry: (To Christiane.) What about my ballet, what has happened to it?

Gilbert: What ballet?

Henry: You know I am leaving for my world tour at the end of May.

Christiane: I hope I can show you the summary before then.

Henry: That's a joke! The summary is all done. Pilar will be here the twenty-seventh...

Gilbert: Pilar!

Henry: And I promised her that everything will be finished before she arrives.

Christiane: Optimist! And what about the music?

Henry: The Brahms *Caprice* is orchestrated and woven into Schubert's *Impromptu.*

Christiane: What a mish-mash.

Henry: It will be wonderful.

(Lawrence enters. Nobody pays any attention to him.)

Gilbert: How secretive she is! I can't stand it!

Henry: She didn't tell me anything about your novel in letters.

Gilbert: That's different. Besides, she's given up that project. Not very sporting.

Christiane: Come on, Gilbert.

Gilbert: Just what is this ballet?

Henry:	That's our little secret.
Christiane:	We'll let you be surprised. (Lawrence coughs.) Hey? You're here? I didn't even see you come in.
Gilbert:	Who is this Pilar? The little Cupie doll who premiered last winter at the Casino de Paris?
Henry:	All I know is that she's remarkably inventive.
Gilbert:	Plaster of Paris poses leave me cold. (Christiane bursts out laughing.) What's the matter with you?
Christiane:	Plaster of Paris poses…where did you find that antediluvian phrase?
Gilbert:	Dance is pleasant sport…harmless and amusing, but no one will ever convince me that it's art.
Henry:	Humpf!
Christiane:	My poor Gilbert, you really hurt our feelings. (To Lawrence.) Did you just get home?
Henry:	(Noticing that Lawrence is there.) Oh! Hello there! How are you?
Gilbert:	(The same, a bit embarrassed.) Yes, hello, how are you? (To Christiane.) And for whom is this ballet intended?
Lawrence:	You're doing a ballet now?
Christiane:	Henry has some connections at the Casino de Paris, but I wonder…
Gilbert:	How awful!
Christiane:	You know they do some wonderful things!
Gilbert:	(With satisfaction.) No, I don't know that.
Henry:	He's a boor.

Christiane:	I'll have to educate him.
Gilbert:	I relieve you from that duty. Personally, I prefer the circus. (To Lawrence.) Don't you?

(Lawrence has taken *The Times* and pretends to read it.)

Lawrence:	Pardon me, what did you say?
Henry:	(To Christiane.) Did you know he was that pig-headed?
Christiane:	It's like you with Marcel Proust.
Gilbert:	(Content.) Aha! He doesn't like Proust?
Christiane:	He refuses to read him. He says that's the surest way not to waste time.
Gilbert:	(Disdainful.) I see. Very clever.
Henry:	(To Lawrence.) Do you like Proust?
Christiane:	(Vigorously.) Lawrence has read him three times from beginning to end.
Gilbert:	That's quite an accomplishment… (To Christiane.) Don't you think it's frightening?
Christiane:	What?
Gilbert:	That we communicate so little…(Pointing to Henry.) He can't stand Proust, and dancing bores me.
Christiane:	(Melancholy.) A broken world!
Gilbert:	(Pointing to Christiane.) What about her?
Henry:	She loves everything, she understands everything.
Gilbert:	She's exceptional.
Henry:	And she knows it.

Gilbert: I'm afraid she does.

Henry: It's our fault. We tell her so too often.

Gilbert: That's got to be bad for her. (To Lawrence.) I hope
                you agree.

Christiane: Don't worry...Lawrence doesn't give compliments.

Henry: That's excellent, a counterbalance.

Gilbert: Women who are too spoiled at home...take, for ex-
                ample, your friend Denise Furstlin.

Christiane: Has Max spoiled her so much?

Henry: It's true, he's always had those bad habits. I knew
                they'd lead him astray.

Christiane: You make me curious; what bad habits?

Henry: We had...No, I prefer not to talk about it.

Christiane: (Disappointed.) Oh!

Henry: Oh well, for a while we had the same mistress. You
                know as students...we were short of funds...and in
                affairs like that there is no professional confidenti-
                ality, so now and then I heard some very strange
                stories.

Lawrence: (Very dryly.) We relieve you from repeating them.

Henry: I wouldn't think of it, my dear friend. I only wanted
                to tell you that Max has always had some very strange
                preferences.

Christiane: I suspected as much. (Gesture of exasperation by
                Lawrence.) You see, Lawrence, just what I was tell-
                ing you a while ago. (To Henry.) But then, why do
                you complain about Denise?

Henry: What do you expect? I don't like publicity.

Lawrence:	Discretion doesn't seem to be one of your domi-nant traits.
Henry:	(Rebelling.) I beg your pardon...
Gilbert:	Come on, all this makes no sense.
Christiane:	Lawrence is right, you know, Henry, it's really not very nice.
Henry:	(Who has gotten up.) Do remember that Pilar ar-rives on the twenty-seventh, and at the end of May I am leaving for six months.
Christiane:	I know...I know.
Gilbert:	(Who has also gotten up.) Think about my suggestion...If you were to write the letters of Francine...And then, I think there should be a third correspondent. Besides, I have another idea. When can we get together?

(The telephone rings.)

Christiane:	(After she picks up the receiver.) Hello! Oh, it's you, Dolores! (Lawrence strikes a pose that says, now what?) Very well, thank you. A week from Wednes-day. Let me see, I really don't know. (To the three men.) You don't see my date book any place, do you?
Lawrence:	Let me remind you of the silver wedding anniver-sary dinner for Uncle Louis and Aunt Alice.
Christiane:	What? I'm sorry, my husband was speaking to me.
Lawrence:	The silver wedding...
Christiane:	He reminded me of a family obligation for that same evening... I wonder...Pardon, you're saying there will be?...Oh...We absolutely must...Yes, yes, we'll manage. You understand that for me this family dinner...my husband can go alone if necessary, it's

| | his side of the family anyway. You are very kind. Dolores…Certainly I will introduce him to you. You must come to the house. We'll set a date. Thank you. A week from next Wednesday. |

(She hangs up.)

Gilbert: Dolores has caught you again, that's too much!

Christiane: Wait a minute! She wants me to meet the Waricourts…You know their little theater on Avenue Henri-Martin. They produced *Fantasia* in a delightful version. Myself, I've always dreamt of acting in a comedy.

Henry: Now it's a comedy!

Gilbert: You're out of your mind.

Christiane: You know, Henry, I might even persuade the Waricourts to produce your little show.

Gilbert: (To Lawrence.) It's not my job to advise you, but if I were you I'd insist that Christiane cancel that engagement. That Dolores person is impossible, believe me, my dear fellow, impossible. To put it bluntly, she's a lesbian.

Henry: Perhaps she's only affecting that lifestyle.

Gilbert: That man, once he sees a chance for his show to be produced!

Julie: (After having knocked.) Madame, there's a lady who is asking to speak with you. She sounds like a foreigner, I can't understand her. Very strange…Is Madame looking for a new cleaning woman?

Christiane and Henry: (Together.) It's Natalia!

Christiane: Madame Antonov?

Julie: Yes, something like that…

Christiane:	Ask her to wait a few minutes; show her into the parlor, will you?
Julie:	Very well, Madame.

(She goes out.)

Gilbert:	(To Christiane, as he leaves.) Do me a big favor; don't go to Dolores's.
Henry:	You're probably wrong to go to Dolores's home, but if you have a chance to meet the Waricourts there…
Christiane:	Yes, yes, I understand. I'll see you later.

(They leave.)

(A silence.)

Christiane:	A bit tiring, isn't it?
Lawrence:	As usual. You will do exactly as you please about that invitation. You know Uncle Louis and Aunt Alice will be disappointed if you are not there, but if that doesn't matter to you…
Christiane:	I could be sick that day…besides, I haven't made up my mind yet. If it really bothers you that I go to Dolores'…just tell me and I'll send her a message….
Lawrence:	You know that I never ask anything.
Christiane:	That's your mistake, Lawrence.
Lawrence:	If I ever tried…
Christiane:	Is it discretion or some less honorable motive that keeps you from ever asking for anything?
Lawrence:	I don't get your point.
Christiane:	Let's say your pride, for example.
Lawrence:	I don't want you to give in to me.

Christiane: That's not a very noble sentiment.

Lawrence: You're perfectly free to go for dinner two or three
                  times a week at that lesbian's house if you like.

Christiane: Wait a minute, no one knows for sure that she's a
                  lesbian.

Lawrence: I won't lift a finger to stop you. I'll leave that to
                  your close friends.

Christiane: Nevertheless, if I were compromised…

Lawrence: You are old enough to judge the consequences of
                  your own actions…

Christiane: (With deep emotion.) Now you are hurting me.

Lawrence: Oh! I don't think so.

Christiane: Then I'm just putting on an act?

Lawrence: No. But you and your friends…your words…you've
                  given up the gold standard long ago.

Christiane: What's that, the gold standard?

Lawrence: No need to define it, we know it exists. Oh! Not in
                  your circle.

Christiane: What do you mean my circle?

Lawrence: Your group of friends.

Christiane: What about your circle then…

Lawrence: I have none.

Christiane: What do you mean? What about your colleagues?
                  (Lawrence laughs.) Why do you laugh?

Lawrence: No, I have no one. That's my strength.

Christiane:	I don't understand.
Lawrence:	Now, you should see whoever it is who's come to call on you.
Christiane:	Let her wait...I assure you, sometimes you treat me the wrong way. There is nothing worse than your leaving me entirely free. You'd do better to tell me frankly what you want. Don't you see? That would be the best way to help me.
Lawrence:	I didn't realize you needed help. You live as you like, don't you?
Christiane:	Are you so sure?
Lawrence:	If you don't like your life, then just change it.
Christiane:	Suppose I need your will to help me change it?
Lawrence:	Of course. So you could complain to your friends about my tyranny.
Christiane:	(Offended.) Is that my style?
Lawrence:	I don't know. I don't eavesdrop.
Christiane:	Do you imagine we talk about you?
Lawrence:	No, I never expected to provide you with an interesting topic of conversation.
Christiane:	You really are strange! Could it be...Oh! You don't trust me...You see, you recognize the fact.
Lawrence:	Your words don't make sense.
Christiane:	You don't let me reach you. You withdraw...you hide...
Lawrence:	From what?
Christiane:	From me...from my tenderness...

Lawrence:	(In a different tone.) Christiane, please, I beg you.
Christiane:	When I saw how you looked just now, when the others were here, I…almost despaired.
Lawrence:	You're dreaming. I was reading *The Times*…Now it seems to me that poor woman has cooled her heels long enough in the parlor. It's becoming rude.
Christiane:	You have no idea what sacrifices I'm ready to make for you…If you are troubled by any of my friends coming here…
Lawrence:	I can tell you one thing for sure, the day I learn that you have "made a sacrifice" for me, something irreparable will have come between us.
Christiane:	Well then? What's the solution?
Lawrence:	Where there's no problem, how can there be a solution?

(He rings.)

Julie:	(Entering.) Madame rang…
Lawrence:	Please show the lady in. I'll leave you.
Christiane:	(Timidly.) You haven't hugged me yet.

(He kisses her coolly, dutifully, and leaves.)

(Natalia enters.)

Christiane:	(Going toward Natalia.) Hello, dear Madame Antonov.
Natalia:	Hello, Madame Chesnay. I hope I am not disturbing you.
Christiane:	You must forgive me for keeping you waiting. I came back only this morning. You know what it's like: people to see, affairs to settle.

Natalia:	I understand, I really do. Vsevolod Ivanovich is afraid. He did not understand what you told him on the phone. He hates the telephone. He thinks it's better that I talk with you.
Christiane:	(Kind of dryly.) Is it still concerning the small apartment?
Natalia:	I have to say he is very nervous these days. As a rule he is always sick in hotels. He cannot sleep. He paces all the time. People complain. It can't go on.
Christiane:	But I promised I'd give him an answer as soon as possible.
Natalia:	(Embarrassed.) He got a telegram from Brussels. They've offered him a house there. But they want an answer right away.
Christiane:	It might be wiser to accept it.
Natalia:	(Disappointed.) Vsevolod Ivanovich does not like Brussels. He thinks Belgian people are thick. He doesn't understand them. He can't digest their food. Then there are the rehearsals at Pleyel Hall. The conductor is lost.
Christiane:	How is that?
Natalia:	So confused. It would be better if Vsevolod Ivanovich could guide him. But if we have to go to Brussels…
Christiane:	We'll see about that. But first, I'll order a cup of tea for you.
Natalia:	(Scared.) I cannot drink tea now. Vsevolod Ivanovich is waiting for me at the hotel. I have to get tea ready for him. He is so helpless.
Christiane:	But that doesn't mean you can't have a cup of tea with me.
Natalia:	I'm afraid he'll lose his patience.

Christiane: Phone him.

Natalia: (Getting herself in deeper.) But maybe he is not in the hotel.

Christiane: So then?

Natalia: Truly, life with a great artist is not always easy. It's better if I can give him an answer.

Christiane: You know my husband will have to make the decision. Would you like to talk with him?

Natalia: But surely if you ask him, he won't say no. Nobody can refuse you anything.

Christiane: But I don't even know if that small apartment would be suitable for you. You haven't seen it.

Natalia: Well, Vsevolod Ivanovich...He said that you had sent him. He thinks it is good enough. I am only charged with asking you if the neighbors are not too noisy.

Christiane: There is an old gentleman and his wife and they are very quiet.

Natalia: (Fearfully.) But maybe they have a radio.

Christiane: Yes, they do.

Natalia: (Passionately.) Well then, Vsevolod Ivanovich is afraid of radios. It's not so much the noise, but the waves enervate him. He can't work with it.

Christiane: But surely, we can't...

Natalia: The doorman said the old couple spends several months in the country...So it wouldn't be so bad.

Christiane: You see.

Natalia:	But he also said that the lady is sick, she might die.
Christiane:	She has been sick for ten years, I think.
Natalia:	But she must not die in the building because Vsevolod Ivanovich can't stand death. Once, in Berlin, somebody committed suicide in the room next to ours. Vsevolod Ivanovich could not work for a whole month.
Christiane:	All that is very complicated.
Julie:	(Coming in.) Madame, Monsieur Antonov would like to see you.
Christiane:	Show him in and then bring us tea.

(Antonov enters.)

Antonov:	Hello, Madame Chesnay. (He kisses Christiane's hand. To Natalia.) I don't understand what is wrong with you. (To Christiane.) Excuse me, Madame, but I have to make a decision. My friend Dortchenko just sent me a telegram from Geneva. (Julie brings in the tea.)
Christiane:	I thought it was Brussels. (Beginning to serve the tea.)
Antonov:	(Annoyed.) Geneva. As usual my wife confuses everything. She is not preciseness itself.
Natalia:	You said Brussels, I am sure of that.
Antonov:	Never.
Christiane:	Anyway, it's not important.
Antonov:	I have to decide. If you can't keep me in the small apartment, I will have to go. What did Monsieur Chesnay say?
Christiane:	My husband and I did not yet have a chance to talk

much about it. He is going to have a cup of tea with us.

Antonov: Madame Chesnay, please tell me…If Monsieur Chesnay does not want me in the apartment, then it is uncomfortable for me to be here.

Natalia: Is Monsieur Chesnay musical too?

Christiane: He knows little about contemporary music. His knowledge stops with Wagner.

Antonov: (Worried.) Maybe he plays Wagner?

Natalia: (In a whisper.) Vsevolod Ivanovich can't stand it.

Christiane: My husband does not play any instrument.

Antonov: (Pointing to the piano.) But maybe you play yourself…

Christiane: Very rarely, don't worry…besides you won't hear it upstairs.

Antonov: Then you agree.

Christiane: I repeat…

Antonov: You just said that I will not hear it. That means, I'll be up there.

Natalia: Later your house will have a plaque.

Christiane: A plaque means nothing to me.

Natalia: You should care because Vsevolod's biologers…

Antonov: Biographer, Natalia.

Natalia: They'll speak about you. Your photograph might even appear in several books. It's kind of nice. We must tell Volodia. He is a great critic. He is writing a book about Vsevolod Ivanovich with a lot of how do you call them?

Antonov:	Pictures.
Natalia:	(In a litany tone.) Vsevolod Ivanovich when he was two years old. Vsevolod Ivanovich's Niania…None of the above have ever existed, but there are lovely photographs. A handsome book, you'll see. To be published first in America.
Antonov:	Volodia says only stupid things.
Natalia:	But it is good publicity. (Meanwhile Julie has served tea.) Today advertising is very important.
Christiane:	Unfortunately.
Antonov:	Don't say unfortunately. Art and advertising are not two things but one.
Christiane:	I'll get my husband. (She goes out.)
Antonov:	I had said Geneva.
Natalia:	I understood Brussels.
Antonov:	Impossible. I hope you didn't say I had visited the apartment.
Natalia:	Of course, I told her.
Antonov:	Stupid you…
Christiane:	(Coming in with Lawrence.) I think you have already met Monsieur and Madame Antonov. (They greet one another.)
Antonov:	I was just saying that art and advertising are not two things but one. Art comes from advertising gone crazy. A compatriot has said that advertising has eaten its object.
Natalia:	(To Christiane in a hushed voice.) I think he's the compatriot. (She bursts out laughing.)

Antonov:	Don't say stupid things, Natalia, Boris Mikhailovich said it.
Natalia:	I don't know this Boris Mikhailovich, but he does not either.
Antonov:	Stop it! Tonight I'll show you his picture.
Natalia:	You can say whatever you want. We don't believe you.
Christiane:	(With feigned seriousness.) But yes…of course, Boris Mikhailovich, why not? I am prepared to like Boris Mikhailovich.
Antonov:	Why, Madame Chesnay?
Christiane:	I'm sure he does not refuse to help when asked.
Antonov:	(Bursting into laughter.) You are right, he never says no…So when can we come?
Lawrence:	(Smiling.) So then you are prepared to….
Natalia:	(Bowing.) We mean if you agree.
Lawrence:	What if I were to say no…
Antonov:	Then we would go.
Christiane:	To London, if I recall correctly.
Antonov:	Did I say London or was it Geneva or maybe Brussels. (They laugh.)
Christiane:	(Wiping her eyes.) I haven't laughed like this in months. In Paris people aren't as jovial as in Russia, before the Bolsheviks I mean.
Antonov:	You don't know how it is with the Bolsheviks. You were not there.
Christiane:	You gave concerts in Moscow last summer, didn't you?

Natalia:	He saw nothing, he did not even go to visit my poor mother in Perm.
Antonov:	Three days on a train…and when you get off. Oh, how you itch! (He puts his hand to his head and scratches it.)
Natalia:	He said they told him that my mother was dead…but she wrote me a letter.
Antonov:	I tell you that letter was not from your mother.
Natalia:	Of course it was from my mother. I recognize her handwriting.
Antonov:	She wanted us to send her sugar and chocolate and other things…I said we should not send anything.
Natalia:	All the same I sent a package. If it got lost, so what? Somebody will eat it. Maybe a Bolshevik, that's true.
Antonov:	I don't want to fatten up Bolsheviks.
Natalia:	Why don't you? You're a Bolshevik yourself. He sometimes says now we should go back to Russia. But I won't go. Three of my brothers were shot, plus five nephews.
Antonov:	We don't know for sure.
Natalia:	I had a prophetic dream. Please don't laugh, Madame Chesnay.
Christiane:	I am not laughing.
Natalia:	When one has had a prophetic dream…(Meanwhile Antonov has opened the piano and is playing.)
Christiane:	It hasn't been tuned for a long time…
Antonov:	It is terribly out of tune…but it's a good piano. Maybe I'll come here to work, if that's all right with you.

Christiane:	I thought you had a grand piano.
Antonov:	(Tapping his forehead.) It's there, my grand piano. I'll have one someday. For the time being I'll rent a piano so I can compose. But when I work on my concerto I shall come here. Well, thanks so much…to both of you. We haven't talked about money yet. But no worry, we'll get along fine on that matter too. I am sure you will have no regrets…
Natalia:	I already told Madame Chesnay that later, there will be a plaque. (She goes out with Antonov. Christiane sees them out and comes right back.)
Lawrence:	That clown amuses me. We deserve to be colonized by buffoons like him.
Christiane:	You know, I don't think he's a fool at all. His wife maybe, but not him.
Lawrence:	Oh!
Christiane:	Anyway, he's brilliant.
Lawrence:	How can you tell?
Christiane:	It seems obvious. Take his remark about art and advertising.
Lawrence:	Nonsense.
Christiane:	I don't agree with you.
Lawrence:	Then explain.
Christiane:	It's an original idea.
Lawrence:	You call that an idea! You mistake a rattling tongue for brilliant thought. Besides, this man is vulgarity in the flesh; that's no sign of great intelligence.
Christiane:	What you find vulgar, I consider unaffected.

Lawrence: The self-centeredness of a spoiled child.

Christiane: For you intelligence consists in wrapping yourself
                    in strictures.

Lawrence: What do you mean?

Christiane: I mean constraints. It seems to me that intelligence
                    should free us.

Lawrence: From what?

Christiane: First of all from ourselves. Antonov does not bother
                    about himself.

Lawrence: No. He just bothers everybody else.

Christiane: That shows he's someone strong, a real personality.
                    That's why I like his music.

Lawrence: His music is just like him. It assaults you.

Christiane: He's not trying to charm you.

Lawrence: He attacks us.

Christiane: Most likely…(A silence.) Why are you smiling?

Lawrence: I don't know, my love.

Christiane: My, that's the first time you've spoken tenderly to
                    me since I've come home.

ACT TWO

Same setting. Ten or twelve days later. It's 10:00 p.m.

(Antonov, Julie in the doorway.)

Antonov:	(In a scarlet bathrobe.) And you don't know when Madame will be home?
Julie:	Madame is out for dinner; but she often goes to the theater afterwards.
Antonov:	(Moaning.) To the theater! What business does she have going to the theater?
Julie:	I don't know if you should wait.
Antonov:	I could always play the piano for a while. But can't we telephone to where Madame is having dinner?
Julie:	I don't know the number. Monsieur Chesnay is at a family dinner.
Antonov:	Telephone Monsieur Chesnay.
Julie:	(Victoriously.) Monsieur Chesnay's uncle doesn't have a telephone.
Antonov:	That is terrible…Upstairs, I thought I would go out of my mind. You didn't tell me that old man and his old lady danced.
Julie:	Their grandchildren come and visit them once a month.
Antonov:	How many grandchildren do they have?…I thought that Parisians decided not to have any more children…Once a month!…I won't have time to recover from one visit to the next…You could tell them there is someone who is very sick. An old lady—say it's an old woman. Besides, Madame Antonov isn't well, most of the time.

Julie: You can tell them yourself.

Antonov: No, that would be unpleasant. If they refuse to stop, what will I do? This is terrible. Please leave me now, and turn the light out as you go.

Julie: (Timidly.) Madame gave me no instructions.

(Antonov opens the door and switches off the light, and the maid goes out. Antonov then goes to the piano, lights a cigarette, and begins to play some violent music, something like a Stravinsky sonata. After a few moments, noise from outside is heard.)

Antonov: What's all that racket? This house is impossible.

(He gets up and goes to the door.)

(Julie enters.)

Julie: (To Henry, who is not yet visible.) Monsieur Chesnay is at his uncle's, I'm sure of that. But I don't know about Madame Chesnay.

Henry: (Appearing.) However, I do know.

Julie: The Russian gentleman is already here. May I ask sir, is this a surprise party?

Henry: No, no, nothing like that; that's passé. Give me the telephone book, will you, I'm going to call. (To Antonov.) Good evening, sir; excuse the interruption please. All this is absurd.

Antonov: (Joyfully.) This gentleman is telephoning Madame. (Henry, having consulted the phone book, dials the number.) It seems to me, sir, that I met you at Madame Morgenthaler's.

Henry: That's right...I beg your pardon...Hello! Is this Senora Dolores de Solveredo? Could I speak with Madame Chesnay? Thank you. I'll hold the line...That's right, sir, we met at that impossible woman's house.

Antonov:	What do you mean impossible? Would you give me the phone, please.
Henry:	Just a moment, please.
Antonov:	(To Julie.) You see, it's quite easy.
Henry:	Hello, is that you, Christiane? Yes it's I, Henry. I am at your house. Are you having fun? There, didn't I tell you? And are the Waricourts there? No, of course not. Listen. Something very annoying has happened. No, not an accident. Nothing involving Claude. Nor your father. Nevertheless something disturbing. I met Denise; she's furious, and I think she's going to stop by here in a little while.
Julie:	Is Madame Furstlin coming, too, sir?
Henry:	Someone's talking here. What? Why are you still there? What are you saying?
Julie:	If Madame Furstlin is coming too, shouldn't I prepare some cakes and some port?
Henry:	Don't you dare. It would be a horrible mistake. (Into the telephone.) Julie is asking me if she shouldn't prepare a light supper. I told her, absolutely not.
Antonov:	I want to tell her something.
Henry:	In any event, I have a piece of advice for you. Fake a migraine headache and get out of there fast. Yes, that's the best thing you can do. Was I right? Of course. The next time, try to listen, my dear Christiane…See you soon. (Henry goes to hang up, Antonov rushes to the phone.)
Antonov:	Don't hang up, Monsieur.
Henry:	But she will be here in a few minutes. You can tell her your grievances then. I can see you obviously have some complaint. Now, my dear Julie, go to bed. We won't need you any more.

Julie:	Are you sure, sir?
Henry:	She insists! I assure you there will be no surprise party. If you really want to know, in a little while there will be a scolding by a firing squad here.
Julie:	If Madame Chesnay is not feeling well, sometimes…
Henry:	No need to worry. That's over too; it won't be happening again.
Julie:	Very well, sir. (She leaves as if against her better judgment.)
Henry:	I have the impression I interrupted you just when you were performing a capital execution, sir. (Pointing to the piano.) Please continue.
Antonov:	(Annoyed.) I don't understand, Monsieur.
Henry:	Yes, it sounded like a dialogue between the guillotine and its victim.
Antonov:	The atmosphere is impossible, sir; one can no longer make music here.
Henry:	Oh! I could very nicely. (He approaches the piano.)
Antonov:	(Stepping in his way.) Monsieur, I beg you. Since we met at Madame Morgenthaler's house, may I ask you a question? I suppose you are a banker, sir?
Henry:	Absolutely not. My father was banker enough for both of us.
Antonov:	Do you know if that lady is solvent?
Henry:	What do you mean?
Antonov:	She commissioned me to compose a ballet for one person…they say it's for a fellow countryman of mine, Seviatsine. I care nothing for him. But I care dearly about my ballet and the four hundred thousand francs Madame Morgenthaler promised me.

That's why I'm asking you, is she solvent?

Henry: Well, I can tell you she has just suffered consider-
            able financial losses.

Antonov: (Painfully.) Who advises these women?

Henry: Sorry. Can't help you there.

Antonov: And what about my interest? What shall I do?

Henry: Finish your ballet.

Antonov: Not on your life. I received an advance of one hun-
            dred thousand francs and I wrote one quarter of the
            ballet. That's all well and good. But if I write any
            more, I lose money.

Henry: In any event, the woman in question owns the first
            quarter.

Antonov: Do you think there are other patrons who would
            pay for the rest of the work?

Henry: Incorporate a cooperative? That calls for some
            thought.

Antonov: Monsieur Chesnay, who is he?

Henry: You know him…

Antonov: No. Madame I know. Monsieur I would not even
            recognize if I met him in the street.

Henry: Don't count on him. Believe me, he's no patron of
            the arts.

Antonov: What's his job?

Henry: Member of the Privy Council.

Antonov: We had that in Russia too.

Henry: I don't think it's the same thing.

Antonov: Madame is very nice, one sees that right away; but Monsieur, is he nice, I don't know.

Henry: Perhaps. He's a gentleman, but no soft touch.

Antonov: (With disdain.) That's fine, very subtle, but decadent too.

Henry: Well, I can assure you, no matter what, he won't give you a sou.

Antonov: But Madame, what if she asks him?

Henry: I think Madame, she will not ask him.

Antonov: (Maliciously.) Perhaps she will ask it…of someone else?

Henry: No chance of that either. She's very nice all right, but not in that way.

Antonov: Who is she nice to?

Henry: Well…sort of nice with a lot of people, really nice with no one.

Antonov: How can that be? When I know her better, I will ask her.

Henry: I warn you not to.

Antonov: I must.

Henry: Why must you?

Antonov: I need to understand. Oh! Don't go imagining something…I've already had enough troubles in Germany with a general's wife—Generaline Von Weber—so I don't want to get involved again. Besides, Madame Chesnay fantasizes too much. That's amusing at tea time, but in bed I like tranquillity…

Henry: Without imagination.

Antonov: Natalia used to be like that; not anymore. She's like
                  an old pair of shoes…Still, some day I ask her. Oth-
                  erwise, it gets on my nerves…and I can no longer
                  work…

Henry: No, you'll just have to think of something else.

Antonov: I'm very disappointed that Madame Morgenthaler
                  has had these losses…I thought maybe I'd marry
                  her.

Henry: And Madame Natalia?

Antonov: If I divorce her, she'll have her children come back.
                  I suppose then she is happy. She laughs all the time,
                  she cries all the time, no matter what. So…how old
                  is Madame Morgenthaler?

Henry: She's a friend of my mother's, a little older than my
                  mother.

Antonov: That doesn't stop me. I will call her Mama, as your
                  Jean-Jacques Rousseau said. Then she is happy. But
                  if she is broke…there is no deal.

Henry: She still has a gorgeous villa on the Riviera, at Cap
                  Martin. A forest of umbrella pines, and a beautiful
                  rose garden.

Antonov: That's delightful…Already the mood is more musi-
                  cal; if you wish, I play.

Henry: I hear someone coming. (He opens the door.) It's
                  Christiane.

(Christiane enters.)

Christiane: Who is there with you, Henry?

Antonov: (Going to meet her.) Madame, pardon me, but why
                  did you not tell me those people upstairs they dance.

And what dances! *Shuh platter*...I thought I'd go crazy.

Christiane:	(Very coldly.) Too bad...
Antonov:	Perhaps you tell them something...You explain there is a sick lady, or something like that...
Christiane:	Unfortunately that is quite impossible.
Antonov:	(Realizing his cause is hopeless.) Perhaps we talk again tomorrow.
Christiane:	Well, not tonight. I am dead tired. You must forgive me. (She collapses in a large armchair without having taken off her coat.)
Antonov:	Good night then, Madame; it's better I come back tomorrow....or perhaps Natalia she will explain.
Christiane:	Whatever you like. Good night.

(Antonov leaves confused and furious.)

Henry:	Take your coat off, Christiane dear.
Christiane:	I'm frozen. So, what's happening?
Henry:	First, tell me about your dinner.
Christiane:	No Waricourts, no one. Just Dolores and me, and a little old lady covered with jewels, an aunt who looked like a stuffed monkey, who shrieked with laughter from time to time for no apparent reason. Don't laugh. A terrible dinner; everything the doctor forbids. I hardly ate anything, but still I have heartburn.
Henry:	No...
Christiane:	After dinner the little old aunt went to bed...and then the heart to heart...Secrets, confessions, muffled exclamations—then questions about my

marriage. How could you? How can anyone? Am I a monster? etc. etc....

Henry: But I thought she had been married.

Christiane: Never consummated. Not even close to consummated. He must have been really frigid....Oh! Let's not talk about it anymore...And now that Cossack with the jeremiads.

Henry: You mean Antonov?

Christiane: Damn!...Since he's been in our apartment, he's been unbearable, like his music. The other evening he came here and pounded on that piano for two hours. I was beside myself...Maybe I should go to Switzerland to live with my son.

Henry: You can't take the altitude; it's bad for your heart.

Christiane: What time is it? Why isn't Lawrence home yet? I'm too warm. (She takes off her coat.) Put that in the vestibule, will you. (Henry takes the coat; Christiane gets up and looks at herself in the mirror.) I certainly look awful tonight. (To Henry, who reenters the room.) And what about Denise? What's happened to her?

Henry: Saturday when I went to their place to hear some new records...wonderful ones from Solesmes, you must hear them...I had the feeling that she was very upset with you. Several very unpleasant remarks. But, just now, when I ran into her, she told me she's disgusted with you and she wants to tell you off before the night is over. She seemed to know you were dining at Dolores's, and made some nasty remarks, but I rebutted them sharply.

Christiane: Why the rush?

Henry: I think she's leaving by car early tomorrow morning. I don't remember exactly what she told me.

Christiane: I think I'm beginning to understand. Bertrand asked me again if he could paint my portrait. He'd mentioned it a while ago, and then let it drop. But last week he was insistent.

Henry: And you accepted.

Christiane: He's improved a great deal, you know.

Henry: That's not the issue.

Christiane: Why would I refuse?

Henry: Come now, Christiane…

Christiane: He seemed to really want to, and there is no portrait of me that's worth looking at…only…yes, yes that must be it…Denise and Bertrand's situation has suddenly gotten complicated.

Henry: How's that?

Christiane: I may be wrong, but it strikes me that's how it's been ever since Max became that little actress's lover.

Henry: Of course! If Max is seriously involved with someone else, Bertrand will want to break off with Denise. Bertrand's afraid Max will ask for a divorce and Denise will then want him, Bertrand, to marry her. But that's not Bertrand's plan. The dear fellow has no intention of doing anything of the sort. So Bertrand's already seeing less and less of Denise; he's keeping as busy as he can with other commitments, and that's why he wants to do your portrait.

Christiane: What a confused mess!

Henry: That's life.

Christiane: (Sadly.) Yes, that's the way our lives seem to end up.

Henry: But let me tell you, you were wrong to accept Bertrand's offer. You're always playing with fire!

Christiane:	Bertrand has no feelings for me.
Henry:	That's not true and you know it.
Christiane:	Henry!
Henry:	What's more, if he weren't in love with you, you wouldn't have accepted...You love to flirt with danger, nothing really bad, but situations involving enough trouble that you ought to avoid them.
Christiane:	That's horrible!!
Henry:	Denise has annoyed you for a while now. Although you take her side if someone else attacks her, you still don't mind upsetting her a bit, all the while telling yourself that you're doing nothing wrong because Bertrand isn't in love with you, and it's a good deed helping a young man to develop his talents.
Christiane:	So that's what you think of me!
Henry:	Don't you see, Christiane, these are the consequences of the kind of life you chose?
Christiane:	Chose!
Henry:	The responsibility for it is mainly yours.
Christiane:	Mine? You think I chose this life. It disgusts me. It makes me sick.
Henry:	Listen. Now you are tired, disgusted, overwrought; nevertheless there are moments when you really enjoy yourself, and then you are quite pleased with your life.
Christiane:	Those moments...I detest them.
Henry:	Come now, admit it. You could have lived an entirely different life. You have the makings of...a great lover.
Christiane:	Sounds like a line from a movie!

Henry: I can feel it. I'm sure of it. I can tell. (A silence.)
          What's more, at times, these needs that life has not
          satisfied surge up, and you feel the pain of remorse.
          Actually, it's more like a cramp.

Christiane: You are awful.

Henry: So, as I said, you like being surrounded by young
          men who admire you, who want you; you couldn't
          live without that atmosphere. However, because
          you're not really a flirt, you feel a certain uneasiness
          enjoying all this...

Christiane: You think that gives me pleasure!...

Henry: Sentiments that you can't really reciprocate, for you
          are basically loyal. That explains your mood swings,
          your flights of fancy, your inconsistencies. You're a
          flirt in spite of yourself. And all I can say is what
          I've told you a hundred times; there's only one solu-
          tion for you.

Christiane: (Profoundly.) I will never leave Lawrence!

Henry: Who's talking about Lawrence? I never mentioned
          divorce. Legal formalities mean nothing. In my opin-
          ion, you will only be a real woman the day you take
          a lover.

Christiane: Well let me tell you, my dear Henry, you don't un-
          derstand anything. In my life there's only one prob-
          lem, by God I'd say...one drama. It's Lawrence. The
          rest is...

Henry: The rest is precisely what interests me.

Christiane: The rest is something that concerns me and me
          alone, and maybe God, if there is a God, and I'm
          not so sure there isn't. I may appear to be just like
          the rest of you, who don't believe in anything, who
          make fun of everything—except suffering and death,
          which terrify you. I'm not saying this against you in
          particular. I'm saying that there's someone in me I
          hardly know, someone who certainly doesn't belong

to your group. There is a part of me that is searching, trying to find herself, and who in rare moments is in touch with herself, in another world, one that is foreign to you.

Henry: But Christiane, do you really think I'm so limited, so insensitive…Why just the other day, listening to the music of Solesmes…

Christiane: (Violently.) It's a long time since anyone has talked about that!

Henry: (Surprised.) Aha! So it is true, what Denise said. Just the mention of Solesmes and you…

Christiane: That's ridiculous!

Henry: And I just happen to have brought you a record from Solesmes…Too bad, I'll just leave it here, and you can do with it what you want…Why, you're crying, Christiane…Can it be true, the idea has occurred to me…I remember when I went to see you at Cimiez, that year you were so sick…

Christiane: (Without answering.) I can't understand how you who know me so well, can judge me so harshly…

Henry: Me, judge you? I who…

Christiane: No, no. Remember our agreement.

Henry: Now listen to me seriously. Just now you said, the only problem, the only drama, is Lawrence. I suppose that means you don't want him to suffer. (Christiane gestures.) I don't know the answer; basically I don't understand him, I never did. Some days, I have to admit, he seems to me to be a very unhappy person. But perhaps he's just someone who's very bored with himself and who is simply incapable of relating to other people.

Christiane: (Heatedly.) And, wouldn't that be enough to make him very unhappy, indeed?

Henry: That's possible, but still…Haven't you ever won-
                dered what causes him to suffer so?

Christiane: (Softly.) Many times.

Henry: My idea is…don't you think his dominant feeling is
                vanity?

Christiane: Pride might be more like it.

Henry: All right…But I wonder if the kind of life you lead
                isn't just the thing that deepens his wound.

Christiane: (With anguish.) But what can I do?

Henry: I'll tell you one thing…if you behaved in a way that
                gave him a more important role in your life, a role
                he could be proud of…

Christiane: What role?…Besides, you're wrong. He's not vain,
                and he's certainly not an actor…He loves me, I feel
                his love for me like a terrible weight oppressing me.
                That his love is mixed with a certain…pride. That,
                I'll admit. But what can I do? I can't betray him,
                and I can't leave him. Nor can I really be his friend.
                If by some heroic sacrifice, which I'm incapable of,
                I were to break off from those he calls my friends
                and create empty time and space around me, that
                wouldn't be a solution, because he can't bear to have
                anyone sacrifice anything for him. Understand, he's
                a man who would never accept even the smallest
                loan, for fear of being in someone's debt.

Henry: There, you see.

Christiane: He would have to believe that I did this for myself
                and almost in spite of him. What's to be done? I
                can't lie, at least not in that way.

Henry: And you're really sure you wouldn't be better off sepa-
                rated?

Christiane: I think he would kill himself. (A silence.) Henry, I

think someone rang the doorbell. Will you go and
see who it is, please.

Henry: It must be Denise. Do you want to see her?

Christiane: Yes. I want to settle this right away.

(Henry goes out and comes back a few seconds later with Denise, who
comes in silently and collapses into a chair, her face in her hands; she
sobs. A silence.)

Christiane: (Carefully.) Well, Denise, Henry told me…(Denise
                    shakes her head to disapprove.) This story of the
                    portrait is ridiculous. If I had only known that it
                    could hurt you.

Denise: (In a flat tone.) That's exactly the point.

Christiane: What do you mean? Henry, it might be better if
                    Denise and I were alone.

Denise: (In a soft voice.) He can stay…(the rest is inaudible,
                    then one hears) one of Bertrand's friends…

Christiane: Have you seen Bertrand? (Denise nods to affirm.)
                    You just came from his place?

Denise: Yes.

Christiane: And what happened?

Denise: It's all over between us!

Christiane: Come now, we all know what those arguments are.

Denise: (Ironically) We all know…do you really know? Have
                    you experienced it…?

Christiane: I can well imagine…

Denise: You "imagine"… For two years my life with Bertrand
                    has been like a dream, no quarrel, no misunderstand-
                    ing.

Christiane:	Yes, but, I remember that last year at Megève…
Denise:	That was child's play. (All of a sudden.) Do you know that he's interested in the de Brucourt girl?
Christiane:	What do you mean?
Denise:	They are almost engaged.
Christiane:	What's this story?
Denise:	He showed me a letter from her…and you, what part did you play?
Christiane:	Don't be silly, Denise. First of all, I don't believe this story of their engagement. And even it were true, how can you blame me?
Denise:	For being what you are.
Henry:	Are you completely crazy?
Denise:	During the ten days Bertrand was in Biarritz, the harm your presence did to us, to our love…Oh, I just realized it today, but Bertrand had already admitted.
Christiane:	Let's face it…It doesn't make any sense. Even if he had some feelings for me…
Denise:	Don't call it feelings. As for Bertrand's feelings…the truth is that Bertrand can't be under the same roof with an attractive woman for two days…without his imagination beginning to work overtime. Usually nothing comes of it, but this time it's quite different. Bertrand could watch you closely and observe you with him (pointing to Henry), with Gilbert, and with the others. He is not as worldly as he looks, and he is very…realistic. The idea that he would be just one of your many admirers did not suit him too well.
Henry:	You see…

Denise:	But your manner with me...with all of us...it's as if you had distilled some kind of poison.
Christiane:	Please explain.
Denise:	The things you say...for instance, the other day when you were talking about the broken world... that kind of sadness that you have no right to feel, much less to complain about, because you live just like we do, you are no better than any of us, you don't believe in anything, you...I realize now all this did upset him and it effectively turned him against me. It's you who made him feel uneasy, anxious to run away...as if anyone can escape, as if we can get away from what we hate about ourselves...Oh yes...there is one way to end everything, but only one. Now it's through you that Bertrand judges me, and he despises me...
Christiane:	I have never judged you; you know that.
Denise:	What difference does it make whether you spoke the words or not?
Christiane:	(Painfully.) No, I just can't understand. What kind of treacherous intention do you pretend I had?
Denise:	Who mentioned intentions?
Christiane:	When I think of my conversations with Bertrand...
Henry:	All these examinations of conscience reveal nothing.
Christiane:	I didn't flirt with him. He didn't tell me any secrets. He never mentioned the de Brucourt girl...
Denise:	That one...
Christiane:	I can't understand why you reproach me...
Henry:	What angers her the most is that there is nothing to forgive.

Denise:	There were moments when I thought I was going be jealous of you. That would have been less painful.
Christiane:	(To Henry.) Do you understand?
Denise:	First of all, if you had been his mistress he would have despised you...Then he would have been free of you.
Christiane:	(Strongly.) I am sure he does not love me.
Denise:	(Bitterly.) Does anyone really love another person? (A silence.)
Christiane:	Denise dear, I am convinced this wedding won't take place. The de Brucourts are very wealthy, very hard to please. Bertrand has no money. Then there is his reputation. Everybody knows that he's been on drugs, that he spent months in a rehabilitation center, and they know which woman paid his expenses...
Denise:	(Crying.) You are despicable. He is a pitiable wreck. Don't you think I've known that from the start?
Henry:	I think Bertrand is a real worry-wart. Some doctor must have told him that he had to clean up his life style. And that's what's happening. Christiane had nothing to do with it. She looks awful, and I think we should let her get some rest...
Denise:	He only had to say the word and I would have asked for a divorce. Max can no longer refuse me.
Christiane:	That would only bring misery to the three of you.
Denise:	(With passion.) You're always so pessimistic, so eager to discourage, to take away a person's desire to live...What are you hiding? What's at the bottom of all this? (She holds her hands.) If we only knew, if for once you would tell the truth, maybe...

(Lawrence opens the door and sees who is there; he is going to leave without a word but Christiane calls him back.)

Lawrence: Oh! I don't mean to intrude on your nice little group!

Christiane: Don't be silly…they're here together by coincidence. Henry phoned me at Dolores's and it was so boring there…

Lawrence: And then Madame Furstlin just happened to arrive. All this seems very natural. Why not drop in for visits at 1:00 a.m.?

Denise: Is it 1:00 a.m.?

Lawrence: (Looking at his watch.) Four minutes to one to be precise.

(A silence.)

Christiane: How come you're so late? Usually evenings end very early at your uncle's.

Lawrence: I left there at 10:30 p.m.

Christiane: And then what?

Lawrence: I went for a walk. The night is beautiful.

Christiane: Denise had an urgent question for me. So did Henry.

Lawrence: No need to explain. (A silence.) I am quite tired from my walk. I hope you'll excuse me if I retire.

Denise: (Abruptly.) Please wait a minute. Before you arrived…

Christiane: Be careful.

Denise: Several of us feel that the kind of life Christiane leads is not good for her. It's not good for either her physical or her spiritual health. You are so busy with your job that perhaps you don't notice. Did she have to go for dinner at that Brazilian girl's house tonight? And to Biarritz for three weeks? So much commotion and agitation...Don't you agree, Henry?

Henry: (Very coolly.) Remember I did not go to Biarritz.

Christiane: You really are too much!

Denise: I'd rather talk in front of her; I hate talking behind people's backs. If she keeps up this pace, in six months she'll have a nervous breakdown.

Lawrence: What's your point?

Denise: I am asking you to use...yes...use your influence to make sure she'll go and rest for two or three months in a quiet place like Switzerland, for example...

Lawrence: I beg your pardon. I am a bit confused. I thought you had come because you had an urgent question to ask Christiane.

Denise: There is something else...well...it's all connected. Even her way of answering...I tell you she worries me.

Henry: All this just doesn't make sense. (Christiane sits down with the dejected, ironic air of a person who is being treated as an object.) Christiane's life is certainly too hectic, too tiring. She's interested in too many things and is so devoted to everything she does...

Lawrence: How interesting.

Henry: She has always been like that. Even before your marriage I remember many crazy days that began at 8:00 a.m. in the hospital and ended after midnight at the theater or a night club.

Lawrence: So you did volunteer work in hospitals?

Christiane: I gave that up when I was expecting Claude. The doctors were afraid of possible contagion, don't you remember?

Henry: They were quite right.

Denise: Moreover, it wasn't your style.

Henry: Not at all.

Denise: Just like when you visited the poor.

Henry: She always hated it.

Denise: You were so relieved the day your mother asked you not to do that anymore. (To Lawrence.) Her mother was so worried, she could imagine Christiane attacked, murdered…

Henry: There are enough women to do that sort of work.

Christiane: (Ironically.) Is it really a job?

Denise: (To Lawrence.) You probably think I should mind my own business, but it's a real concern for her friends.

Lawrence: We are deeply touched by your solicitude, aren't we, Christiane?

Denise: You are making fun of me.

Lawrence: What an idea, of course not.

Denise: .   Just as you came in I was telling Christiane that there is something in her attitude we can't explain.

Christiane: Don't you think that's enough?

Lawrence: Very interesting.

Denise: Maybe I should not talk like this in front of her, but it's done now. And I don't think I would have been brave enough to write to you. Besides, she would have read my letter anyway.

Lawrence: Or you could have written to my office. How complicated!

Denise: With a friendship that goes back twenty years, there are things one just can't do. That's the way it is with you, darling Christiane.

Christiane: (Ironically.) Darling!

Denise: Something even you are not quite aware of...

Lawrence: Maybe you'll be so kind as to give us the address of a specialist?

Denise: What do you mean?

Lawrence: Well, maybe a psychoanalyst? As I know Christiane —excuse me if I sound pretentious in front of friends like you—she'll be delighted to confide...

Christiane: You're out of your mind.

Denise: If you ask me, psychoanalysis is a joke. (To Christiane.) Do you remember Jacques Meyer Wurmser, Katy's younger brother, who was in school with us at Villiers? He went to work in Vienna after he failed his Medical Boards for the third time. All we know about him is that he makes love to all his patients. Maybe it's good for them...All the same it's a strange way to practice medicine. No, I think Christiane simply needs to rest and find herself again. It would be nice if you could go together to a very quiet place...you could hear her confession.

Lawrence: (Ironically.) What a wonderful idea. What a superb friend you are.

(Denise and Henry get up to go.)

Henry: (To Denise.) Do you have your car?

Denise: Of course not! Max uses it night and day.

Henry: In that case, I'll take you home.

Denise: Thanks.

Henry:	(In a low voice.) I knew you could be nasty but not to that point…

(They leave. Christiane sees them out and comes back to the living room right away.)

(A silence.)

Christiane:	I just can't understand why you came back so late.
Lawrence:	It was so stuffy at Uncle Louis's. I needed some fresh air.
Christiane:	Two hours walking. Where did you go?
Lawrence:	I went to the park. I walked several miles.
Christiane:	You could have been attacked. A few minutes ago you were talking about a secret meeting you thought we'd organized. That's absolutely false. Don't you believe me?
Lawrence:	Does it matter?
Christiane:	It's important for me to know that you trust me.
Lawrence:	I realize that.
Christiane:	I was probably wrong not to go with you to Uncle Louis's. Were they offended that I didn't come?
Lawrence:	They asked very politely how you were.
Christiane:	The evening at Dolores's was awful…I would have been much happier at your uncle's and aunt's. They go back to prehistoric times, but I love them. I had to go to Dolores's, in order to meet the Waricourts. It was important for Henry. But as it turned out, they didn't come.
Lawrence:	What a shame!
Christiane:	You know I don't like to hurt anybody.

Lawrence:	Do you think anyone does?
Christiane:	(In spite of herself.) Yes. Denise, for instance.
Lawrence:	(With a feigned surprise.) Oh! How is that? What about her concern for you?
Christiane:	Were you taken in?
Lawrence:	A friendship of twenty years! What a loss!
Christiane:	Yes…No…I can't say. To tell the truth, it's not a surprise. The only surprising thing is that I find it quite normal.
Lawrence:	Anyway, the disappointment did not deprive you of your talent for expressing your own point of view.
Christiane:	(Still in her thoughts.) A real bond…not a simple habit…a tie not shaped by time, and that time cannot undo…a friendship. Let's face it, I think I have no friend, no real friend. You, Lawrence, you could have been my friend. You still could be, I assure you. But you don't want to. Your refusal to accept anything from me for fear it would appear that you'd asked for something is killing me. You could have helped me. You could have made me less selfish, but instead you leave me to my own resources. And when I am on my own, I am not worth anything. Maybe I even become evil. Denise's accusations were almost absurd, yet deep down she was not completely wrong.
Lawrence:	I don't see where you are going with all this ruminating, and it's very late.
Christiane:	Your attitude reveals a resentment so deep that you can't even talk about it. It's rooted so deeply it pervades your whole being.
Lawrence:	So many secrets in this house. So many locked closets and nobody seems to have the keys.

Christiane:	If I was unfair to you, and that may be, I beg your pardon with all my heart.
Lawrence:	Unless there are things I don't know about, I don't see how you could feel guilty. But if you'd like a general absolution, I am more than willing to give it to you.
Christiane:	(Deeply.) You're not being fair. You know exactly what I'm talking about. Knowing how you felt about me when you asked me to marry you, I should have refused. Today I see that. At the time, though, I believed the opposite. I had seen such terrible things all around me. My mother was miserable. My brother was dying. I asked myself, "How could I add to the world's misery by thinking only of myself?" So much suffering. Moreover, I did not lie to you, I did not deceive you about my feelings for you. I thought your love might awaken mine. I knew of cases in which this happened. I reasoned as best I could. I swear I did my best. But now I realize it was a mistake. The real courage would have been to leave you to your sorrow. You might have recovered very quickly. I was too proud to admit that. Now I see clearly that we can be honest in words while dishonest in acts. On my part our marriage was not an honest act. Because I married you, you can't get over me. I ask your forgiveness for that.
Lawrence:	(In a dull tone.) You are not telling me anything new and I still think it was unnecessary to…
Christiane:	The silence of our life is crushing me. I can't breathe. But it seems that for you there is no other way it could be.
Lawrence:	What more do you want? It seems to me that there is a lot of talking in this house.
Christiane:	If we could, for instance, figure out where we stand.
Lawrence:	In our assets, you mean. Sometimes you really are your father's daughter. Your examples, your comparisons…Unfortunately, I don't believe in this

kind of accounting …official records. The other kind, the only true kind, cannot appear in any ledger. It is entirely hidden…invisible. Furthermore, when you recall in a very moving way—no irony intended—our marriage, you still refer only to book-keepers' accounting. The other accounting, the real one, is beyond words. When your…your ex-friend was just casting her very nasty allusions about I don't know what secret, I wonder if she wasn't onto something.

Christiane: (In an anxious tone.) But there is no secret.

Lawrence: I'm not so sure about that. Anyway, it's no dramatic secret. I am sure nobody has any compromising letters to blackmail you. But there are other kinds of secrets.

Christiane: But, does there have to be a secret?

Lawrence: Please understand that all these insinuations are no surprise to me. Don't think I am that naive.

Christiane: I wouldn't.

Lawrence: Your crazy restlessness probably hides…

Christiane: What?

Lawrence: I don't know exactly…probably an obsession…

Christiane: (Shuddering, then collecting herself.) But remember at the time of our wedding, Denise was in Morocco.

Lawrence: I am not talking about our wedding.

Christiane: All right, then…

Lawrence: We are talking about our situation here and now.

Christiane: So, what about it?

Lawrence:	I am not asking anything of you. All I can say is that it's strange you would think me so blind, and moreover imagine that this blindness could help our relationship. That reveals a fear that is hardly worthy of you and that offends me.
Christiane:	So we should…
Lawrence:	There is no "we should." You know you are free. But are you using your freedom intelligently? In fact I realize…you misjudge me badly. If before you left for Biarritz, instead of talking about your childhood friend, you had honestly told me, "There will be someone there at Biarritz who is attractive to me…"
Christiane:	Oh, so that's what I should have said?
Lawrence:	Always your way of twisting my words. I just mean that if, at the time, you had simply acknowledged, courageously admitted…
Christiane:	That would have made us closer?
Lawrence:	At least it would have done less to separate us than inventing a lie that I could not believe.
Christiane:	And who should I have picked as my favorite? Henry? Gilbert?
Lawrence:	I know you keep your distance from those uninteresting gigolos.
Christiane:	Oh!
Lawrence:	You kind of like their stupid flatteries, but that's a far cry from having any real feeling for them…
Christiane:	(Not really controlling her sarcasm.) You enlighten me about myself. I see I can't hide anything from you.
Lawrence:	What do you mean?

Christiane:	(More seriously.) Henry, whom you underestimate, was just saying how…perceptive you are. In fact, just now…
Lawrence:	You were talking about me?
Christiane:	In passing. He was telling me how very intelligent you are. Yes, well, it's true I should have been more honest with you. And since Denise…I wanted to spare you. In fact I realize now that I went about it the wrong way. I was very clumsy indeed.
Lawrence:	Let's say: a bit cowardly.
Christiane:	If you prefer… Fortunately it's not too late.
Lawrence:	Remember though, that the confidences one shares during the night one often regrets by daylight. I learned that in the old days…when I had friends.
Christiane:	(More and more confident.) No, darling, I am sure I won't be sorry. I know what I am doing. I should have told you ages ago. All of a sudden it seems so easy…Yes, I realize now that it's you who should be my friend, the one to whom I tell everything.
Lawrence:	What an honor!
Christiane:	It's when I want to spare you that I hurt you. Something extremely painful has happened to me. It was in Biarritz that I started to realize…
Lawrence:	(Very coolly.) We have not been husband and wife for a year, now.
Christiane:	(Indignant.) Lawrence, how could you imagine? That's horrible!
(A silence.)	
Lawrence:	(Ashamed.) I beg your pardon…Besides…I did not suspect you.

Christiane: So.

Lawrence: (With a vague gesture.) I am…one is very much alone.

Christiane: From now on we must be together, not side by side but with one another.

Lawrence: If only that were possible…

Christiane: You'll see.

Lawrence: And to seal this new intimacy?…Paradoxical though it may be.

Christiane: We mustn't be always preoccupied with ourselves, watching ourselves like fascinating objects. You seem to be always scrutinizing yourself.

Lawrence: I've always been like that.

Christiane: And I'm that way too, when no one helps me…

Lawrence: No, you…when you're excited, happy, you're not self-conscious. But as for me, it's a kind of disgrace. I'm the opposite…Now about Biarritz…was it someone whom you met there?

Christiane: In any event, I hadn't paid any attention to him until then.

Lawrence: What about him?

Christiane: Not then, not now.

Lawrence: How's that?

Christiane: I don't think I interest him, not the least bit.

Lawrence: Is he totally insensitive?

Christiane: He's someone with whom I have very little in common, and whom I really don't like.

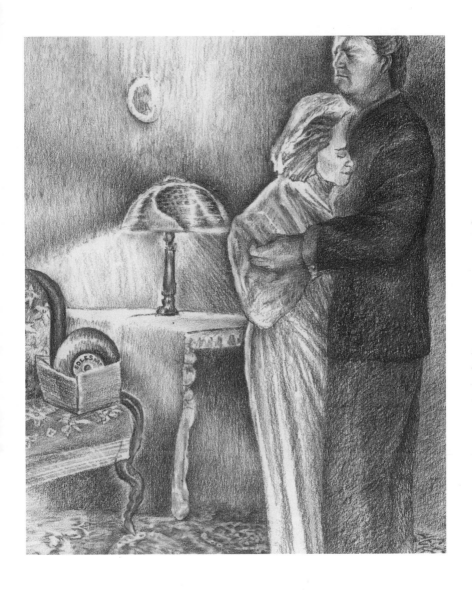

Lawrence:	Then it's just…physical?
Christiane:	I can't explain it.
Lawrence:	My poor darling!
Christiane:	(Pressing close to him.) Lawrence, I'm so ashamed.
Lawrence:	(Softly.) Who is it?
Christiane:	No, I can't.
Lawrence:	What's more, I think I've guessed.
Christiane:	That can't be.
Lawrence:	When you asked me the other day if he could live upstairs…
Christiane:	(Surprised.) Oh!
Lawrence:	It's Antonov, isn't it?
Christiane:	(After a long while, adjusting to the lie.) Yes, it's he. (She kneels next to Lawrence, hiding her face in her husband's chest.)
Lawrence:	(With tenderness, still showing a certain self-satisfaction.) Yes, it's sad…yes, pitiful. (Christiane sobs inarticulately.) You'll see, I think I'll be able to help you.
Christiane:	We'll be together.
Lawrence:	Come now, in an hour it will be dawn. (He notices the package that Henry has left on the chair.) What's this?
Christiane:	Oh that! It's a record Henry brought me.
Lawrence:	A dance record?
Christiane:	Hardly…It's religious music…a record from Solesmes.

ACT THREE
Same setting. Two weeks later. It is 2:00 p.m.[1]

(Christiane, Augsburger, Lawrence)

Christiane:	(Somewhat dryly.) Come now, Daddy, you mustn't take that disappointment so much to heart. I warned you: I never trusted that person.
Augsburger:	That person!
Christiane:	I think you have deceived yourself about her feelings for you.
Augsburger:	Ach! Ach! You always were biased. I don't know if it was jealousy or what…
Christiane:	Me, jealous!
Augsburger:	Among women…
Christiane:	It turns out that I was right.
Augsburger:	When I think that if I could have afforded the Carlton, nothing would have gone wrong.
Christiane:	Just an excuse.
Augsburger:	Money is a plague.
Christiane:	That's something you never would have said when you were rich.
Lawrence:	Listen, Christiane!
Augsburger:	(To Christiane.) You are not being kind. Remember your poor old father may not be with you much longer.
Lawrence:	Are you sick?

1. The time for this act is not given in earlier versions, but is the translator's editorial addition here.

Augsburger: My sickness has no name.

Christiane: You see…

Augsburger: (With pride.) The doctor told me my arteries are those of a man of twenty.

Lawrence: Bravo!

Augsburger: Still, I'm sometimes uncomfortable.

Christiane: So is everyone. When I have a migraine…

Augsburger: That's different. After seventy, discomfort is a warning sign.

Christiane: Go on a diet. Your housekeeper's cooking is much too greasy.

Augsburger: Lucy used to take such good care of me. But I won't talk about her any more, she doesn't deserve it. What about my grandchild? How is he doing?

Christiane: No news at all since we left La Clusaz.

Augsburger: No news is good news. But I'm sad that he is staying there another year. If he were here I could take him to the circus and to the movies. That would be fun. When he does come home, maybe he won't have a grandfather anymore.

Christiane: Listen, Daddy. We can't always be thinking only of our own pleasure. We let him stay in Switzerland because his health improves there.

Augsburger: In my day, children were healthier than they are nowadays. No one thought of sending them to the mountains. Besides, that must cost you a fortune.

Christiane: You know we have money in Swiss banks and Lawrence is very generous.

Augsburger: Before the holidays your husband talked only about Claude's starting school here.

Christiane:	Circumstances change.
Lawrence:	Claude couldn't have passed the entrance exams. All he does is sleigh ride and skate. Beyond that…
Christiane:	He likes to read.
Augsburger:	Well, I'm off to my sad home….I had an antique dealer come and look around. He made me some interesting offers for a few things. It costs so much to live these days. But I'd like your opinion. It does concern you. After all, when I'm gone I don't want you saying I sold your inheritance.
Christiane:	I'm not like that!
Augsburger:	I'd like you to take a look.
Christiane:	Is it urgent?
Augsburger:	The appraiser is coming back this evening.
Christiane:	I'll stop by in a while then.
Augsburger:	See you later.

(He leaves.)

Lawrence:	I think you were a bit hard on your father.
Christiane:	Oh?
Lawrence:	Even if his mistress is only a habit…at his age, it's no fun.
Christiane:	(Ironically.) I wasn't aware you had such a compassionate nature.
Lawrence:	You are strange.

(Christiane gestures.)

Christiane:	Daddy has an exasperating habit of self-pity. It bothered me so much during my mother's illness. He

	thought only of himself. You would have thought he was the one who deserved all the pity.
Lawrence:	That's human nature.
Christiane:	That's how men are especially. In any event, your change of attitude toward him is so strange. You who never could stand him...
Lawrence:	Certainly he gets on my nerves, but we just have to overcome some feelings.
Christiane:	My goodness, Lawrence, you are well on your way to perfection.
Lawrence:	You don't look well, my dear.
Christiane:	I haven't had a good night's sleep in a while, and sleeping pills don't help anymore.
Lawrence:	I think we made a mistake in coming directly back to Paris. We should have gone to the Italian Lake district for a couple weeks.
Christiane:	(Violently.) Thanks a lot. (The phone rings. Christiane picks up the receiver.) Hello. Yes, that's right. Is your phone out of order? I can barely hear you. Your voice is hardly recognizable. Yes, we spent a few weeks near our son. He's wonderful. We've decided to leave him there another year. What a question, of course we miss him. There's nothing he wants more than to stay in Switzerland. Whenever he saw us coming it put him in a bad mood, which of course was delightful. Yes, it's probably quite natural. And your little boy? How is he? He spent the whole summer with Max? But you? What did you do? Were you on your favorite islands, Les Porquerolles? You could have at least sent me a postcard. You thought I was mad at you? (Deeply saddened.) You know I don't hold grudges. You have a question to ask me? Then stop by if you like, but come right away because I'll have to go out later. See you. (She hangs up.)

Lawrence: Are you reconciled?

(Gesture by Christiane.)

Christiane: These days we can't even completely break off a friendship. Another sign that it's a broken world.

Lawrence: I don't get it.

Christiane: (With subtle irony.) You are more settled than I am, Lawrence. Oh, that's no reproach. Of course you need certain conditions, but once these are satisfied, you are content. As for me, I'm the opposite…

Lawrence: So what?

Christiane: To be at ease! What a compromise in a world such as this!

Lawrence: (With some bitterness.) To hear you talk, you give the impression that it's the sight of the atrocities one sees these days that overwhelms you.

Christiane: With good reason!

Lawrence: Yes, but you and I know that our problem is slightly different. By the way, all the time we were in Switzerland I made no reference at all to our troubled relationship. I hope you will give me credit for that. But I must say that recently your mood has changed considerably. It's quite natural. Even your attitude toward your father can by explained only by that obsession. Yet neither you nor I pronounced the name of that fellow during all that time…

Christiane: You are too much.

Lawrence: I think this reticence is not worthy of us. I read just a few minutes ago in the *Geneva Herald* that he's now giving concerts in Switzerland.

Christiane: That's what he wrote me.

Lawrence: He wrote you here?

Christiane: I got a letter from him the day before yesterday.

Lawrence: Aha!

(A silence.)

Christiane: Would you like to read it?

Lawrence: Not at all.

Christiane: It must be in my purse.

Lawrence: I don't see why…

Christiane: Yes, yes.

(She opens her purse; takes a letter, offers it to Lawrence.)

Lawrence: Are you sure?…

Christiane: (Somewhat bitterly.) Yes, of course.

Lawrence: I assure you, I'd rather not read it.

Christiane: As you wish. (She puts the letter back in her purse and closes it.) Now, he seems determined to get a divorce.

Lawrence: What about his wife?

Christiane: What can she do? Besides, I am not sure that they really are married.

Lawrence: Oh!

Christiane: They probably thought that some doors would be closed to them if they didn't pretend to be married. How foolish!

Lawrence: So?

Christiane: He will be married to Madame Morgenthaler before the end of the year.

Lawrence:	She's accepted?
Christiane:	She must be on cloud nine.
Lawrence:	He'll be unfaithful?
Christiane:	I'd be surprised; she must have laid down her conditions.
Lawrence:	Does he know... how you feel?
Christiane:	What do you mean?
Lawrence:	Have you told him what you thought of his plans?
Christiane:	It would have been useless...Besides...it doesn't really matter.
Lawrence:	(With eager curiosity at first, then very controlled.) Do you think?...No, it's nothing.
Christiane:	(To herself.) My God!
Lawrence:	(Sympathizing) Do you feel badly?
Christiane:	No.
Lawrence:	(With mixed feelings.) Someone so unworthy of you...so inhuman, so insensitive.
Christiane:	Exactly...so good riddance!
Lawrence:	No generosity.
Christiane:	Who is generous?
Lawrence:	Without integrity.
Christiane:	His character is in his music.
Lawrence:	I'm not so sure about that. Even his admirers are starting to wonder...Have you read Cyril Tverski's article in the *Musical Review*?

Christiane: If only he had somebody close to him who under-
                   stood him…

Lawrence: You know he cannot take criticism. He wants
                   only…adoring fans.

Christiane: Yes, but blind adoration…well, maybe that's won-
                   derful.

Lawrence: Not everybody can do it. You, for instance, you could
                   not…I know you.

Christiane: Are you sure you know me?

Lawrence: I foresaw what is happening right now.

Christiane: (With a hidden irony.) Oh?

Lawrence: My only fear was that you might not have the cour-
                   age to confide in me. That would have been a ter-
                   rible shame.

Christiane: Seriously…why?

Lawrence: Don't you agree you feel better now that you told
                   me?

Christiane: Whatever you say.

Lawrence: We should not keep anything from each other. So
                   now, I won't hesitate to ask you the question I wanted
                   to ask a while ago.

Christiane: Go right ahead.

Lawrence: Does Antonov suspect the sort of…interest you have
                   in him?

Christiane: (Intensely.) What do you want me to say?

(A silence.)

Lawrence: (With some hesitation.) But I am just asking you to
                   tell me the truth.

Christiane:	All of a sudden you seem to hesitate.
Lawrence:	No. Even if I should learn that you declared to him your…your folly…
Christiane:	My love.
Lawrence:	It is the same thing.

(A silence.)

Christiane:	Well, yes, I did.
Lawrence:	How so?
Christiane:	One day, probably a week before we left…I wrote him a letter which he never answered.
Lawrence:	And in this letter?
Christiane:	I told him the truth.
Lawrence:	You threw yourself at him.
Christiane:	(Hiding her face in her hands.) Exactly.
Lawrence:	Have you seen him since then?
Christiane:	Two or three times.
Lawrence:	And he did not mention your letter?
Christiane:	Not once.
Lawrence:	Perhaps the letter got lost.
Christiane:	No.
Lawrence:	How do you know?
Christiane:	I gave him some addresses he wanted in a postscript.
Lawrence:	So?

Christiane: I know he used them…

Lawrence: That is too much…But if he had answered the letter…

Christiane: I was at his mercy.

Lawrence: Do you realize?

Christiane: Yes.

Lawrence: Surely you must have experienced some strange sort of base satisfaction.

Christiane: Pleasure? You know very well that it's not I who feels that sort…

Lawrence: Do you mean that brute…?

Christiane: Well, yes…I was talking about Antonov…No, no, Lawrence, no angry words. He will probably come to visit us soon, maybe even today, and you must make sure that everything goes smoothly among the three of us.

Lawrence: (After a silence.) I don't understand.

Christiane: You just said you know me. But, do you even know yourself, Lawrence?

(Denise enters.)

Christiane: (Going to greet her.) You look awful.

Denise: (In a somber tone.) It doesn't matter.

Lawrence: I believe you want to speak with Christiane. I'll leave you two together. (He goes out.)

Christiane: Have you seen a doctor?

Denise: It's not a medical problem. Your prediction was wrong. Bertrand is going to marry that de Brucourt girl. And that's not all…

Christiane:	(Looking at her.) Why, Denise, your pupils are dilated...you haven't...?
Denise:	Yes, I tried to, but failed as in everything else.

(She looks around her.)

Christiane:	(With tenderness.) You know I really don't blame you.
Denise:	Thanks. But that's not enough...
Christiane:	For what?
Denise:	To keep going. This time I think I've had it.
Christiane:	You scare me.
Denise:	Oh, it's only talk. Max said that I scared him, too.
Christiane:	You see each other?
Denise:	Occasionally a friendly visit. He's not mean.
Christiane:	Of course not.
Denise:	And besides, not everybody can be nasty. You and I can't be. Perhaps that's why the others are beginning to show some consideration.
Christiane:	Who are you talking about?
Denise:	People from Eastern Europe. Oh you, you can't understand. You're true to your name.
Christiane:	You're crazy. I don't believe in anything, otherwise...
Denise:	Well? (A silence.) What I wanted to ask you...oh, perhaps it's indiscreet, but I can't get it off my mind...During these past weeks when I was all alone on my favorite island at Les Porquerolles, I thought a lot about you, about our childhood, our youth, and what happened afterward...It may simply be

curiosity, surely it is. But I'd still like to get it straight…That young man you were seeing all winter at Cimiez, Jacques Decroy…didn't he become a priest?

Christiane: A Benedictine monk at the Abbey of Solesmes.

Denise: Didn't you care for him a little, even a lot more than just as a friend. (A short silence.)

Christiane: (With a disinterested air.) He was exceptionally intelligent.

Denise: Of course. That means you don't want to tell me anything.

Christiane: There's nothing to tell.

Denise: So be it.

Christiane: Did you come here to ask me that silly question?

Denise: A chance to see you once more…once more before I go…

Christiane: Where are you going? What's the matter with you that you can't stay put? Henry left for Chile a few weeks ago, but of course he has business interests there…

Denise: As for me, I have no interests anywhere.

Christiane: (Suddenly frightened by this tone.) Listen, Denise…You don't mean…?

Denise: (In an artificial tone.) Why shouldn't I spend the winter in Tunis or Morocco?

Christiane: Oh!

(Gilbert enters.)

Christiane: Gilbert, I thought you were visiting your mother at Saint-Lunaire.

Gilbert:	Let me explain. Some fantastic luck. But I have to make some important decisions, immediately.
Christiane:	What can these state secrets be?
Gilbert:	Well, I showed Demetriopoulos the little play we wrote last winter. He's very interested. So we'll have to elope. You must come with me to Saint-Lunaire where Demetrio is sponging off his family.
Christiane:	What a dreamer; you must be joking.
Gilbert:	We have to strike while the iron is hot. If you ask Demetrio yourself, I'm sure he will say yes.
Christiane:	Will you please excuse me. I promised I'd go over to my father's. He lives close by. Would you be kind enough to wait for me? (To Lawrence, who has just come in.) Would you visit with Gilbert a few minutes while I go next door to Daddy's? Gilbert is just back from Saint-Lunaire with a story of film-making that sounds completely crazy. (To Denise.) Shall we go out together?
Denise:	I have my car. I'll drop you off at your father's.
(They exit.)	
Gilbert:	(Offers a cigar to Lawrence, who refuses it. They sit down.) It seems that I've arrived at a bad time. Am I interrupting something?
Lawrence:	(Flatly.) No, but…actually it's not a very good time.
Gilbert:	I sensed it right away. Is she sick? She looks pale.
Lawrence:	She's not sleeping well these days.
Gilbert:	So? And what about the vacation in the mountains?
Lawrence:	That wasn't so great either. It didn't do her much good.
Gilbert:	I'd thought you'd go away for a while in September,

perhaps to the Italian Lakes or even to Annecy. Last year we went there with my sister, it was so restful. We simply spent our days on the lake.

Lawrence: To tell you the truth, it's hard to picture Christiane canoeing.

Gilbert: I'll say. It would be murderous to rough up her delicate hands…But…you can rent boats with oarsmen. And the climate is so…(timidly) soothing! If, however, she is inclined to do the plays, I beg you, please don't stand in her way…That wouldn't be fair…She's so gifted, she really is exceptional. Anyway, you don't need me to tell you. You know better than I how wonderful she is…Just between the two of us, Demetrio plans…

Lawrence: Go on…

Gilbert: To give her the leading role.

Lawrence: Oh really!

Gilbert: You know people realize more and more that professional actors…well…with professionals there's always something not quite natural…

Lawrence: Is that so?

Gilbert: And that's easy to explain, if you think about it.

Lawrence: Well, I can't say I've really thought about it.

Gilbert: Don't you like the movies?

Lawrence: Once in a while, perhaps a good documentary.

Gilbert: Oh, no, I love films; but documentaries bore me. They make me feel like I'm back in school.

Lawrence: Well, I see our viewpoints differ.

Gilbert: A fantastic fantasy that comes alive without ceasing to be a dream…Nothing but film can create that.

Absolutely nothing. That's certain. That's why Christiane's idea...But she will explain it to you better than I can.

Lawrence:

I'm afraid she won't explain anything to me. She's so preoccupied these days. Her thoughts are miles away, I fear.

Gilbert:

Is she worried about something?

Lawrence:

Isn't everybody?

Gilbert:

About politics, of course, but she doesn't read the newspapers. Fortunately. (A silence.) I feel something's wrong. I should have written. But after my conversation with Demetrio, I was ecstatic...as happy as a child...

Lawrence:

How very nice. Christiane will be pleased when she thinks about that.

Gilbert:

It's too bad she'd need to think about it so much...

Lawrence:

Well, she has other things on her mind right now.

Gilbert:

I'd like her to be free from worry, from everything that makes her sad...When she laughs, it's wonderful. But that seems to happen less and less. Tell me, has she made up with Denise Furstlin? I'd heard they had quarreled.

Lawrence:

You know Christiane's relationships are always hard to follow. I just don't have the time to try and keep up with them.

Gilbert:

But she is such a faithful friend. Once in a while her head gets turned by some newcomer but she gets back on track very fast. She has such good judgment.

Lawrence:

I dare say it must be very consoling for her to know she's appreciated so much.

Gilbert: I just don't know what would happen to us without her. It's as simple as that.

Lawrence: Who exactly is in your little group?

Gilbert: Henry, Bertrand, myself, Sabine Verdon, Alice Wertheimer…

Lawrence: Is Monsieur Antonov part of it?

Gilbert: Oh no…I just can't stand that odd ball…He is so indiscreet, so full of himself…

Lawrence: Well…that might be a case where Christiane's judgment fails her.

Gilbert: You're wrong there…just the other night she really made fun of him, and right in front of me. Of course, she does admire his music, that's not the problem…

Lawrence: Oh, really?

Gilbert: But she can't stand him. I assure you. You can believe me. (Lawrence does not answer; under the weight of this silence:) Did you by any chance imagine?…

Lawrence: I imagine nothing.

Gilbert: You'd be barking up the wrong tree.

Lawrence: Let me point out that I have no special reason to believe you.

Gilbert: Am I to understand that somebody else?…

Lawrence: Christiane herself.

Gilbert: (Flabbergasted.) What are you talking about?

Lawrence: (Very dryly.) This subject is extremely painful to me. So let's drop it.

Gilbert:	That's impossible. He is exactly the kind of man she can't stand. Nor can any other woman, I imagine. Let's face it, he is ridiculous.
Lawrence:	Do you think no woman could love that kind of a man?
Gilbert:	Love!…Well, there are some creatures who want to be walked over…but not Christiane…
Lawrence:	Don't you think a woman who has had too much admiration may be fed up with it to the point that she craves a man who is hard, heartless, even cruel…
Gilbert:	How can that be?
Lawrence:	Not only do I think that; I know it for a fact.
(Julie enters.)	
Julie:	Monsieur Antonov would like to know if Madame is home.
Antonov:	(Entering without waiting for an answer.) Madame is not here?
Lawrence:	My wife is out. But we thought you were in Switzerland.
Antonov:	I just landed and have to go back tonight. I got terrible news.
Lawrence:	Madame Antonov.
Antonov:	She does not exist.
Lawrence:	(Dumbfounded.) How's that?
Antonov:	A long time ago we went to see the pope but there was no…how do you say this here…there was no marriage license. I am going to marry Madame Morgenthaler in a few days on the bank of a Swiss lake. Ida believes in lakes. I don't like them. There are mosquitoes, and one hears…*Die Lustige Witwe*

	or something like that. But we have to be ready to make concessions, don't we?
Lawrence:	What about Madame Natalia?
Antonov:	One of my friends, who is almost six feet tall, was supposed to take her to Brussels. He told her that her mother had just arrived there. I think she didn't believe him. While he was buying the tickets at the station she disappeared. He telegrammed the news.
Lawrence:	What happened to her?
Antonov:	Who knows?
Lawrence:	That's terrible. We must call the police.
Antonov:	If I were a believer, I would light a candle to be sure I'll never hear from her again. But our apartment is locked up. The doorman's son told me he saw smoke. What if she burnt my music…I beg you, does Madame have another key?
Lawrence:	The doorman's wife has a key…
Antonov:	But she is at her mother's in the country. How come they all have mothers?
Lawrence:	She shouldn't have taken the keys with her.
Antonov:	Her son is stupid. He says he doesn't know.
Lawrence:	You judge rashly. This young man has a scholarship. He may one day be president.
Antonov:	If you don't have another set of keys we'll have to get a locksmith. (Pointing to Gilbert.) Maybe this gentleman will take care of that?
Gilbert:	Sorry. I don't know any lock pickers.

(Antonov wrings his hands.)

Antonov: I was wrong. I must find Natalia and get the keys…but there isn't time.

(Natalia enters.)

Antonov: (Leaps towards her, yelling.) The key…

Natalia: Don't you touch me.

Antonov: The key.

Natalia: I don't have it anymore…

Antonov: My music.

Natalia: (Calmly.) The choice is yours. If you marry that cow, you will never see your sheet music again. Torture is not allowed in this country, so no one can make me tell where I have hidden them. I will only say that they are in a very damp place…(Screams from Antonov.) And the paper they use for sheet music now is not like it was before the war. Humidity will ruin it.

Antonov: (To the two men.) It's unthinkable that in a civilized country something like this can happen. The rocks should cry out…

Gilbert: My dear sir, the rocks have seen worse in other countries, civilized or not.

Lawrence: In any event, we can't help you. So please take this pathetic discussion elsewhere.

Natalia: I will not stay with him alone.

Lawrence: Madame. Ask the policeman on the corner to protect you. He's big and strong.

Antonov: Sir, you forget the sacred dignity of art and the unalienable rights of artists.

Lawrence: You're out of date, sir. I wouldn't have thought you'd be such a reactionary.

Natalia: (Viciously.) A counterrevolutionary! They don't write
                    the life stories of reactionaries. And they don't put
                    historic markers on their houses either.

(They leave.)

Gilbert: How can you, even for a moment, think that this
                    clown…

Lawrence: I agree with you that if Christiane had seen him just
                    now…however, I'm still not sure. A few chords
                    played dramatically might have impressed her again.

Gilbert: Nonsense.

Lawrence: Monsieur Desclaux, do you ever go to exhibitions
                    of paintings? Do you force yourself to admire these
                    hollow women, painted both full face and profile at
                    the same time? Some people like that kind of art.
                    To call it "snobbism" explains nothing, believe me.
                    We are witnessing a radical transmutation…A dis-
                    traught society is experiencing a total disintegration
                    of humanity. This is more dangerous than commu-
                    nism, or are they related? I wonder.

Gilbert: An exhibition, a concert, that's something else.

Lawrence: No, it's the same thing. There is something sexual
                    in all this. (With a kind of fierce fervor.) Basely
                    sexual.

Gilbert: There cannot be anything base in Christiane's world.
                    May I ask her about it?

(Christiane enters.)

Lawrence: (Coldly.) How could I prevent you? (To Christiane.)
                    You just missed a comic interlude, Christiane. Your
                    friend will tell you all about it. I'll leave you now. I
                    know you have serious business to discuss. (He goes
                    out.)

Christiane: You look completely deflated, my dear Gilbert.
                    What's happened?

Gilbert:	Antonov.
Christiane:	What about him?
Gilbert:	Your husband told me…No, I can't…
Christiane:	Why don't you tell me instead what Demetrio said?
Gilbert:	You are changing the subject.
Christiane:	Me, changing…?
Gilbert:	So it is true?
Christiane:	What's true?
Gilbert:	Your husband thinks that this big ape attracts you. He's obsessed with the idea…The proof is, he even confided in me!
Christiane:	(To herself.) That's despicable!
Gilbert:	He says that you told him yourself…Christiane, is it true?
Christiane:	(After a while.) I am not sure I understand your question.
Gilbert:	Did you really admit it?
Christiane:	Lawrence cannot lie.
Gilbert:	So?
Christiane:	Yes.
Gilbert:	And was it…?
Christiane:	I don't have to tell you anything more.
Gilbert:	(His face contorted.) It's horrible…How could this barbarian, with no class, no nobility, no beauty…he attracts you…? No, I can't believe it.

Christiane: (Weakly.) How can you imagine what goes on in…a woman's mind?

Gilbert: Then you agree it's some kind of mental fixation…at least your heart isn't…no, I can't accept even that…I just can't believe it.

Christiane: Believe whatever you like, Gilbert dear.

Gilbert: But, first, why did you tell him?

Christiane: We always try to be honest with each other.

Gilbert: But there have been so many things you never told him about…I've noticed that countless times.

Christiane: Just trifles or mere details.

Gilbert: That's not so. Even as we speak, I feel you are uneasy, embarrassed…look at me. Why do you turn away? Now, I am going to tell you the truth.

Christiane: (Instinctively.) No!

Gilbert: What are you so afraid of?

Christiane: You, you have no right to question me. I'm not accountable to you. What happens between my husband and me…It's not your business. Just think… just think about it, you are too much.

Gilbert: (Deeply.) No, it's because I love you.

(A silence.)

Christiane: Gilbert, it's I who lied…yes, I lied to my husband. I feel the same way about Antonov as you do. He means nothing to me. He could disappear tomorrow and I would not give it another thought.

Gilbert: So what is this all about?

Christiane: I swear to you what I just said is the truth. But the rest…I can't explain it to you.

Gilbert: I beg your pardon, but…

Christiane: You don't believe me?

Gilbert: (Humbly.) If you lied to him, how do I know you
                are not lying to me now…Just a while ago you told
                me you never lied to him, now you tell me you
                did…It's too much… I can't believe you anymore.

Christiane: (Very moved.) My dearest Gilbert!

Gilbert: What reason can there be…Christiane, explain to
                me! First of all your husband, I don't understand
                him at all.

Christiane: No.

Gilbert: Just now when you came in, his face suddenly be-
                came so hard, so strange…

Christiane: You're mistaken.

Gilbert: Maybe he is in pain…I don't know…but if he is
                suffering, he seems to take pleasure in it.

Christiane: That's crazy.

Gilbert: I feel that everything that happens is his fault.

Christiane: (Abruptly.) That's not true. Just think for a mo-
                ment…

Gilbert: Just your way of denying it…

Christiane: I cannot allow you to accuse Lawrence.

Gilbert: I'm not accusing him. What could I accuse him of?

Christiane: No one can reproach him for anything except…a
                lack of self-confidence.

Gilbert: And that's why you lied to him?

Christiane: It's not hard to guess, just think for a minute…

Gilbert:	(Pounding his forehead.) Oh! Was it to put him on the wrong track…in case he was suspicious?
Christiane:	Yes.
Gilbert:	Then?…
Christiane:	It was very selfish of me…It would have been terrible if he had suspected the truth.
Gilbert:	The truth!
Christiane:	Yes, you understand, he could have…
Gilbert:	Christiane! If you tell me this truth, will it leave me without hope? (Christiane is frightened by Gilbert's anguish. She pauses a minute, in silence; then as if hypnotized, yielding to a new compulsion, she raises her head and stares at Gilbert.) No?… Go ahead, tell me the truth…But Christiane… Christiane… Am I to believe? (full of hope) Dare I hope? (bitterly) Now you are deceiving me…it's not possible.

(Lawrence enters.)

Lawrence:	(Enters quietly. To Christiane.) The mail just came. There's a letter from Claude.
Christiane:	Oh!
Lawrence:	Terribly scribbled as usual, with a big ink spot on it. They should have made him rewrite it neatly.
Christiane:	I don't think they read his letters.
Lawrence:	There's also a death notice. I wonder if it wasn't sent to us by mistake. Some Benedictine monk, a Dom Maurice. Does that sound like anyone you know? Died July 16th, age 33, at the monastery of Solesmes.
Christiane:	(Painfully.) It must be someone I knew years ago. At a time when he wasn't thinking of entering religious life.

Lawrence: (With a certain irony to Gilbert.) Are your projects
                       progressing well?

Christiane: (With no emotion.) The scene is set. The climax is
                       coming.

Lawrence: I'll leave you then. (He goes out.)

Christiane: (In an outburst to Gilbert.) Gilbert dearest,
                       don't abandon me.

ACT FOUR
The same setting. Four months later.

(Christiane, Henry, Gilbert)

Henry: And what is Max going to do with the child?

Christiane: He'll send him to boarding school.

Henry: Does everybody know that Denise...?

Christiane: No...They were discreet...spoke of a stroke. So they all convinced themselves they knew she'd always had high blood pressure.

Henry: And Bertrand, how did he take it?

Christiane: Hard to say. He left for Egypt with his new wife.

Henry: As for Max, I suppose...

Christiane: Max, he's a survivor.

Gilbert: Why did you look at me when you said that?

Christiane: Not so, I assure you.

Gilbert: Am I not "a survivor"?

Christiane: Not yet, but who knows?...Anyway, don't torture yourself. There's not much chance.

Gilbert: For what?

Christiane: That any woman would overdose for you.

Gilbert: (Ironically) That's consoling!

Henry: Poor Denise...I can see her slouched in that armchair, you remember, the night of the surprise party...yes, that's how I always picture that night last April...Still, who will miss her, poor thing? Did she kill herself because she thought no one cared?

	Or did she do it because she hoped someone would care?
Christiane:	Probably for both reasons.
Henry:	That's logical. (Gesture from Christiane.) This whole affair is rather atrocious.
Christiane:	For six weeks it has left me with feelings of oppression that are just beginning to go away…Especially since I should have known…It's as though I hadn't wanted to…Please don't dwell on the subject. Those feelings might come back…
Henry:	Since I never got the letter you sent to Valparaiso… it's only now that those feelings hit me…Poor Denise!
Christiane:	They say one doesn't suffer…in a way…it's wonderful.
Henry:	But afterwards…if there is an afterwards?
Gilbert:	Heavens! What are you getting at?
Christiane:	(To Henry.) Sometimes I wonder, since murder haunts the heart of a murderer…and suicide is murder too, maybe its victim is likewise haunted…
Gilbert:	How awful!
Christiane:	Don't think about such things, my dear. (Henry shivers.) I'd be happy if they never crossed your mind.
Gilbert:	Don't worry.
Christiane:	What amazes me, Henry, is that you…It must be marvelous not to have any imagination.
Gilbert:	Are you talking about me? And my scenarios…?
Christiane:	Yes! You fabricate scenarios, we understand and live them.

Henry:	Now it's my turn to be intrigued.
Christiane:	No need to be.
Gilbert:	With all that you still haven't told me where we're to meet tomorrow evening.
Christiane:	Oh, that's right…Let's see, I'll be at Marie Louise's until 7:30 p.m.
Gilbert:	That's fine.
Christiane:	Will you be prompt?
Gilbert:	Probably more so than you.
Christiane:	The other day I would have waited for you if you'd been late.
Gilbert:	But I explained to you.
Christiane:	I was only teasing. Bye bye. (Clearly Gilbert cannot leave.) You will be late for your fitting.
Gilbert:	If you knew how boring these fittings are.
Christiane:	But you will look ravishing in that outfit.
Gilbert:	On top of everything else, you are making fun of me.
Christiane:	I never make fun of you.
Gilbert:	Maybe when the day's over I'll meet you at Madame Clain's.
Christiane:	You know Lawrence will be with me.
Gilbert:	Your husband makes social calls?
Christiane:	His boss's wife.
Gilbert:	Fine! See you tomorrow.

| Christiane: | That's right, seven-thirty at Marie Louise's. (He goes out.) |

(A silence.)

| Christiane: | Now tell me more. |

| Henry: | I've told the story so many times, I've lost touch with the event. |

| Christiane: | How very sad. |

(Silence.)

| Henry: | I can't understand why she killed herself. You were friends and on good terms again, weren't you? |

| Christiane: | Yes, after we came back from Switzerland. At least I thought we were. |

| Henry: | But Bertrand wasn't interested anymore. |

| Christiane: | That makes sense, since he was engaged… |

| Henry: | In the end, she might have done what was best. |

| Christiane: | Your trip did not make you any more cheerful. |

| Henry: | I agree that after what I've seen I'm not cheerful. |

| Christiane: | I know coffee rots on the docks in Rio de Janeiro, and wheat is used to fuel locomotives, while people starve in Russia and China. |

| Henry: | (Ironically.) You are very well informed. |

| Christiane: | It's not necessary to go around the world to know what's happening. |

| Henry: | You are strange…Are you happy or desperate? |

| Christiane: | Depends on the day. |

| Henry: | On the whole? |

Christiane:	Rather happy…yes, happy.
Henry:	In this famous letter which I did not receive but which you sent me care of general delivery at Valparaiso, did you tell me also the latest about you and Gilbert…
Christiane:	Well, finish your sentence.
Henry:	And what has happened.
Christiane:	What?
Henry:	No, I guess not, those are things one doesn't write about.
Christiane:	What happening, Henry?
Henry:	After all I had wished for it to happen…at least I thought… I wished it…(A silence.) And you don't even bother to lie about it.
Christiane:	No. I wouldn't lie to you. There's no reason…life is difficult enough. Maybe I should have…Do you hold it against me too?
Henry:	I don't hold anything against you. I'm just aware that I am very unhappy. It's stupid.
Christiane:	Henry!
Henry:	Yes, I probably did not see clearly what was happening to me.
Christiane:	We never can, it's impossible.
Henry:	What?
Christiane:	Lucidity. And if it ever existed, it would be a curse.
Henry:	How can you say that, you of all people?
Christiane:	If you only knew…

Henry: (Painfully.) Well, I don't think I want to know. What I understand is plenty.

Christiane: Still, I must tell you someday…Oh! not now…the beginning of this story is still too painful for me.

Henry: Is it really a story?

Christiane: All that I can say today is that one day I made Gilbert believe that I loved him…when it was not yet true.

Henry: Why?

Christiane: Then a mysterious thing happened. The flame that my declaration aroused in him became too much for me and I was drawn into it. It caught hold of me like fire, touching me, enveloping me, inflaming me from within.

Henry: You say that so sadly…

Christiane: Because it's something my conscience has not yet accepted. When I am with you, for instance, I try to explain it that way but I'm not convinced. But when I am with him then it's different. Those are the true times, I am sure.

Henry: That's terrible.

Christiane: No, it is…it will be wonderful.

Henry: When will it be wonderful?

Christiane: When we will have gone away together forever…

Julie: Madame, Monsieur Antonov is here.

Christiane: Show him in.

Henry: Do you still see that boor?

Christiane: He has married Madame Morgenthaler.

Henry: Come on now!

(Antonov enters.)

Christiane: (Giving him her hand.) Well, you're back already?
                    You know my friend, Monsieur Braunfels.

Antonov: I think I know, I have no memory…Oh! Yes, I know
                    now. (They shake hands.) We left Capri, Madame,
                    what an ordeal! It was terrible.

Christiane: Capri, terrible?

Antonov: Oh, the temperature was pleasant, all right. But the
                    landscape! It was like walking through an album of
                    post cards.

Henry: It's Capri's fault.

Antonov: One can't compose music there. It's too much.
                    "Dolce Napoli," "Sancta Lucia," it drove me mad.

Christiane: It wouldn't be the first time.

Antonov: (Bristling.) Certainly, Madame, a musician's nervous
                    system is very fragile, you must admit.

Christiane: You sent me a card from Venice.

Antonov: There I felt like I was walking in a pastry shop.

Christiane: What a thought!

Antonov: I saw an airplane factory somewhere. I didn't visit
                    it, but I saw it. I did admire that.

Henry: You must get along very well with futurists.

Antonov: Monsieur, you are insulting me.

Henry: (He gets up.) Good-bye, Christiane. See you soon?

Christiane: Soon? Yes, certainly. I won't show you out. (He goes
                    out after having bowed to Antonov.)

Antonov:	Madame, it's not working. Perhaps I made a false step. Yes, that's probable, I made a mistake.
Christiane:	Which one?
Antonov:	I'll give you just one detail…Ida won't give me a checkbook. What an embarrasing situation for an artist.
Christiane:	Well, what do you expect? She doesn't trust you…At least two of her former husbands were indicted for financial misconduct.
Antonov:	(With disdain.) Probably bankers.
Christiane:	One was a journalist, the other a theater director.
Antonov:	What theater?
Christiane:	The Folies something or other…
Antonov:	These Folies are a hard act to follow… Besides, she didn't tell me. There is a rabbi in her family. He built a fence because I wrote *Pogrom*.
Christiane:	What do you mean he built a fence?
Antonov:	He became distant and formal.
Christiane:	Oh, you mean he took offense.
Antonov:	Never mind. That's not important. Ida says now that if I don't change the title she will not pay for the choirs. That's blackmail. What am I going to do, now tell me?
Christiane:	Does the rabbi's opinion matter so much?
Antonov:	(Mysteriously.) I'll let you in on a secret. Ida has heart problems. Sometimes she has shortness of breath.
Christiane:	So what?
Antonov:	They say Jews don't believe in immortal life. That's

not so. Ida is afraid of going to a bad place in her afterlife. She gives a lot of money to Jewish humanitarian organizations. And you know she's not all that rich! It's unreasonable.

Christiane: Dear Antonov, why do you always confide in me? You ask me to come to your rescue every time you're in trouble. You know that touches me very much.

Antonov: I thought you might talk to Ida. She admires you, she is even a little jealous of you, which is not a bad thing.

Christiane: Jealous?

Antonov: I have been your tenant and she wonders…

Christiane: How awful!

Antonov: (Hurt.) How so?

Christiane: What about Natalia?

Antonov: I haven't heard from her. Maybe she can't afford a postage stamp. It is sad but satisfying nonetheless. Ida takes care of the children. You asked me a question that I have been wondering about myself. You are an attractive lady. I think I am attracted. If I were still living in your apartment, it could be trouble. Perhaps I think so much of you I could not work. But now we live far apart, which makes things easier.

Christiane: Listen…This has nothing to do with what we were just talking about…but it is funny. Do you know how one of my friends described his reaction to hearing your *Études for Orchestra* performed at the Champs-Élysées Theater?

Antonov: (Worried.) What is it?

Christiane: It sounded like old cleaning ladies viciously beating their faded old carpets making filthy dust fly in all directions.

Antonov: (Furious.) Why old carpets? Why faded? Why filthy? It has to be a deadly enemy who said that. Tell me his name. You have to…

Christiane: No, no, no.

Antonov: Maybe it's yourself. Anyway, it's horrible. I cannot sleep if I do not know who said that.

Christiane: Calm down.

Antonov: And to think I was going to dedevote my jazz symphony to you!

Christiane: Just a tip, we say dedicate, not dedevote.

Antonov: Now I may not be able to write a note for two weeks.

Christiane: So, sue me for damages. (To Lawrence, who comes in.) Lawrence, would you kindly show Monsieur Antonov out.

Antonov: It is not necessary… What an ordeal! I never knew.

(He goes out.)

Christiane: (With a sigh of relief.) Oh darling…! What a good riddance. I could see a proposal coming. Can you believe it?

Lawrence: (Flabbergasted.) What else?

Christiane: Didn't you notice? He has gotten even homelier. One of the ugliest puppets whose strings I've ever pulled.

Lawrence: He should have had the decency never to show his face in this house again.

Christiane: Decency…from him?

Lawrence: I know. But…what did he tell you?

Christiane: The news is, he finds me attractive. Even to the point, that it could be dangerous for his work if we lived close by. That remark just clinched my decision to get rid of him. He's finished.

Lawrence: I don't follow your reasoning.

Christiane: It's very simple. I can't stand him, that's all there is to it.

Lawrence: Are you that bitter?

Christiane: Me? Oh no, believe me, I wouldn't give him that satisfaction.

Lawrence: You are an enigma. When I recall…

Christiane: It is wiser not to remember anything.

Lawrence: Easier said than done.

Christiane: Practice makes perfect. (A silence.)

Lawrence: I just looked at Claude's most recent letters. They're disgraceful.

Christiane: He's only eleven. His grammar mistakes are no tragedy. There are so many worse things that could happen.

Lawrence: I don't see anything happening.

Christiane: That's because you're not very perceptive.

Julie: There's a lady asking to see Madame. (She gives Christiane a calling card.)

Christiane: (Trying to conceal a shiver.) Thank you.

Lawrence: Who is it?

Christiane: She says she needs me to give her some information?

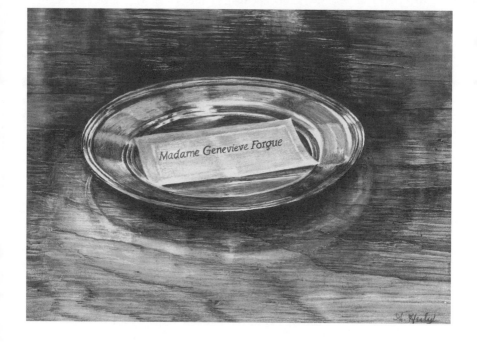

Julie: I don't know, Madame.

Christiane: Oh yes, now I know what it's about. Genevieve Forgue's husband has the same sickness that was my mother's last illness; I imagine she has come to ask me what I think of the specialist who treated her. She wrote me about it.

Lawrence: Forgue? What family is that? Where are they from?

Christiane: They are from Nice…We saw a lot of them when we had our villa at Cimiez. You may show the lady in, Julie. Please leave us alone, this will no doubt be very painful for her…

Lawrence: After that we'll go to Madame Clain's, as we've planned.

Christiane: (Nervous.) Yes, I think so. (Genevieve comes in, escorted by Julie.) My husband, Madame Forgue. (Lawrence leaves after having bowed to them.)

Genevieve: I just stopped by. I hope I am not disturbing you.

Christiane: Not at all…It's very moving to see you again after all these years…you haven't changed much at all.

Genevieve: It's very moving for me too, Christiane.

Christiane: How is your husband?

Genevieve: About the same.

Christiane: Is he bedridden?

Genevieve: Yes. It was very difficult to bring him here.

Christiane: Did you come to see a doctor?

Genevieve: Once again.

Christiane: What do the doctors say?

Genevieve:	They are not sure of their diagnosis. In any case, they don't give me much hope. Chances are he will be permanently paralyzed.
Christiane:	That's terrible! Does he know?
Genevieve:	He doesn't accept it. He cannot…A man like him just can't cope with that…
Christiane:	I only saw him the day of your wedding, but I can imagine…so strong, so active. It's too hard to accept. (A silence. With a different voice.) I thank you for answering my letter so quickly, especially when my letter to you was so late. It was August when I received the announcement. For weeks I didn't have the courage.
Genevieve:	Yes.
Christiane:	Even in my letter I couldn't say anything. Maybe you thought…
Genevieve:	No, I understood. There was a…a silence between the sentences that did not escape me.
Christiane:	Is that true?
Genevieve:	Have you ever thought of going to Solesmes, now that…
Christiane:	No, never…I'm a nonbeliever.
Genevieve:	Who knows, really?
Christiane:	Yes, who knows? I have asked myself that same question…But if you knew my life!
Genevieve:	Do you accept it?
Christiane:	(Dumbfounded.) What do you mean?
Genevieve:	Your life, do you accept your life?

Christiane:	(Half-whispering.) I'd say rather that I put up with it. It's very like me, in that respect. But now, tell me about your brother, Genevieve…For me…
Genevieve:	(As gently as possible.) I know.
Christiane:	What do you mean?
Genevieve:	I have always known. Yes, when you were together at Cimiez, you were different from the others. Yes, you were different…I can't explain it…Silent, as though you were overwhelmed.
Christiane:	(Very softly.) Overwhelmed…you are so right.
Genevieve:	When I saw you the day before he told you he was going to become a Benedictine, and then I met you again the day after you heard the news, I no longer had any doubts. You didn't have to tell me. Those two images remain fixed in my memory. One was the picture of joy, of trust…the other…
Christiane:	So you…you're the only one!
Genevieve:	Your parents, your friends didn't suspect anything!
Christiane:	We didn't see many people at Cimiez. Mother probably suspected something. But I fell ill shortly after that. No doubt the sickness was a consequence, but nobody caught on, and I certainly wasn't going to enlighten them. Oh! You just can't imagine…at the very time he told me he wanted to become a monk, I was about to tell him I loved him…Yes, it was a beautiful, such a beautiful love, just as you guessed…It overwhelmed me…That instant traumatized my whole existence. Since…since then, I am no longer myself…I don't even know who I am. (A silence.) I don't know why I told you this secret; I had sworn I would never tell anyone…
Genevieve:	I think I understand that you did what you had to.
Christiane:	It's as if I just destroyed myself. This secret, it gave

	me a kind of strength; now I no longer have it. Oh! It would be better… Genevieve, please, would you leave me alone?
Genevieve:	No, because I have some news for you. It's because you sensed this that you've told me the truth.
Christiane:	I hardly know you…You frighten me… Something in your eyes scares me. You know something that will break me.
Genevieve:	Christiane, my brother knew you loved him.
Christiane:	He knew!
Genevieve:	He knew it later when to understand was no longer dangerous for him, because the time to hesitate was over…he could no longer be tempted.
Christiane:	Why do you call it temptation? We could have been so happy. (She bursts into tears.) I can't understand why all this was sacrificed…I don't want to…I cannot…
Genevieve:	My brother carried your love like his cross during the last months of his life. He offered it….
Christiane:	That's impossible…How could he suddenly see, after having been so blind…I was going to say: while he was alive?
Genevieve:	We'll never know. But I can tell you that as of a certain date, yes, a very precise day, in the notes he wrote each morning, which he had neither the time nor the will to destroy, he indicates deep concern about you…I have the feeling it began after a dream he'd had…
Christiane:	(With a kind of hope.) When was it? Maybe if we can find a…a coincidence.
Genevieve:	Quite an ordinary dream, I suspect, nothing exceptional like a vision or anything like that. Christiane, you have to understand that the dream didn't trouble

him, but it was as if it awakened in him…how can I say it…a sense of a mysterious responsibility toward you…yes, a kind of spiritual fatherhood. At some point he realized that the same act by which he gave himself to God might have meant despair for you…who knows, even perdition. That just mustn't be. So from that moment, he prayed fervently that light would come to you…

Christiane: (Passionately.) I hate all that…

Genevieve: Christiane, don't you feel that a part of you, maybe the most precious, perhaps the only precious…

Christiane: (Ironically.) My soul.

Genevieve: That's right, your soul. Was it ever present in your life?

Christiane: (In spite of herself.) No, not my soul, a mere caricature of my soul. A false charity that only inspired lies. A fake love that was maybe…(A silence.) It's as if a sudden light has come upon me but I cannot yet see it. Genevieve, are such things real? (She looks at her pleadingly.) You are like everybody else, like everybody I meet, your face tells me nothing; only that look…the one that frightens me. I remember, in the old days we thought you were kind of slow and had too much patience, as if you didn't feel anything. You didn't get our jokes. That always annoyed me, but Jacques would only laugh when I told him…And then when I learned Jacques' plans…I couldn't stand you because you did not look sad. And then your marriage. Everybody said: Genevieve is marrying a playboy. That too seemed…but we never really understand, we never really know someone…And now it's you who hand me this burning torch, this truth which could kill, and with which I must live. Who sent you, Genevieve? Tell me, who?

Genevieve: (Softly but with deep seriousness.) The mere fact that you are asking, Christiane…Would poor Denise Furstlin have ever asked that question?

Christiane:	Why are you bringing up Denise?
Genevieve:	I learned about her suicide a few days ago, just by chance. And although I can't explain why, that news prompted me to come here to tell you what you just learned. Before that I hesitated. I was not sure I should tell you.
Christiane:	So that's the connection.
Genevieve:	The truth is a connection, too.
Christiane:	(Bitterly.) You are too sure of it. Everything is simple for you, I know. We don't live on the same earth. The world I live in is a broken world...
Genevieve:	Maybe, but it hasn't captured your soul! You just said...Sadly, I am not any stronger than you, believe me. If you only knew...(In a whisper.) I can't stand the prospect of the months and years ahead for my husband and me. I almost told my husband the truth about his health, because I was sure he would kill himself and that would have been a big relief. Yes, I thought of it.
Christiane:	And so?
Genevieve:	I prayed, oh! without fervor, just routinely... The temptation faded. But I'm sure it'll come back, I know it will...Christiane, you must pray for me.
Christiane:	Pray?
Genevieve:	You have a patron now.
Christiane:	Genevieve, does he see me?
Genevieve:	He sees you, and right now you know it. (The two women hug each other in silence.)
Lawrence:	(Coming in.) I am sorry, but if you really want to go with me...

Genevieve: I've stayed too long, forgive me.

Christiane: (With a deep seriousness.) Genevieve, I'll try to do what you want.

Genevieve: (With simplicity.) Thank you.

(Christiane goes out with her for a minute; Lawrence paces nervously.)

Lawrence: (Annoyed.) What effusiveness!

Christiane: She just gave me the greatest gift I could ever receive.

Lawrence: A leather desk set?

Christiane: Not exactly.

Lawrence: Of course not. Are we going to Madame Clain's?

Christiane: I'm very tired all of a sudden.

Lawrence: I thought you would be. All right then, I'll go alone.

Christiane: Please stay here with me.

Lawrence: What?

Christiane: I'll call this evening and express our regrets.

(A silence.)

Lawrence: A while ago, why did you say that I'm not perceptive?

Christiane: Did I upset you?

Lawrence: What were you talking about?

Christiane: (Seriously.) Are you sure you want to know? (A silence.) I'm sorry. The fact is, we are both afraid of the truth. You are afraid to hear it, and I am afraid to tell it. Perhaps that's because telling the truth involves hearing it...

Lawrence: I don't understand. You sound so different, not like your usual self.

Christiane: That's because something happened here, this past half hour. Something unexpected...a kind of miracle.

Lawrence: You really are carried away.

Christiane: I assure you, that word is not too strong! Why look at me so harshly, Lawrence?

Lawrence: I don't trust...miracles...In any case I don't think you'd better tell me anything more about it.

Christiane: Why not?

Lawrence: I don't know what's just happened, but I am afraid I wouldn't appreciate this...gift at its true value, and that might spoil your pleasure in it.

Christiane: It's not a question of my pleasure. You're deceiving yourself...You are terrified. Admit it. Lawrence, you are very weak, and if I hadn't sensed that, I think I never would have married you. But, your biggest fault is that you won't admit your weakness. As if I might take advantage...

Lawrence: I've heard that reproach many times before.

Christiane: But have you ever had the courage to accept it? That, you see, is your worst weakness.

(A silence.)

Lawrence: (Painfully.) You may be right.

Christiane: What came in here just now with that poor woman...was a spirit of truth.

Lawrence: A spirit of truth!

Christiane:	It has moved you too, otherwise you wouldn't have admitted that I might be right. You see, Lawrence…
Lawrence:	Even your voice has changed.
Christiane:	I was never in love with Antonov…
Lawrence:	Christiane!
Christiane:	In fact you are the one who forced me…
Lawrence:	Explain!
Christiane:	Gradually I began to realize that you couldn't bear to see me, what shall I say, so popular, so appreciated. Instead you would rather have seen me humiliated.
Lawrence:	That's not true!
Christiane:	Remember…Oh! I can't explain exactly how I got this impression, but it came to me, as clear as can be and experience proved me right. My plan worked. That's what is so terrible. It succeeded better than I ever would have dreamed.
Lawrence:	I…I pitied you.
Christiane:	Oh no, take a closer look. What you call pity was really your vanity's revenge. So petty you can't even admit it. But, at the same moment, I must confess…I despised you. That kind of pitiful compassion was like a horrible caricature of what I so desperately longed for. And from that day on, I felt so completely alone. There was no recourse possible. Not even in the depth of my own heart. In shaming you, I shamed myself even more… At that precise moment, Gilbert came to tell me once again that he loved me. Countless times before I had resisted his advances in a lighthearted manner, with a joke or a shrug of the shoulders. But suddenly he took on infinite value in my eyes. I needed him. I could no longer resist his advances.

Lawrence:	(With a cry of distress.) Oh, no!…
Christiane:	Not out of love, Lawrence, but out of longing for love.
Lawrence:	Don't say another word. I can't bear it. (A silence.) Do I really deserve this?
Christiane:	All I know is, I deserve what I am suffering right now. I am ashamed not only for myself, but for both of us.
Lawrence:	(Bitterly.) Both of "us," does that exist?
Christiane:	Your fault is my fault; your weakness is my own. My…sin, if that word means anything, you are part of that too.
Lawrence:	"Sin!"…Obviously, her visit…
Christiane:	We are not alone, no one is alone…there is a communion of sinners…just like there is a communion of saints.
Lawrence:	How is all this connected with her visit? What did she want?
Christiane:	(Troubled.) I can't explain it to you…I promise you later on I will.
Lawrence:	Oh, there's still another secret…Well anyway, now…You are free…If you want to make a new life for yourself with that other man…I won't try to stop you.
Christiane:	(Profoundly.) Lawrence, I am your wife.
Lawrence:	I don't know…I don't understand…you betrayed me, and I never ever suspected you.
Christiane:	But along with that confidence I inspired, there was another feeling, wasn't there…a kind of hate?…You sometimes wished I were dead, didn't you…?

Lawrence:　　　　You must understand, if I had lost you...I could have grieved at least. My suffering could have had some expression. Your presence stifled it. And now...

Christiane:　　　(Solemnly.) I swear to you that now I belong only to you. I have been freed... It's like an unbearable nightmare has ended. Now it all depends on you...

Lawrence:　　　　(In a kind of trance.) It's as if you are coming back to me from the dead...

Christiane:　　　(Humbly.) I will try to live up to those words.

Two Drama Critics' Commentaries
on
The Broken World

Henri Gouhier's Critique
in
L'Europe Nouvelle, 20 janvier 1934

and

Marcel Belay's Commentary
in
La Mort dans le théâtre de Gabriel Marcel
Paris: Vrin, 1980

Translated by Katharine Rose Hanley

Henri Gouhier
L'Europe Nouvelle, 20 janvier 1934, pp. 66-67
Le Courrier de Paris. "Le monde cassé" de M. Gabriel Marcel.

"At the heart of these four acts lies a question much deeper than any pragmatism: What does it mean to exist? Gabriel Marcel's response is the most meaningful effort of our time to restore to realism its philosophic merit."

At the heart of *The Broken World* [1] lies, in the most vital sense of the term, an uneasiness. "Don't you have the feeling," asks the heroine of the play, "the impression that we are living...if it can be called living...in a broken world? Yes, broken like a watch that has stopped. The mainspring is gone. To all appearances, nothing has changed. Everything is in place. But if you bring the watch to your ear, and listen...you don't hear anything.... The world, what we call the human world...it must have had a heart at one time; but that heart, it appears, is no longer beating."

The impression of life hovering over a void is what creates the drama; it directs the movement of the four acts and raises them to a balance essentially tragic, if indeed tragedy means the transfiguration of a drama through the intervention of a mysterious power beyond everyday natural events, be it historic destiny, fate, or God.

At center stage are the main protagonists, Christiane and her husband, Lawrence. A very French, very Parisian daughter of a German Israelite, Christiane has an intelligence that is curious, lucid, and penetrating; she loves and understands everything. She has only to yield to her friends' solicitation for them to acclaim her as an intellectual. One wants her to coauthor a novel, another a ballet. Actually, it's the stage that attracts her most and, if she dared, she would make her acting debut, not just on stage but in film. Her behavior is irreproachable, but her conduct is not the consequence of any preordained code. Morality, she says, is a sort of diet each individual must invent on his or her own, without a doctor and without prescriptions. "Normal," she asks herself, "what can that mean?" Still, her intellect adapts more quickly than her heart to the freethinking atmosphere that has become the rule in her circle. She accepts as a matter of fact the sense of emptiness that underlies her life, but she cannot accept it like other facts, because it casts a shadow that no pleasure can dissipate. Christine has married a "maître des Requêtes du Conseil d'Etat," an upper-class gentleman who holds a position of distinction and power, an elite member of the Tribunal that judges the French Government. He is a gentleman of distinction who is isolated between his strictly professional milieu and his wife's milieu, which his entire being refuses with a haughty, ironic violence. Lawrence, it must be noted, does not have a sense of the broken world. He judges the world as decadent, but he is too much outside it to feel its emptiness. He decries a disorder, not a void. Downstage of them, Denise's tragic story unfolds. A childhood friend of Christiane's, she is one of those creatures doomed to fail who, while waiting, parades her lover under her husband's nose. Christiane has communicated the sense of the broken world to her, but she refuses to accept it because she senses its hidden logic; such an idea announces either death or another life. Christiane is a revolting paradox because she looks at life without faltering. Denise knows all too well, after her lover has deserted her, the dizziness that nothingness produces, so she suspects that her friend's uneasiness is somehow strangely shielded from despair. Her suicide is death by the void; all breathable air is withdrawn.

Other characters of similar importance in the play are two of Christiane's admirers, Philippe [Gilbert in the 1950 version] and Henry. Philippe [Gilbert] writes novels and sketches scenarios. His talent is a conscientious imagination. He is a decent, healthy young man with no metaphysical concerns. Henry displays to the world a distinguished intelligence, worthy of the great sights his travels provide. Parisian society gives him the impression not so much of a broken world as one where people want to break something. Besides, it is obvious that if Christiane would only love him, he'd quickly convert to a more settled life.

Further downstage, more distant from the center of the drama, are two gentlemen whose antics cause them to appear as comic figures. These are Christiane's father, whose age has diminished neither his accent nor his vital energy, and Antonov, the great Russian musician who's in vogue, a genial artist who knows that valuable publicity is given to the exotic and eccentric. Stuck with an aging mistress who serves him devotedly, he pursues a better match because a solid fortune would be a good sign of predestination. Finally, in the background, offstage, we find: Biarritz before the crash, the enervating strains of jazz, the snobbism of the Revolution and the new pedagogy; and there are several silhouettes who appear briefly—a tricky psychoanalyst; Dolores, the lesbian; Max, who is gay; Denise's lover, Bertrand, a Don Juan turned gigolo by his morphine addiction.

No doubt all these people have personal lives; thus Bertrand heard the cracking of a breaking world through Christiane's soul; his marriage was an escape, or better yet a refuge. Nevertheless, if Antonov and the others have their dramas, they are not the ones the author has chosen; they figure in the drama as creating a social reality that exists in them by their choice, and that gives rise to a certain dramatic situation.

The drama Gabriel Marcel explores is that of Christiane and her husband. No communion is possible between Lawrence and his young wife; he can neither follow her in a lifestyle that he despises, nor can he participate in her sense of a broken world, since he does not know this world interiorly. Knowing that Christiane has married him without love, his sense of justice and courtesy create a duty for him to leave her absolutely free. There is never any question of a reproach, never any advice, never a request. Now, Christiane has a profound sense of the seriousness of human responsibilities; she is a spouse and a mother. Even without love she cares for this man from whom she expected something—an energy, a firmness of purpose, a friendship, a strength that would perhaps have helped her true personality to emerge.

Is it not possible for Lawrence to recognize his tactical error? But there is more at stake here than tactics. Here it is no longer sufficient to define someone by his social functions; Marcel is not painting a bourgeois gentleman, but Lawrence, a man in whom love and pride are strangely mixed. The hero loves; he knows that to love means to give, but for him giving is an activity that glorifies the giver. Obstinate in his determination to respect Christiane's liberty, he declares that he is ready to help her if she feels too strongly the temptation to slip, if, for example, Antonov…. Such lack of understanding leaves Christiane's wounded soul only a desparate irony. Yes, a diabolical force pushes her toward the grotesque but genial musician. Yes, she humiliated herself to the point of confessing her love for him. Yes, she is miserable because she waits in vain for a response from him….Thereafter Lawrence surrounds her with a compassionate tenderness; he suffers, but with a bitter satisfaction, the savior proud of *his* salvation. His vanity lets the secret slip in front of Philippe [Gilbert], the psychologist who pretends to understand women…. Christiane feels totally alone. Suddenly Philippe's [Gilbert's] simple love, free of pride, takes on in her eyes an infinite value; she will give herself to him.

The sentiment of a broken world doesn't founder in confusion. It has come from too long ago, as the last scenes show, taking us back to the time when Christiane as a young girl loved Jacques Decroy. Was that love recognized by the one who, as a very young man, entered a Benedictine monastery? Still, he had left in Christiane's heart an unrequited longing, and when she listened to the records of music from Solesmes her emotions were more than artistic. Now, at the moment when she's really slipping, the sister of this now holy man comes to tell her that Dom Maurice, shortly before his death, recognized what Jacques Decroy had not seen. His personal journal revealed that he had been troubled by the thought that his own sacrifice might have meant despair and even perdition for another. Until the end of his life he carried that disappointed love as his cross….Hearing this account from a woman whom life had not spared of its harshness, one who knew the cost of sacrifice, Christiane feels the flame of her youthful love rekindled but now sustained, illumined, and oriented by that of this man of God. The deceased, from beyond death, gives her the will and the loving friendship that liberates her authentic being. The sentiment of a broken world was the reverse image of a certitude lived as inward assurance.

Reduced thus to an abstract schema, the broken world might seem like an artificial hell, an easy setting for a conversion. But in the play these are real live men and women; their faces are not masks. Those who pass before our eyes are human beings, their misery is ours. This play, it must be said, deserves to be staged. If a reading gives the impression of a reality richer than any conceptual analysis, an intelligent production would overcome any apparent discontinuities that even the simplest and most nuanced of texts cannot avoid. While awaiting a theatrical production that will give this play its full dramatic power, it is possible to sense its spiritual greatness in the study of the pages that follow *The Broken World* under the title "Concrete Approaches to Investigating the Ontological Mystery."

In publishing both a play and a metaphysical meditation in one volume Gabriel Marcel wanted to affirm the unity of his work and thought. However, to interpret his work in terms of philosophic theater or thesis theater or a forum for ideas would be a radical mistake. Marcel doesn't start with an idea that on the one side he clothes in a dramatic fiction and then on the other side argues philosophically.

Before the theater and before the philosophy, there is the drama; before the author and before the dialectician, there is the person facing reality, experiencing his dramatic condition of being alive, suffering, loving, and dying. At the beginning there is a dramatic situation that can be *represented* or *understood*. The theater and the philosophy are not two demonstrations of the same idea, but rather two transcriptions of one searing reality.

The Broken World can stand on its own independently, but the metaphysical meditation gives it a touching transparency. Through the rupture in her world, Christiane felt pass the breath of despair. Her response of recoiling was not an instinctual fear of death, but rather a desire for life—an exigency for being—that idealist philosophy represses but whose validity Gabriel Marcel has already established in his *Metaphysical Journal*. The play's inspiration is by no means apologetic; its nature is purely ontological. One can discuss the metaphysical solidity of certain attitudes and issues, but not merely dismiss them as artificial means of a Christian dramatist. Underlying the four acts there is the question that goes beyond all pragmatisms: what does it mean "*to exist*"? Marcel's response is one of the most masterful efforts of our time to restore to realism its philosophic value.

If one always situates a problem in front of *oneself*, the problem of being can never be posed, because I can never detach myself from being in order to take my distance from it. Gabriel Marcel calls "mystery" that inability to be reduced to a "*problem.*" However, to say that being is a *mystery* is not a way to close off inquiry or debate; on the contrary, we must explore being where it is, and that is not interior to a concept, nor interior to an intuition—no knowledge can circumscribe being; rather, it is being that holds all knowledge. I attain it when my attention, reflecting back upon itself in recollection, feels its existence stirring to a naked consciousness.

Then a world opens, a world that Gabriel Marcel sketches in an exchange I cannot even evoke. To all those attuned to the spiritual, these pages will bring a witness wherein lucidity becomes a form of generosity; to some, they will show a way.

—Henri Gouhier

---

[1] *Monde cassé*, pièce en 4 actes. Desclée, de Brouwer et Cie., Paris, 1934.

Marcel Belay
La Mort dans le Théâtre de Gabriel Marcel
Paris, Vrin, 1980

Marcel Belay's essay on *The Broken World* was published in *La Mort dans le théâtre de Gabriel Marcel* (*Death in the Theater of Gabriel Marcel*), Paris, Vrin, 1980, pp. 89-96. To begin his essay (pp. 89-90), Belay quotes from Gabriel Marcel's summary presentation of *The Broken World* published in *Théâtre et Philosophie* (*Theater and Philosophy*), (Recherches et Debats) (Research and Debates), Paris, 1952, pp. 36-37. Page references in square brackets allow readers to examine in this book's translation the passages from *The Broken World* that are cited in Marcel's summary and Belay's commentary. [Translator's note.]

Christiane is married to an extremely reserved and correct gentleman, who is not at all communicative, and to whom Christiane's friends pay no attention whatsoever. This Maître des Requêtes au Conseil d'État* is a serious bore, the kind one often prefers to ignore. Christiane realizes that her husband suffers obscurely from this situation, but he has too much pride to admit it, and when she tries to get close to him, when she admits that she is ready to make this or that small sacrifice for him, he withdraws. He does not want charity. Is he jealous? She never has given him cause for jealousy; she is faithful to him. Still, she will discover that this jealousy is rooted in a self-love that has been deeply wounded. Her brilliance, her successes, overshadow him precisely because he goes unnoticed everywhere. What remedy will cure this shameful sickness of the soul? Christiane, enlightened by a friend, leads him to believe that she is infatuated with a man who rejects her, an extremely egocentric and crude Russian musician. As soon as Lawrence feels that his wife is humiliated and miserable, it's as if his soul can breathe again. Christiane, in lying, gives him an artificial lung. It is with a feeling of horror that she sees the success of this strange therapy. But, in the long run, such a lie can only bear bitter fruits. Disgusted with her husband and with herself, Christiane falls into the arms of an attractive but shallow young man who has loved her for a long time. She gives herself to him without love, out of nostalgia for love. This also is not done in truth. Yet it is later, when she is perhaps on the verge of sinking irreparably into sin, that she receives a revelation.

---

* Lawrence Chesnay is the official who determines the agenda of the Tribunal that judges the government of France. In most countries outside of France, there is no exact equivalent to the Conseil d'État or its Maître des Requêtes.

Evidently Christiane sought to distract herself, to forget. This is because, before she married Lawrence, she was passionately in love with a young man who, at the very moment when she was going to tell him of her love, announced to her that he was entering a monastery, that he was going to become a Benedictine monk. This remained an open wound for her. Christiane married Lawrence as one drowns, without hope, without love, with only a sort of pity that she now judges unjustifiable; pity can become a temptation. And now, just at the moment when she's ready to run away with her lover, she receives a totally unexpected visit. Her visitor is none other than the sister of the Benedictine, of whose death she had heard several months earlier. That news left her feeling desperate and helped to precipitate her downfall, just as the announcement that he was joining the Benedictines had determined her marriage. What is Jacques' sister, this Genevieve whom everyone used to find so boring and whom Christiane hasn't seen for fifteen years, coming to tell her? It appears from some notes that were found in Jacques' monastery cell after his death that he had become aware, but only later on, of Christiane's love, perhaps as the result of a dream. It's as if this dream had awakened in his soul the sense of a mysterious responsibility. At a given moment in his life, he saw that the very act by which he had given himself to God had perhaps meant for Christiane despair—who knows, perhaps even perdition. He found this idea intolerable. So from that moment on, he prayed fervently that she in turn might be enlightened. Thus, a mysterious connection revealed itself to Christiane, a connection of which the broken world has lost awareness. She feels herself transported to a level where lying is no longer possible. She confesses to Lawrence that she deceived him after having lied to him out of pity. At first, Lawrence rebels like a child. But then suddenly, if only for an instant, he is overcome by this fire, by this illumination.

> Christiane: I swear to you that now I belong only to you. I have been freed…It's like an unbearable nightmare has ended. Now it all depends on you….
> Lawrence: It's as if you are coming back to me from the dead…
> Christiane: I will try to live up to those words."[BW, IV, p. 152].

> — Gabriel Marcel

Commentary:

This presentation doesn't mention Christiane's friend Denise Furstlin. Yet Denise's drama is of particular interest to us, because it ends in suicide. Contrary to other characters in Marcel's theater, who talk about suicide, Denise actually does take her own life with no warning other than veiled allusions.

What is Denise's situation? She is a victim of the broken world. Married to Max, a débauché with whom she has not been intimate in a long time, she wants a divorce so she can marry her lover Bertrand, a drug addict whose detoxification cure she has financed. Max previously opposed a separation, but no longer objects as he now has his sights set on another woman. But it's Bertrand who becomes more and more distant. Denise finally learns that he has set his sights on an extremely wealthy young woman. Denise tries in vain to win him back. His rejection transforms her life into a nightmare that cocaine and heroin can't end. "She's superfluous like everything else...." So, even the affection she feels for her young son doesn't hold her back. She kills herself to escape an existence that was becoming a desert of solitude [III, p. 114]. Denise's suicide is death by a void; any life-giving air has been withdrawn. "Did she kill herself because she thought no one cared? Or did she do it because she hoped someone would care?" Christiane replies: "Probably for both reasons."[IV, p. 129-30]

Desperation can push one to throw oneself into the arms of death as one cries aloud into the night, both to break the awful silence and to release the pain of knowing that one's cry goes unheard.

Before her disappearance, Denise accused Christiane of having turned Bertrand against her. "The things you say...for instance, the other day when you were talking about the broken world...that kind of sadness that you have no right to feel, much less to complain about...I realize now all this did upset him and it effectively turned him against me..." [II, p. 88]. Bertrand had good reason to be disgusted with the life he was living. He should have wanted to change his situation. So he gave up Denise, who represented this senseless life for him.

But Christiane also seemed to go along with this broken world. Is she so very different from the other women in her group? "...[Y]ou live just like we do, (Denise asserted)...you are no better than any of us..." [II, p. 88]. Apparently, that is the case. She is caught in a whirlwind of frivolous busyness. The phone is always ringing. She's invited to cocktail parties, to shows, to society benefits. Rarely does she refuse anything. She has so many different activities. She is coauthoring a ballet and a play. She's even planning, with her friend Gilbert, a novel in the form of letters in which roles are reversed; she will write the man's letters and Gilbert the woman's. When she goes on vacation to the Riviera, she is immediately surrounded by a flock of admirers.

How to explain, then, that this life, where she goes from one triumph to the next, seems to be fractured, disconnected, dead, and leaves her with a feeling of profound melancholy?

"Don't you have the impression that we are living…if we can call that living…in a broken world? Yes, broken like a watch that has stopped. Its mainspring no longer works. To all appearances nothing has changed. Everything is in place. But if you put the watch to your ear…you hear nothing. Remember, the world, or what we call the world, the human world…used to have a heart. But it seems that heart has stopped beating…Everyone has their own little niche, their own little thing, their own petty interests. People meet, or more accurately, bump into each other. That makes quite a racket. But there's no center, no life, anywhere." [I, pp. 46-47]

Indeed, one day she even confided to her friends, "I may appear to be just like the rest of you, who don't believe in anything…there's someone in me I hardly know, someone who certainly doesn't belong to your group. There is a part of me that is searching and who in rare moments is in touch with herself in another world, one that is foreign to you." [II, pp. 83-84]. Isn't this latter world the one in which transcendence lets itself be felt? In fact, Christiane is not so sure that God doesn't exist. She in no way shares the skepticism and blasé disbelief of her friends.

She discovered this world with the blossoming of her love for Jacques Decroy. For her, his lost love lingers like a haunting melody. Of course she tries to escape it in busy distractions. But all it takes is some unexpected connection—like hearing the Gregorian chant recorded at Solesmes—and her pain sharpens acutely again. This path of suffering leads her toward that mysterious region of herself that is her longing for communion.

So lack of communication with Lawrence becomes unbearable for her. She decides to do everything she can to get closer to him. She suspects that, if he remains withdrawn, always focused on himself, it's because he feels inferior to her. This she sees as a kind of weakness. So, out of a "false charity," she fabricates a lie. She confesses that she is infatuated with Antonov, a coarse sort of man, who has, she claims, humiliated and rejected her. She wants Lawrence to see her as a creature who needs him, his understanding, his support…. Unfortunately, however, hearing this confession, Lawrence cannot hide the triumph of his ego's vanity. He shows Christiane a kind of condescending pity, a repulsive caricature of the genuine love she hoped would bond the two of them.

After this fiasco, Christiane's lot is one of total isolation. Jacques Decroy has just died in his monastery. She had never seen him again, nor had they ever corresponded. Nonetheless, especially in her darkest hours, just to be able to think of him was a sort of *viaticum*…but now, he has gone! No doubt, it was to draw herself back from the dizzying pull of nothingness that she fell into the arms of Gilbert Desclaux, a young man who was constantly professing his love for her. She was fond of him, but she let him believe she was in love with him. "Then," she explained, "a mysterious thing happened. The flame that my declaration aroused in him became too much for me and I was drawn into it." [IV, p. 134]. Why was she "caught up, enveloped, inflamed," if not because in seeing Gilbert passionately transformed, she saw herself, as in other days she had been in Jacques' presence? Probably she let herself believe that soon she would once again experience what she had formerly known. But adultery grieves her conscience and does not satisfy her heart. She must fight off despair, and she is tempted to follow Denise's escape route. "They say one doesn't suffer...in a way...it's wonderful" [IV, p. 130]. But she's not certain that suicide ends everything. "Sometimes I wonder, since murder haunts the heart of the murderer...and suicide is murder too, maybe its victim is likewise haunted...." [IV, p.130]. The pull of death, counterbalanced only by the fear of possible punishment, would that have vanished, if, as planned, she broke off completely from her family and went away with Gilbert?

She does not throw herself into this adventure that would have led to her complete perdition. It is her conversation with Genevieve Forgue that dissuades her from it and completely changes her attitudes. Let us try to understand what she could have experienced.

Christiane has sworn that she would never talk to anyone about the love she felt for Jacques and the despair she experienced when he told her he was going to become a monk. Now she finally yields her secret to Genevieve, but she immediately laments: "It's as if I just destroyed myself. This secret gave me a kind of strength; now I no longer have it" [IV, pp.143-44].

It is no doubt true that what we don't tell anyone remains locked deep within us and is capable of nourishing us. But then, why did Christiane tell her story? She felt obscurely that her guest, too, had something to reveal to her.

Indeed, Genevieve revealed to Christiane the place she held in Jacques' thoughts during the last months of his life. Moved in the depth of her soul, Christiane weeps, evoking what might have been. "We could have been so happy" [IV, p. 144]. And this happiness was sacrificed for the sake of a vocation whose sense remains incomprehensible to Christiane. Learning that Jacques had suffered and prayed so that she too might be enlightened doesn't console her in the least. Instead, it disgusts her. "I hate all that" [IV, p.145].

Still, she doesn't stiffen in an attitude of refusal—because a whole part of herself, "the most precious, the only precious" [IV, p. 145], her soul, is not a stranger to this mysterious world where Jacques' prayer and self-gift make sense. She first enters this world with a question. "[A]re such things real?" [IV, p. 145]. And, suddenly, a light breaks through. Her eyes, at first, cannot look into its brightness. She can only behold its reflection in the radiance of Genevieve's face, shining with a spirit of truth. In contemplating it one can only accept the truth in oneself. Genevieve is there so that Christiane may receive "this burning torch, this truth that could kill and with which [she] must live" [IV, p. 145].

Christiane dares to confront her own misery because Genevieve, her guest, does not dissimulate hers but admits that, faced with the prolonged incurable illness of her husband, her courage has often faltered. Once she even was on the verge of telling him how serious his condition was, knowing that with such news he would kill himself. To overcome this homicidal temptation, she resorted to prayer, simple but persevering prayer. And now she will count on Christiane's prayer, for she has an intercessor very close to God, namely Jacques. Genevieve acknowledges her weakness with humility, while quite simply affirming her faith. Thus Christiane has an insight that weakness and faith together can create indissoluble bonds. "We are not alone," she will soon say to Lawrence, "no one is alone…there is a communion of sinners…there is a communion of saints." [IV, p. 151].

It is a communion from which the dead are not excluded. As a matter of fact, it is they who are its artisans. Christiane asks if Jacques sees her. Genevieve replies: "He sees you, and right now you know it" [IV, p. 146]. Yes. Jacques is there, invisible. And it is in the mystery of this presence that the deep friendship and understanding between these two women is born. The reality of this presence is indistinguishable from the light of truth from which Christiane no longer hides. It is also in this light that Lawrence and Christiane will become reconciled, recognizing that they have been separated by the same sin.

In Lawrence's eyes, Christiane is a new creature. "It's as if you are coming back to me from the dead…" [IV, p. 152]. Perhaps he will one day realize that this regeneration is a grace of God, operating through the intermediary of a loved one from beyond death.

—Marcel Belay

Concrete Approaches to Investigating the
Ontological Mystery

Address Delivered January 21, 1933,
to the
Philosophical Society of Marseilles

by

GABRIEL MARCEL

Translated and with a
Foreword and Notes by
Katharine Rose Hanley

Foreword

In his introduction to the first edition of *The Broken World* and "Concrete Approaches to Investigating the Ontological Mystery," Marcel affirmed that it was a personal question, his own existential search, that he clarified and came to terms with. He formulated his quest, on the one hand, through dramatic imagination in the play *The Broken World*, and on the other hand, through the critical clarification of reflective philosophic inquiry in the essay. Together these two works of entirely different literary genres form the keystone of Marcel's thought.

Etienne Gilson rightly observed that the philosophic essay "Concrete Approaches to Investigating the Ontological Mystery" is to Marcel's work what the *Introduction to Metaphysics* was for that of Henri Bergson. This essay certainly is of central importance, and it can be an ideal introduction to Marcel's philosophy, for it provides readers with a succinct overview of the questions, method, and main themes of his thought.

Yet one should approach this text with balance. Reading this essay is no easy task, but a thoughtful consideration of it can lead to a most gratifying and enlightening experience. It is hoped that some preliminary comments may facilitate readers' appreciation of it.

Let us address some of the text's difficulties, which need not detain all readers. First of all, the author's style, his obvious erudition, and the influence of his immediate audience on the development of the essay may present some difficulty. "Concrete Approaches to Investigating the Ontological Mystery" was addressed to a live audience of professional philosophers. So, even from the very first page, it contains numerous allusions to ideas of various philosophers and their schools or traditions. In some instances, moments of debate or ongoing dialogue occur to challenge or correct positions of thinkers well known to that particular audience. Basically, Marcel's style is to reason in dialogue with others, and he was presenting his newly evolved method of philosophic inquiry to an audience many of whose objections he himself could well anticipate. So he engaged and took seriously the questions and challenges that could come from philosophers of other traditions, particularly the idealism so popular in France, England, and Germany at the end of the nineteenth and the beginning of the twentieth century. Again, these allusions need not detain all readers, but footnotes are supplied to briefly identify the personalities or schools mentioned.

Besides the difficult challenge of Marcel's erudition and his allusions to the immediate philosophic and intellectual culture of his day, there is the challenge he presents by inviting all readers to involve themselves in the process of philosophizing. Marcel's style of reasoning in dialogue form applies not only to professional philosophers, but also appeals to all readers, inviting them to become involved in the process of reflective analysis of experiences so they can critically clarify the meaning and value of their lives in light of their own intelligence and in relation to their own experience. Marcel's style, inviting people to participate actively in the process of philosophizing, presents a demanding challenge, yet if one enters into the process, the reading becomes easier and meaningful dialogue with Marcel's ideas develops into a fascinating and life-enlightening conversation.

As we approach this essay it can be helpful to hear it as if it were a musical composition. Marcel himself was a musician who improvised piano compositions, many of which were preserved through his wife's notation of them. With this in mind, we may listen to this essay as we would to a musical composition. Music, it may be noted, affects us physically, emotionally, mentally, and spiritually. Music resonates at the deepest center of our being. It is also important to note that when we listen to music, memory plays a central and active role. When we hear music we naturally retain and interconnect various notes in our memory so that we hear not just isolated sounds but rather a melody line or a musical phrase. Memory likewise plays an important role in our hearing of a whole composition, a symphony for example, wherein we hear each movement as distinct but nevertheless resonating in relation to the movements preceding or following it. This image can help us anticipate and then enter into the flow of Marcel's essay.

"Concrete Approaches to Investigating the Ontological Mystery" has the architectonic structure of a musical composition in three movements. The first movement, through several concrete approaches, introduces and opens up the question "Who am I? - Is Life (Being) empty or full?" The second movement searches out an appropriate method for investigating this question. It introduces the distinction between the quasi-scientific approach of problem solving and the deeper approach of reflective clarification of mysteries in which the very being of the questioner is involved as that person seeks to discover a meaning and value to life. Then it identifies recollection and reflection as central to the process of clarifying such mysterious dimensions of human life. The third movement is one of vision wherein Marcel clarifies perspectives of insight that emerge in response to ongoing pursuit of the question "Who am I? - Is Life (Being) empty or full?". There we find Marcel's explanation of the essential perspectives of insight that constitute his vision. Readers will recognize such now-familiar themes as authenticity/inauthenticity, presence, fidelity, creativity, hope, despair, I-Thou, suicide, death, and life. Readers will also recognize that the determination of the meaning and value one gives to human life is influenced by one's freedom. So Marcel also examines the fundamental attitudes and predispositions that influence the different choices people make and then the interpretations they give to various aspects of the human situation. In this sense Marcel sees that freedom is the logic of metaphysics. He also recognizes, however, that the meaning of one's life can be created in a dialogue of freedom and grace.

As was indicated earlier, Marcel respects the dignity of his interlocutors and thus expects active involvement from his readers. He speaks conversationally, referring to experiences in his own life and insisting on introducing concrete approaches that enable others to encounter whatever reality is to be discussed. In this way Marcel encourages readers to be in touch with these or similar situations in their own life experience. This *experiential* encounter with the realities under investigation assures that it is the reality itself given as *data*, i.e. as present to the conscious attention of a cognitive, affective, incarnate investigator which provides the evidential basis for valid and realistic interpretations. Thus interpretations are drawn from actual data and not from mere theories or theoretical arguments taken from outside sources. In another way, Marcel also invites his interlocutors to be part of the process of *critically reasoned analysis*, i.e. the entertainment of challenging questions, objections, and alternative interpretations and the understanding of the fundamental attitudes that give rise to these. Marcel's goal is that each partner in the dialogue, through recollection and reflective clarification, arrive at a rich deep encounter with a given mystery and a clear personal grasp of its meaning and value.

This approach to philosophy asks a great deal of readers, yet it offers a proportionate reward. Admittedly, the process followed by Marcel meets the criteria for true and valid interpretations reached through phenomenological investigations. But perhaps of even greater import is the fact that Marcel's dramatic and concrete approaches enable us to get in touch with realities that are or may become most gratifying dimensions of our lives.

Those who have already experienced the drama of *The Broken World* can enter more easily into the mysterious dimensions of human life that are explored dramatically in the play and examined philosophically in the essay. For, as Gaston Fessard observed, Marcel's is a theater of communion; by the magic of theater the actors communicate as subjects both what they are living and what they live by. This enables members of the audience to experience in the forum of their own consciousness the mysterious reality that is affecting the lives of the characters on stage. Thus those who have experienced the drama and begun to reckon with some of the questions it raises will more easily enter into the questioning of mysterious dimensions of human life explored in the essay of philosophic reflection.

For example, familiarity with Christiane's evocation of the sense of living in a "broken world" and the play's gradual disclosure of what contributes to this facilitates fathoming what the more abstract terms, such as "ontological uneasiness," or an "ontological need," or "a need for being" refer to. Dramatic experience of the painful sense of "distance" rather than "presence" that characterizes relationships among the various characters until the final scenes of *The Broken World*, and of the anxious attempts of Christiane and others to find diversion from the shallowness of their lives in somewhat hollow activities, primes readers to identify what "Concrete Approaches to Investigating the Ontological Mystery" refers to in more general terms as "a life centered on functions." Again the dramatic experience helps us sense more vividly how a life centered on functions or a life defined in terms of its least common denominator can lead one to rebel and ask, as the ontological exigency urges us to do, the essay's question, "Who am I?—Is Life (Being) empty or full?"

Once the essay establishes recollection and reflection as its method of philosophic inquiry and moves into positive description of concrete approaches to investigating the ontological mystery, readers find themselves more at home with the themes investigated. In fact, the phenomena of death, emptiness, suicide, and despair are tragically present in our world today as part of a consciousness of life without meaning or value. Superficiality and fragmentation of relations impoverish our human world. In today's world there is definitely a need to inquire into our most authentic human possibilities and to clarify what our realistic hopes for fulfilled lives can be. Thus readers will be intrigued to consider such themes as presence, belonging, creative fidelity, availability, and hope, which Marcel explores and clarifies. Many find these themes attractive, and find Marcel's investigation of them heartening and enlightening.

His investigation of these themes, or dimensions of authentic human life, is compassionate and balanced. His investigations are by no means simple or naive. His interpretations are always circumspect and critically weighed. He sees clearly that the logic of freedom is at the heart of metaphysics. Yet he also recognizes the influence one's fundamental attitudes or predispositions can exert on one's choices and interpretations of life. Thus he not only clarifies various themes such as presence, belonging, intersubjectivity, or creative fidelity, but he also goes further and brings to light the predispositions requisite for such authentic attitudes to occur.

For example, he explores the nature of availability and unavailability and notes their significance in influencing one's willingness or ability to be present rather than distant, impersonal, or absent. He notes that egocentrism is the root source of the inability, just as other-directedness is the root source of the ability, to live intersubjectivity as *being with and for others.*

There is a Marcelian purposefulness in unearthing the various root sources of the attitudes people adopt that influence the different responses they can give to questions about life's meaning and value. Marcel clarified two aspects of that purposefulness. He mentioned the first goal—to express compassionate understanding—when he commented that as he advanced in years he came to prefer his theater because it conveyed a spirit of fraternity (or understanding and kinship); it says "you are understood." The second goal he mentioned in commenting on his early predilection for theater. He pointed out that dramatic imagination in the light of theater had enabled him to open up a path for freedom in his life. Gradually he realized that for himself and also for some others reflection in the light of theater can help to sort out and evaluate, from among the gamut of choices with various underlying fundamental attitudes and predispositions, a way enabling them to discover a path for their freedoms to create authentically fulfilling human lives.

As Marcel explained on many occasions, his theater was always prospective as a first mode of inquiry that followed the path of dramatic imagination and was neither composed nor intended as a forum for illustrating or proving philosophic theories. Yet *The Broken World* and "Concrete Approaches to Investigating the Ontological Mystery," two works of quite different genres, when taken side-by-side, seem to show the scenery as it would appear on alternate sides of a traveled route. But Marcel noted that it was the first time ever that his dramatic exploration and philosophic investigation were like two paths that scaled the same height. He commented that this had never happened before, because prior to his evolution of this new experiential and reflective approach, the idealistic philosophy in vogue in his day was too confining and could not provide categories adequate for working with experiences and questions seeking insight into life's meaning. But now finally *The Broken World* enabled him to communicate the experience and "Concrete Approaches to Investigating the Ontological Mystery" allowed him to analyze and interpret it philosophically.

So it should not be surprising that, after we have first read *The Broken World* and then studied "Concrete Approaches to Investigating the Ontological Mystery," we cannot help but find in the characters and the drama of their life situations concrete presentations of some of the insights Marcel later articulates as themes in the philosophic essay. It is especially characteristic of Marcel's dramas that they focus on situations of living relationships among people. Artfully he brings to light deep and poignant aspects of the mystery of intersubjectivity, and he wisely shows that life's meaning and the quality of these relationships can evolve through a dialogue of freedom and grace.

Coming now full circle we can again take up the image of music. Marcel once said that in his communication there were three concentric rings:

music, theater, and philosophy. Music was the innermost and deepest; theater next, situating people in relationships of dialogue and conflict; and the outermost was philosophy, addressing these issues in more abstract and general terms. He elsewhere gave notice that his theater is a privileged gateway into his philosophic inquiry, and he asserted that those with an affinity for music have a favorable predisposition for understanding his thought.

Marcel did not try to write a systematic or didactic exposition of his thought, or to leave a skeletal presentation of his main lines of argument. He declined even to refer to "his" philosophy. Rather he felt like Jaspers, one who, having traveled through a certain country, calls out to others who venture to explore that territory also. He is comfortable with being one who has found a way and charted it to guide others who may choose to explore that same region on their own.

It is hoped that now, having experienced the drama of *The Broken World* and having been attuned to the style and flow of "Concrete Approaches to Investigating the Ontological Mystery," readers will find the essay not only a challenging but also an exciting and gratifying introduction that provides a comprehensive overview of the questions, method, and main themes of Gabriel Marcel's thought. Marcel developed these themes more fully and in greater detail in later plays and philosophic works, especially in *The Lantern, Dot the I's, Creative Fidelity, Homo Viator, Presence and Immortality,* and *Humanity against Mass Society.*

Concrete Approaches to Investigating the Ontological Mystery

Address delivered January 21, 1933, to the Philosophical Society of Marseilles.

Numbers and letters in the text represent endnotes, which begin on p. 198. The letters following each number indicate the area or areas of interest that a particular note addresses. Thus, "i" indicates notes offering "identifications"; "d" indicates notes relating to "drama"; "ph" indicates notes referring to "philosophy"; and "t" refers to comments about "text." This system of referencing is intended to facilitate a quick recognition of notes corresponding to a reader's particular interests. [Translator's Note]

I am well aware that the words *Ontological Mystery*, which I have chosen for the title of this meditation, may disconcert nonphilosophers and even shock professional philosophers. The latter customarily relegate mysteries to theologians or to popularizers of either mysticism or the occult, Maeterlinck, for example. (1i) Moreover, for philosophers formed in the context of idealism, the word *ontological* has fallen into disrepute, and for nonphilosophers it has only the vaguest of meanings. (2i,ph) The term is familiar to philosophers formed in scholastic thought, but they habitually reserve the term *mystery* for mysteries of revealed religions.

Thus I am well aware of the resistance I shall meet and the criticisms I shall incur. (3ph) Nevertheless, it seems to me that only this terminology is adequate to designate the ensemble of perspectives I am going to sketch, and whose importance is central. Those who have already read my *Metaphysical Journal* (4i, ph) will easily recognize that the fundamental theses I shall propose are the result of a whole philosophic and spiritual evolution pursued throughout that *Journal.*

Instead of beginning with abstract definitions and dialectical argumentation that are sure to discourage my audience, I prefer to start with a sort of global and intuitive characterization of persons for whom any sense of being or the ontological is lacking, or who—more exactly—have lost all consciousness of having had any such dimension to their lives. This is the way most modern men and women are, and if a need for a sense of being affects them at all, it is only in a muted way, as some vague uneasiness. I often wonder if a psychoanalysis—one deeper and more nuanced than what has been developed to date—would not succeed in revealing the morbid effects engendered by the repression of this sense, this need so unfortunately misunderstood. (5i, ph)

Today's world is characterized, it seems to me, by an orientation misdirected by the notion of function, and here I use the word *function* in its generally accepted sense, which includes both vital and social functions. The individual tends to consider him or herself, and likewise tends to appear to others, as merely an agglomeration of functions.

For historical reasons that are very deep and are thus far only partly understood, the individual has been inclined increasingly to regard him or herself as merely an aggregate of functions whose hierarchical order appears problematic, or in any event subject to contradictory interpretations.

First of all there are the vital functions; it is hardly necessary to point out the reductionist influence on the concept of humanity exercised by historic materialism on the one hand and Freudian theories on the other.

Then there are the social functions: the function of consumer, the function of producer, the function of citizen, etc.

Between these two there should be, at least theoretically, a place for psychological functions. But we notice that the properly psychological functions are all too often interpreted either in terms of vital functions or in terms of social functions so that their autonomy as psychological functions becomes precarious and their specificity is contested. In this respect, Auguste Comte, (6i) aided by his total misunderstanding of the human psyche, foretold the future in refusing to give psychology any proper place in the classification of the sciences.

We have been speaking abstractly until now, but, in matters such as these, it is easy to pass directly into the most concrete experiences.

I often ask myself, with anxiety, what might be the consciousness or inner life of a particular employee of the metropolitan transit authority, for example, the conductor who guards the doors or inspects the tickets. We must see that everything in and around him or her conspires to equate this individual's identity with his or her functions, and I have in mind not only the professional functions as an employee, or a member of a labor union, or a voter, but also the vital functions. The frightful expression, *the use of one's time,* is in this context most significant. Precise amounts of time are allotted for various functions. Sleep also is a function, one that must be carried out if other functions are to be performed properly. And it's the same for leisure and relaxation. We can well imagine a health-care specialist prescribing that a person needs so many hours of recreation per week. It is simply a psycho-organic function that can no more be neglected than the sexual functions, for example. No need to elaborate further; this brief sketch paints the picture. We see emerging the notion of a kind of vital schedule whose details will, of course, vary according to countries, climates, occupations, etc. But what is important is that there be a schedule.

There is no doubt that elements of disorder and rupture can occur: all sorts of accidents, sickness. It follows quite logically then—and it's what happens in America and, I believe, also in Russia—that an individual is scheduled for periodic check-ups like a clock or a watch. The hospital then functions as a preventive maintenance or repair shop. What's more, it will be from this same point of view of regulating functions that essential questions like birth control will be considered.

As for death, from this objective and functional point of view it appears only as ceasing to function, falling into total uselessness, becoming sheer *waste* to be discarded.

There is no need to stress the atmosphere of suffocating sadness secreted by a world whose main axis is functions. Just consider the heartbreaking image of a person who has been retired, or the very similar image of Sundays in cities where pedestrians have the air of people withdrawn from life. In this kind of world there is something sinister and mocking about the tolerance shown toward retired people. (7d)

A world such as this is a sad spectacle not only for the one who observes it; there is, moreover, the unspoken and intolerable uneasiness felt by those who see themselves reduced to living as if they were nothing more than their functions. This uneasiness is sufficient to show that there is an error or at least an abusive interpretation that an increasingly inhuman social order and philosophy (which, if it has formed that order, has also built on it) have tried to inculcate into defenseless minds.

I have had occasion to write, provided this be understood in a metaphysical and not in a physical sense, that the distinction between the full and the empty is more fundamental than that between the one and the many. And it is in the present context that the significance of this remark becomes evident. Life in a world centered on function leads to despair because such a world is empty, it rings hollow; and if such a life resists despair, it is only inasmuch as there come into play from within and in favor of that existence certain hidden forces that the individual is not yet able to recognize or name. However, a fundamental blindness tends inevitably to diminish the potential action of these forces and finally to deprive them of their leverage. (8d)

I note that on the one hand this sort of world is saturated with problems; on the other hand it is determined to leave no place for mystery. In a little while I shall explain technically the meaning of this fundamental distinction between problem and mystery. (9ph,t) For the moment I want to point out that to eliminate or to try to eliminate mystery is, in this functionalized world we've described, to apply to events that rupture the course of human existence—birth, love, death—the psychological and pseudo-scientific category of the *purely natural*, a concept that should itself be subject to careful critical study. For this category is merely a vestige of a degenerate rationalism in which the cause accounts for the effect, that is, totally explains it. In a world of this kind, there is nonetheless an infinite number of problems, because the causes are not known to us in detail; therefore, there is room for an indefinite number of investigations. Besides the theoretical problems, there are also innumerable technical problems linked to the question of finding out how the different vital and social functions—which one has inventoried after having labeled them—can be exercised without impairing one another. The theoretical and technical problems are interdependent because the theoretical problems arise from definite techniques, and, conversely, technical problems can only be solved where a certain theoretical knowledge has already been established.

In a world such as this, the ontological exigency, the need for being, weakens precisely to the extent that on the one hand the personality fragments, and on the other hand the category of the *purely natural* triumphs and what we must call the powers of amazement or the capacity for wonder atrophy. [The French word *émerveillement*, I hasten to say, is not adequate. The French language does not have an equivalent of the German *wunder* and the English *wonder*, which attest to the possibility of a sort of vital circulation between the miracle and one's amazement.]

Finally as to this ontological exigency, can we not now approach it directly and attempt to define it? Actually this is possible, I fear, only to a limited extent. For profound reasons that will gradually appear, I suspect that this exigency possesses the peculiar character of not being able to be completely transparent even to itself.

If we force ourselves to translate this exigency without modifying it, we will be led to say something like this:

There must be—or there must have been—*being*; everything cannot be finally reduced to the interplay of successive and *inconsistent* appearances—this word *inconsistent* is essential—or, as Shakespeare has phrased it "a tale told by an idiot." I aspire avidly to participate in some way in this being, and perhaps this exigency itself is already a degree of participation, no matter how rudimentary. (10d,ph)

A similar exigency, let us note, is already at the heart of even the most radical pessimism. Pessimism makes sense only if it means that there must assuredly have been being; now, however, there is not—and, as a result, I who make this declaration am nothing. (11d,ph)

As for defining more precisely what the word *being* means, let us all agree that this is extremely difficult. I will just propose this approach: being is what resists—or would be what would withstand—an exhaustive analysis of the data of experience that would try to reduce them progressively to elements that are increasingly devoid of any intrinsic value or significance. (It's an analysis of this kind that is pursued, for example, throughout the theoretical works of Freud.) (12i)

When in *The City* (*La Ville*) the pessimist Besme (13i) states that "nothing is," he wants to affirm precisely that no experience withstands such an analysis. And it will always be around death, considered precisely as a manifestation, an evidence of this ultimate nothingness, that this sort of reverse apologetic of absolute pessimism gravitates.

A philosophy that refuses to give serious consideration to this ontological exigency is indeed possible, and modern thought as a whole tends toward just such an abstention. But here it is important to distinguish two different attitudes that one might confuse and consider to be the same. One is an attitude of consistently reserving judgment; this would be the attitude of agnosticism in all its forms. The other, bolder and more coherent, would tend to see the ontological exigency as a remnant of an outdated dogmatism that the idealist critique has discredited once and for all.

The first attitude appears to me to have an exclusively negative import. In fact, it merely corresponds to a certain intellectual politics: *The question will not be asked.*

The second attitude, on the contrary, pretends to be based on a positive theory of knowledge. It is impossible to give a detailed critique of such a philosophy here. I will only mention that such a philosophy, it seems to me, tends toward an unconscious relativism, or even more toward a monism of values that ignores the personal in all its forms, that ignores the tragic, that denies the transcendent and tries to reduce it to caricatures that misrepresent its essential characteristics. I will point out that because of the fact that such a philosophy continually stresses activities of verification, it consequently ends up by ignoring *presence*, that interior realization of a presence at the heart of love that infinitely transcends any possible verification, because this presence occurs within an immediacy that places it beyond any conceivable mediation. This will become clearer to a certain extent through what follows. (14ph)

I, for my part, judge that the ontological need can only be reduced to silence by an arbitrary, dictatorial act that mutilates spiritual life at its very roots. Such an act is always possible, and our conditions of existence are such that we can really believe that we have accomplished it, and this is something that we must not forget.

These first reflections on the ontological need, bringing to light its indeterminate character, reveal an essential paradox; to formulate this exigency first of all engages me in a labyrinth of problems: Does being exist? What is being? But I cannot reflect on these questions without seeing a new abyss open up under my feet. I who am questioning being, can I be sure that I am?

Yet surely, I who articulate this problem, I should be able to remain *outside* of it—whether that be *before* or *beyond* the problem that I state. In reality, however, it becomes clear that this is not the case; reflection shows me clearly that this problem inevitably invades this theoretically preserved arena. It is by a fiction that idealism in its traditional form seeks to maintain a consciousness outside of being that can affirm or deny being.

Consequently I cannot exempt myself from also asking: Who am I, I who inquire about being? What qualifies me to undertake this investigation? If I do not exist, how can I expect to successfully carry out investigations? And even granted that I *may* exist, how can I be sure that I *do* exist?

Contrary to what might automatically come to mind, I think that in this context the *cogito* is of no help to us. Despite what Descartes might have thought, if he gives us an indubitable principle, the sole certainty with which it provides us concerns only the epistemological subject as organ of objective cognition. (15i,ph) The *cogito*, I have written elsewhere, guards the threshold of validity and nothing more; the proof of this lies in the indeterminateness of the *I*. The *I am*, it seems to me, presents itself as an inseparable whole.

One objection remains to be foreseen: either the being referred to by the question "What am I?" concerns the knowing subject, in which case we are precisely on the level of the *cogito*; or what you call the ontological exigency is merely the extreme point—if not a fallacious transposition—of what is simply a vital need that should not concern the metaphysician.

But isn't the error primarily one of arbitrarily separating the question "*Am I?*" from the ontological *problem* taken as a whole? Actually, neither one nor the other can be approached in isolation; they can only be approached jointly and simultaneously. Moreover, as we shall see, taken together they prevent one another from being considered and dealt with *as problems*.

I must also say that the Cartesian position is, in fact, inseparable from a dualism that I reject without hesitation. To pose the ontological problem is to inquire about the totality of being and about myself as a totality.

Moreover, and in a correlative manner, it is legitimate to ask whether this disassociation of the intellectual from the vital, with its consequent arbitrary depreciation or arbitrary exaltation of the vital, should not be refused. We do not mean to deny the legitimacy of introducing distinctions within the unity of a living being who thinks and who attempts *to think his or her own being*, but the ontological problem only presents itself beyond those distinctions and to each of us taken in his or her most comprehensive unity.

If we seek to summarize the situation in which we find ourselves at this point in our reflection, we shall observe that we are in the presence of a certain orientation (*élan*) toward an affirmation which, in the final analysis, appears to be impossible to establish, since it is not until it has been made that I can consider myself qualified to articulate it. (16ph)

Let us note that this situation would not occur if I were actually facing a problem that needed to be solved. In such a case, in fact, I work on what's given, but at the same time everything happens, everything authorizes me to proceed as if I didn't have to pay any attention to this self who is working, as if this self were merely a factor that is presupposed and nothing more.

In the case of questioning being, however, what I will call the ontological basis for questioning takes on decisive importance. For as long as I stay within the realm of mere speculation, I seem to be engaged in an endless regression. Yet, by the very fact that I conceive the impossibility of putting an end to this regression, I transcend it in some way. I recognize that this regressive process remains interior to a certain *affirmation that I am rather than one that I utter.* In articulating it, I break it, I fragment it, I am on the verge of falsifying or betraying it.

One might say, in a language inevitably only approximate, that my inquiry into being presupposes an affirmation in regard to which I would be in some way passive *and of which I would be the stage rather than the subject.* But this is only a limit idea, and one that I cannot realize without contradiction. I am inclined toward the affirmation or the recognition of a participation that has the reality of a subject; this participation cannot, by definition, be the *object* of thought; it could not function as a solution, but rather is situated beyond the world of problems: it is meta-problematical. (17ph)

Conversely, one can see that if the meta-problematical can be affirmed, it must be as transcending the opposition between the subject who would affirm being and being *as affirmed by this subject*—and as in some way underlying their opposition. To admit the meta-problematical is to acknowledge the primacy of being over knowledge (not of being *as affirmed,* but rather of being *affirming itself*); it is to recognize that knowledge is enveloped by being, that it is in some manner interior to being, perhaps in a way analogous to what Paul Claudel was trying to explain in his *Art Poétique* (*Poetic Art.*) (18i) From this point of view, as opposed to what epistemology strives vainly to establish, there really is a mystery of knowledge; knowledge derives from a mode of participation that no theory of knowledge can account for because the theory itself presupposes this participation.

At this point, the distinction between problem and mystery can be clarified. A mystery is a problem that encroaches upon its own data, that invades the data and thereby transcends itself as a simple problem. A series of examples will help us to give meaningful content to this definition. (19ph)

It is evident, obviously, that there is a mystery of the union of one's body and mind; the indivisible unity that is never quite adequately expressed by such phrases as: *I have a body, I use my body, I feel my body,* etc. is exterior to any kind of analysis and can in no way be reconstituted by any synthesis that begins with logically prior elements; the indivisible unity of body and soul is not only given, I will even say it is *giving* in the sense of what I will call the presence of me to myself, a presence that is only inadequately symbolized by the act of self-consciousness. (20ph)

We see immediately that there can be no hope of drawing a clear line of demarcation between problem and mystery. For a mystery placed before reflection tends inevitably to degrade itself into a problem. (21t, ph) This is strikingly manifest in the case of the problem of evil. (22ph)

In fact, I am inevitably inclined to treat the problem of evil as a disorder I contemplate whose causes, reasons for being, or hidden purpose I attempt to sort out. How is it that "this machine" functions in such a defective manner? Or is it perhaps that the apparent flaw is due this time to a real defect in my perception? The real disorder in this latter case lies in me, but it remains objective for my thought that discovers and studies it. But evil that is only stated or observed is no longer the evil that is suffered; quite simply it ceases to be evil. Actually I only really perceive it as evil to the extent that it *touches* me, that is to say, the extent to which I am *involved,* in the sense of being implicated in the affair. It is this implication that is fundamental here, and I can only abstract from it by an unjustifiable fiction, because by this act of abstraction I proceed as if I were God, and a God who only contemplates. (23ph)

Here we see clearly that the distinction between what is within me and what would be merely in front of me breaks down; it dissolves under the power of a second-level reflection. (24ph)

But it is, without a doubt, in the case of love that we best see the distinct frontier between the *within myself* and the *before myself* vanish.

Perhaps it might even be possible to show that as a matter of fact the realm of the meta-problematical coincides with the realm of love, and that love is the only starting point for understanding a mystery like the union of body and soul, which in some manner it expresses.

Besides, it is inevitable that a reflection that is not itself reflected upon, in attacking love, tends to lose what is meta-problematical, to interpret it in terms of abstract notions like the will to live, the will to power, the libido, etc. Moreover, as the order of the problematic is the realm of the verifiable, it will be extremely difficult—perhaps even impossible—to refute such interpretations without placing oneself on a different level, where, to tell the truth, these objections simply lose their footing. And at the same time an assurance is given to me, a guarantee is mine—and this assurance envelops me like a protective cloak—that to the extent that I really love I do not have to be concerned about these demeaning reductionist interpretations.

One will ask: What then is the criterion of real or true love? One must reply that there is no criteriology except in the realm of objects and what can be problematized, but already from a distance we see the eminent value that from the ontological point of view must be assigned to fidelity. (25ph)

Here is another, more immediate, more particular example, which seems appropriate to clarify the difference between a mystery and a problem.

You may have an encounter that has a deep and lasting, albeit indeterminate, effect upon your life. Everyone can have had the experience of what such an encounter can mean from the spiritual point of view. Yet this is something that philosophers communally ignore or disdain, probably because the encounter affects only the individual as a person; it is not universalizable, it does not concern thinking beings in general.

It is evident that such encounters present, if you will, a *problem*, but it is equally clear that the solution to the *problem* falls short of the only question that matters. If, for example, someone says to me "You met that person at a certain place because he or she likes the same type of countryside as you, or because his or her health requires that he or she receive the same treatments as you yourself do," one sees right away that the explanation is not there. Crowds of people were with me at Florence or Engadine who supposedly share my tastes, and in the spa where I go for health treatments there are a considerable number of people who have the same health problems as I do. But the presumed identity of taste or of illness does not *bring us close* (26t,ph) in the true sense of the word; these similarities are not adequate to account for the intimate affinity, unique in its kind and essential to any encounter, which is at issue here. At the same time it would go beyond the limits of valid reasoning here to treat this affinity itself as a cause and say: "It's precisely this affinity that has determined our meeting."

Hence, I find myself in the presence of a mystery, that is to say a reality whose roots go far beyond what is, properly speaking, the problematical. Will we avoid the difficulty by saying that there is nothing here except a question of fortunate coincidence, or good luck? Immediately from deep within myself there arises strong protest against this hollow phrase, this ineffectual negation of something that I sense at the very center of myself. But here again we find the initial definition of the mystery as a problem that trespasses on its own givenness: I, who inquire about the meaning and the conditions of possibility of this encounter, cannot place myself outside or opposite it; I am engaged in this encounter, I depend on it, I am in some manner interior to it, it envelops and comprehends me— even if I do not comprehend it. Therefore it is only through a sort of denial or betrayal that I can say: "After all, it could have never happened at all, and nevertheless I would still be who I was and who I am now." Nor should one say: "I was changed by this encounter as by an exterior cause." No, the event developed me from within, it acted upon me as an interior principle within myself.

However, this is very difficult to understand without distortion. Inevitably I shall be tempted to react against this feeling of the interiority of the encounter, and tempted by my own probity. Tempted, because from a certain point of view I must judge by what is the best part—the safest and most reliable part—of myself.

Indirectly, these clarifications risk reinforcing in listeners' minds a preliminary objection that I want to address as directly as possible now.

This meta-problematical, they will say, is still a content of thought; hence why not inquire about its mode of existence as such? What assures us of its existence? Is this not itself problematic to the highest degree?

My response to this is as categorical as can be: to think the meta-problematic is to affirm it as indubitably real, as something I cannot doubt without contradiction. We are in a zone where it is impossible to disassociate the idea itself from the degree of certitude it carries. For this idea *is* certitude, it *is* its own assurance, and to that extent it is something other and more than an idea. Moreover, the term *content of thought,* which figures in the objection, is as deceptive as can be. For a content is, after all, an extract derived from experience, whereas only an approach that detaches or liberates us from the experience enables us to rise to the level of the meta-problematical or of mystery. What is called for is a *real* disengagement, a *real* detachment, not an abstraction that can only be a fiction recognized as such. (27ph)

And this brings us at last to recollection, for it is in recollection and in recollection alone that this disengagement is accomplished. I am, for my part, convinced that no ontology is possible, that is to say, no apprehending of the ontological mystery to any degree whatsoever, except for a being who is capable of recollecting him or herself—and by this to bear witness to the fact that he or she is not purely and simply a living thing, a creature thrown into life with no hold on it. (28d,ph)

We must note that recollection, which has been given very little attention by professional philosophers, is very difficult to define, if only because recollection transcends the dualism between an act and a state of being precisely because in recollection these two otherwise opposite aspects are reconciled. The word itself says what it means. Recollection is essentially the act whereby I collect myself as a unity; but this gathering together, this concentration is also a relaxation, a letting go. It involves *abandoning to...,* *relaxing in the presence of...,* without it being possible for me to specify in any way the substantive reality that these prepositions refer to. The path stops at the threshold...

What's more, this question, like so many others, will be reduced to a problem, and in this case it will be the psychologist who will attempt to accomplish this transmutation. Yet, suffice it to say that psychology is in no more of a position to shed light upon the metaphysical significance of recollection than on the noetic value of the act of knowing.

It is in the womb of recollection that I take a position—or more exactly that I put myself in a state that allows me to take a stand—with regard to my life. I withdraw from it in some way, but not as the pure knowing subject; *in this retreat I bring with me what I am and what my life perhaps is not*. Here we perceive the distance between my being and my life. I am not my life, and if I am able to judge my life—a fact I cannot deny without falling into a radical skepticism that is nothing more than despair—it is on the condition that I can first of all encounter myself within recollection that is beyond all possible judgments, and, I will add, beyond any possible representation. Doubtless the process of recollection is what is least spectacular in one's soul; it does not consist in looking at something, it is a retrieval, a renewal. It might well be asked, I merely note in passing, whether we ought not to see in recollection the ontological foundation of memory, the effective principle of unity that is beyond representation and is the very basis of the possibility of remembering. The English expression *to recollect oneself* is very revealing.

One will ask: Is recollection not after all the same thing as the dialectical moment of turning back to oneself or the *Für-sich-sein* that is at the center of German idealism? (29i)

To tell the truth, I think it is not. Entering into oneself does not mean to be for oneself and to have in view some sort of intelligible unity of the subject and the object. On the contrary, I will say, we are here in the presence of the paradox of mystery whereby the self into which I return ceases, precisely to that extent, to belong to itself. "You are not your own." (30i) That great statement of Saint Paul here conveys a significance that is both ontological and essentially concrete; it is what best expresses the reality we are exploring at this moment. Some will ask: Isn't that reality an object of intuition? Isn't what you are calling recollection the same thing others call intuition?

Here again, it seems to me, one must be extremely prudent. If it is possible here to speak of an intuition, it is an intuition that is not or cannot be given as such. The more an intuition is central, the more it fills the depth of the being that it illumines, the less susceptible it is precisely to reflect back on itself or to apprehend itself.

If we reflect beyond that to ask what an intuition of being might be, we see that it is not—that it cannot be—susceptible to figure in a collection, to be catalogued as an experience or some kind of an *Erlebnis* (31i) that on the contrary always presents the quality that it can be at times integrated, at times isolated and, as it were, laid bare. It follows that any effort to commit that intuition to memory, to picture it for oneself, I shall say, can only be vain. In this sense, to speak of an intuition of being is to invite us to play on a silent piano. This intuition cannot be brought out into the light of day, for the simple reason that the intuition is not something one possesses. Here we arrive at the most difficult point of our discussion; instead of using the term *intuition*, (32i) it would be much better to say that we have to deal here with an assurance that underlies the development of all thought, even discursive thought. From this it follows that we can only approach it through a movement of conversion, that is to say, by a second reflection: that reflection through which I ask myself in what way and on what basis the initial process of reflection was possible, which reflection itself postulated the ontological, but without realizing it. (33ph) This second reflection lets recollection become self-conscious to the extent that recollection can be thought.

It is certainly most annoying to have to use such abstract language when in truth one is dealing not with a dialectic *ad usum philosophorum*, but with what is most vital, and, I will say, most dramatic in the rhythm of a consciousness seeking to become conscious of itself.

It is this dramatic aspect that we now want to clarify.

Let us recall what I indicated right from the start: The ontological exigency, this need for being, can in fact deny itself. On a certain level, one's being and one's life do not coincide; my life, and by refraction every life, can appear to me as forever inadequate to something that I carry within me, something that in some sense I am, which, however, reality seems to resist and exclude. Thus despair in all its forms is possible at any time and to any degree of intensity. Such betrayal, it seems, is counseled if not imposed by the very structure of a functionalized world. And the spectacle of death that this world presents can be regarded from a certain point of view as a continual invitation to denial, to absolute betrayal. One could even say that, in this sense, the permanent possibility of suicide is an essential starting point for authentic metaphysical thought. (34t, ph, d)

Perhaps some will be surprised to find such emotionally charged, fashionable words as *suicide* and *betrayal* in the midst of a calm and abstract analysis. This is no concession to sensationalism. I am firmly convinced that it is in drama and through drama that metaphysical thought becomes conscious and defines itself concretely. Jacques Maritain (35i), in a lecture delivered at Louvain (36i) two years ago, on the topic of Christian Philosophy, said, "There is nothing easier for a Philosophy than to be tragic, it need only yield to the weight of the human condition," which doubtless refers to the early speculations of Martin Heidegger. (37i) I find, on the contrary, that philosophy naturally inclines toward realms where the tragic dimension, it seems, has simply disappeared, evaporated by its contact with abstract thought. This can be verified in the thought of many contemporary idealists. (38i) Because they ignore the person and sacrifice it to I know not what ideal truth, to what anonymous principle of pure inwardness, they are unable to grasp the tragic dimensions of human life that I have alluded to above; they exile them along with illness and all that is akin to it to some disreputable suburb where a philosopher worthy of the name doesn't deign to go. But this way of thinking, as I have said, is intimately bound up with a rejection of the ontological need. In effect, they are the same.

If I have stressed despair, betrayal, and suicide, it is because we find in these the most obvious expressions of a will to negation brought to bear effectively on being.

Take despair, for example. It is the act by which one despairs of reality as a whole, as one might give up totally on another person. Despair announces itself as the consequence or the expression of a certain *balance sheet*; "Insofar as I can evaluate reality—and after all what lies beyond my ability to appreciate is for me like something nonexistent—I find nothing that withstands a process of dissolution that develops at the heart of things and which my reflection enables me to recognize and measure." At the root of despair I believe that there is always this affirmation: "There is nothing in being to which I can give credit, nothing that I can count on, no security." It is a declaration of complete insolvency. (39ph)

By contrast, hope implies just such credit. Contrary to Spinoza (40i), who it seems to me has confused two distinct and very contrary notions, fear is the opposite of desire, not of hope. The negative correlate of hope is that act which construes things for the worst, which the attitude of *defeatism* illustrates strikingly, an attitude that is always at risk of deteriorating into a desire for the worst. Hope consists in asserting that there is at the heart of being, beyond all data, beyond all inventories and all calculations, a mysterious principle in connivance with me, which cannot but will what I will, at least if what I will is really worth willing and is, in fact, willed with my whole being. (41ph)

We are now at the heart of what I call the ontological mystery, and simplest examples will be the best. To hope against all hope that the person whom I love will recover from an illness that is devouring her and which is considered to be incurable is to say, it is not possible that I am alone in willing her recovery, it is impossible that reality at its very depths is hostile or only indifferent to what I declare to be a good in itself. It is useless to cite *examples* or refer to *cases* of a sort intended to discourage me; beyond any experience, beyond all probabilities, all statistics, I affirm that a certain order *will be* reestablished, that reality *is* with me in willing that it be so. I am not just wishing, I am asserting; and this is what I will call the prophetic resonance of genuine hope.

Some may say, "In the vast majority of cases, this is an illusion." But besides the fact that it is of the essence of hope to exclude mere consideration of cases, we must show here that there is an ascending dialectic of hope, by which hope rises to a transcendent level that is beyond all possible empiric disproof, the level of salvation, as opposed to the level of success no matter what form it may assume.

This in no way alters the fact that the correlation between hope and absolute despair remains until the very end. They appear to me to be inseparable. The world we live in, so centered on functions, facilitates and can even seem to recommend an absolute despair, but it is only in a situation such as this that invincible hope can arise. What's more, this is why we can never be too grateful to the great pessimists in the history of thought; they have pushed to the limit an interior experience that had to be realized and whose radical possibility should not be glossed over by any sort of apologetic. These thinkers prepared us to understand that absolute despair might be what it was for Nietzsche (on an infra-ontological level, and, moreover, in an area strewn with mortal perils): the springboard for the highest affirmation. (42i)

At the same time, it remains certain that, to the extent hope remains a mystery, as Charles Péguy (43i) saw so well, this mystery can be misunderstood and converted into a problem. Hope, then, is treated as a desire clad in illusory judgments that disguise an objective reality whose true nature one prefers to ignore. What happens here is what we have already observed in connection with encounter and with love. It is because a mystery can and in a sense must logically degrade itself into a problem that an interpretation like Spinoza's, with the confusion it involves, must itself, at some given moment, be proposed. As long as one stays short of the ontological level, such an attitude is not susceptible to any critique. This is a very important fact and must be stressed. As long as my attitude toward reality is that of someone who is not involved, but I consider myself responsible to prepare as precise a report as possible (and this is by definition the attitude of the scientist), I am justified in addressing toward this reality a kind of mistrust, in principle, that has no limits to its application. Such is the attitude of the laboratory scientist who would in no way prejudice the results of the analyses he or she is conducting and who can readily imagine *the worst* possible outcome, since on this plane the very notion of the worst is devoid of all sense. But an investigation of precisely this sort, rigorously comparable to that of an auditor of accounts, is carried out short of the realm of mystery, the order where the problem encroaches on its own data.

Effectively, when I inquire about the value of life, it is a serious paralogism (44i,t) to imagine that I can maintain this disengaged attitude: it is truly a mistake to think that I can carry out this inquiry as if my own life were not at issue.

From this it follows that between hope, genuine hope in the heart of the one it inhabits, and the judgments cast upon it by someone who remains a prisoner of objectivity, there is the same barrier that separates pure problems from pure mystery.

Here we are at the nodal point of our subject, where some particularly intimate connections can be traced.

The world of the problematical is the world of desire and of fear, which cannot be separated from one another; it is also the world of the functional or functionalizable that I defined at the beginning of this meditation; finally it is the world where techniques of whatever kind reign supreme. There is no technique that is not or that could not be put directly at the service of a given desire or a given fear, and conversely every desire and every fear will tend to create techniques geared to its own ends. In such a world despair will consist in recognizing the ultimate ineffectiveness of techniques, but without being willing or able to place oneself on another level where all techniques are recognized as incompatible with being's fundamental characteristics, which by their very nature escape our grasp (at least for as long as our grasp encompasses the world of objects and this alone). Therein lies the reason that we may appear to have entered into the age of despair: we have not ceased believing in techniques, that is, envisioning reality as an ensemble of problems, and yet, at the same time, the *global bankruptcy* of techniques as a whole is as clearly discernable as are its *partial* successes. To the question: "What can humans accomplish?" we still reply: Humans are capable of what their technical abilities can accomplish, but at the same time we cannot but recognize that technical achievements are unable *to save us from ourselves* and even appear susceptible to conclude the most sinister alliances with the enemy that each one of us carries within ourself.

Being *taken over by techniques,* as I have said, means becoming increasingly incapable of controlling them and becoming powerless *to govern one's own power.* For this control of one's own power, which is the realization in the realm of the active life of what I have called second reflection or reflection at the second power, can only find its center or its source of strength within recollection. (45ph)

Some will object, saying that those most completely imbued with belief in techniques are forced to recognize that there are vast domains over which techniques have no control. But what matters is not this observation but the way one's mind interprets it. We are forced to admit that we have no control over meteorological conditions, but the question is whether or not we judge it desirable and just that such control be given to us. The more one's sense of the ontological tends to disappear, the more the one who has lost it will see his or her claims as limitless, extending to a sort of cosmic governance, because he or she will become less and less capable of inquiring about the credentials he or she has to exercise such authority.

It must be added that as the disproportion grows between the claims of technical intelligence and the fragility, the persistent precariousness of what remains of its material substratum, the more the permanent possibilities of despair at the heart of that intelligence will increase dramatically. In this sense there really is a close dialectical connection between an optimism of technical progress and a philosophy of despair that the former seems to inevitably secrete—and there are plenty of illustrations of this in our world today. (46t)

One might say: Well, after all, this optimism in technological progress is animated by a great hope. How can this be reconciled with an ontological interpretation of hope?

We must respond, I believe, that, speaking from a metaphysical point of view, *the only genuine hope is one based on what does not depend on us,* one whose wellspring is humility, not pride. And here one is led to consider another aspect of this unique mystery, which I am endeavoring to bring into focus from different standpoints. (47ph)

The metaphysical problem of pride, of *hubris,* which the Greeks perceived and which was one of the essential themes of Christian theology, seems to me to have been almost totally misunderstood by modern philosophers who are not theologians. It was an issue left to moralists. But from my viewpoint, it appears, on the contrary, to be an essential question, perhaps even the most vital issue. Just reading the definition Spinoza (48i) gives to *superbia* in his *Ethics* (III, def. XXVIII) is enough for us to see how completely he missed the point. "Pride," he writes, "is the exalted opinion of ourselves that self-love gives to us." This is in fact a definition of vanity. Pride consists in finding one's strength solely in oneself; the prideful person withdraws from a certain communion of beings, thereby tending to fracture it. Thus pride operates as a principle of destruction.

That destruction can also be directed against oneself. Pride is in no way incompatible with self-hatred; it can lead to suicide, and this, it seems to me, is what Spinoza failed to see.

At this point a massive and very serious objection might be raised.

Perhaps some will say to me: Isn't what you are attempting to justify ontologically nothing else but a kind of moral quietism that satisfies itself with passive acceptance, resignation, inert hope? But then, what becomes of the human dimension in peoples' lives, the person acting as a responsible agent? Isn't action itself censured insofar as it implies a self-confidence that is already akin to pride? Finally, isn't action itself a sort of degradation?

I will point out that this objection implies a series of misunderstandings.

First of all, the idea of inert hope is, to my mind, a contradiction in terms. Hope is not a listless waiting, it is something that underpins yet overarches the action, but which inevitably degenerates or disappears when action ceases. I perceive hope as the prolongation into the unknown of an activity that is central, that is, rooted in one's being. Hence its affinities, not with desire, but with one's will. The will also carries within itself a refusal to calculate possibilities, or at least a refusal to be stopped by such a reckoning of probabilities. From all this then couldn't one define hope as an act of will that applies itself to what does not depend upon itself?

We have an experimental proof of this connection in the fact that it is the most militant and active of saints who have brought hope to its highest degree of realization; this would be inconceivable if hope were a mere velleity of one's soul. What has confused the issue here, as in many of the higher forms of morality, is a certain stoic representation of will as a rigid stiffening, whereas on the contrary will is relaxation and creation.

The word *creation* occurs to us here for the first time; it is, however, the decisive word. Where there is creation there is not, and there cannot be, degradation, and to the extent that techniques are or involve a creation, they are not a degradation. Degradation starts at the moment that creation begins to degenerate into self-imitation, becoming mesmerized and rigidly fixated on itself. And we can see here the origin of certain misconceptions that I warned against in regard to recollection. (49t, ph, d)

Great is the temptation to confuse two distinct movements whose opposition our spatial metaphors do not allow us to differentiate clearly enough: the shriveling, the contraction, the absorption with oneself—which are inseparable from the arrogance of pride and even symbolize it—could not be mistaken for the humble withdrawal that is appropriate to recollection and through which I come into contact with my ontological bases.

There is good reason to think that this retreat, this recollection, is a precondition for even aesthetic creation. Aesthetic creation, like scientific research, excludes in fact that act whereby one's *ego* fixes itself at the center of one's life, locks its focus rigidly on itself, and it is this act that is ontologically pure negation of being.

It may seem that here I come so close to Henri Bergson's thesis as to coincide with it. (50i) However, I do not think that this is actually the case. Bergson's habitual terminology almost always gives the impression that for him the essence of creation is its inventiveness, its sparkling innovation. But I wonder if attention concentrated too exclusively on this aspect of creation doesn't lead one to lose sight of its ultimate significance, namely, its rootedness in being. It is here that the notion of *creative fidelity* intervenes, a notion difficult to grasp and above all to define conceptually because of its underlying and unfathomable paradox, and because it is at the very center of the realm of the meta-problematical.

It is important to note that it seems difficult to save fidelity in a Bergsonian metaphysics because fidelity always risks being interpreted as a routine, as a mere compliance in the pejorative sense of the term, maintained as an arbitrary safeguard *against* the power of renewal that is the spirit itself.

I'm inclined to think that there is something in this misinterpretation of the values of fidelity that profoundly vitiates the notion of static religion as presented in *The Two Sources of Morality and Religion*. (51i) And here a brief meditation on creative fidelity, of which I can only sketch the main lines, might be helpful in presenting an indispensable clarification on this matter.

Fidelity is actually the opposite of inert conformism; it is the active recognition of something permanent, not formally as a law, but ontologically. In this respect, fidelity always relates to a presence or to something that can and should be maintained in us and before us as a presence, but which by this very fact can just as well be completely unacknowledged, forgotten, obliterated, and here we see reappear that shadow of betrayal, which, if you ask me, envelops all our human world like a sinister poisonous cloud.

Won't some say that we normally speak of fidelity to a principle? But we still need to discern if this doesn't involve an illegitimate transposition of fidelity from another order. A principle, insofar as it reduces itself to an abstract statement, can exact nothing from me, for it owes its very reality to the act by which I sanction or proclaim it. Fidelity to a principle—merely as a principle—is idolatry in the etymological sense of the word; it can even be a sacred obligation for me to renounce a principle from which the life has withdrawn and to which, I am well aware, I no longer adhere. For in continuing to conform my behavior to it, it is ultimately myself—myself as a presence—that I am betraying.

Fidelity is so far from being an inert conformism that it implies a vital and constant struggle against the forces that incline us toward interior dispersion and also toward sclerosis of habits. Some will say that is only a kind of active conservation, the opposite of creation. On this point, I am convinced that we must explore much more deeply the nature of fidelity and of presence.

If presence were merely an *idea* in us, whose nature would be nothing more than that, then the most we could actually hope for would be to conserve that idea in us and before us, as one keeps a photograph in a drawer or on a mantelpiece. But what is proper to presence—precisely as presence—is that it is uncircumscribed, and here again we encounter the meta-problematical. A presence is a mystery precisely to the extent that it is presence. Now, fidelity is that presence actively perpetuated; fidelity is the renewal of the benefit of presence—of its virtue, which consists in a mysterious incitement to create. There, once again, consideration of artistic creation can be a great help to us, because if aesthetic creation is conceivable, it can only be because of a certain presence of the world to the artist—presence to the heart, mind, and very being of the artist.

If, then, creative fidelity is possible it is because fidelity is ontological in its principle, because it draws on a presence that itself corresponds to a certain hold that being has on us, because it increases and deepens almost unfathomably the influence of this presence throughout the course of our lives. This seems to me to have almost inexhaustible consequences, if only for what pertains to the relations between the living and the dead.

It is appropriate to again emphasize that a presence to which we remain faithful is not an effigy of a vanished object that we carefully preserve. An effigy is after all a reproduction, a diminished reduction; it is metaphysically *less* than the object. Presence, on the contrary, is *more* than the object, surpassing it in every sense. Here we are at the start of an exploration that ends with death appearing as a *test of presence*. This is an essential point upon which we need to concentrate our attention.

Some will say: What a strange way to speak of death! Death *is* a certain phenomenon definable in biological terms; death is *not* a test.

We must respond that death is what death signifies, and what it means for a being situated at the highest spiritual level we can attain. It is obvious that the death of a Mr. or Ms. So-and-so, which I read about in the newspaper, who is nothing more to me than a name, is for me only an object of notification. It means that I have to cross out this name from among the list of people I can address, to ask them a question or to give them information. It is entirely different with someone who has been given to me as a presence. In this case it depends upon me, upon my interior attitude, to hold onto that presence that could degenerate and become a mere effigy.

Some will reply: What you have there is just an expression in unusual and needlessly metaphysical language of a very common psychological experience. Obviously it depends upon us to a certain degree as to whether or not the dead live on in our memory. But that existence is completely subjective.

I believe that we are dealing with something that is actually quite different, a reality that is infinitely more mysterious. When one says, "It depends upon us whether the dead live on in us," one is still thinking of an idea as a diminishment or an effigy. One admits that the object has disappeared but that an image of it remains that we can maintain in the sense that a housekeeper or a maintenance person keeps an apartment or a house in good repair. It's obvious that this type of maintenance has no ontological value. But if fidelity is creative in the sense I have tried to define, then it's an entirely different situation. A presence is a reality, a certain influx; it depends upon us whether or not we remain permeable to this influx, but not in fact to summon it forth. Creative fidelity consists in actively maintaining oneself in a state of permeability, and we see that there occurs here a sort of mysterious interchange between this free act and the gift given in response to it. (52d,ph)

Here we must expect an objection that is the converse of the preceding one. Someone will say to me, all right, you stop embellishing with metaphysical vocabulary what is just an ordinary psychological phenomenon, but only to gratuitously assert an unproven thesis and one that exceeds all possible experience; this is the case at the moment when you substitute for the neutral and ambiguous term *presence* that of *influx*, which is infinitely more compromising.

To reply to this objection, I believe it is necessary once again to refer back to what was said earlier about mystery and recollection. As a matter of fact, it is only on the level of the meta-problematical that the notion of influx can be appropriately understood. If "influx" were to be taken in an objective sense, that of the result of a physical force, we would find ourselves confronted not with a thesis of metaphysics but of physics, which would effectively give rise to all sorts of objections. When I say that a being is given to me as a presence or as a being (which amounts to the same thing, for the other is only a being for me if he or she is a presence), this means that I cannot treat the other as if he or she were simply placed there, positioned in front of me; there arises between the other and me a relationship which in a certain sense goes way beyond the conscious awareness I may have of it. The other is not only before me, the other is also within me; more exactly, the physical categories are transcended, they are no longer accurate or illuminating. The word *influx* expresses, although in too spatial a fashion, the kind of enrichment from within that happens the moment presence occurs. Of course the temptation will be great, almost irresistible, to think that this discernible presence can only be a presence of an object, but with that we fall again beneath the level of mystery to the problematic level, and in that case the protestation of an absolute fidelity resounds: "Even when I can neither touch you nor see you, I feel it, you are with me, it would be a betrayal of you not to be assured of this." *With* me: let us notice here the metaphysical character of this word *with*, which has so rarely been acknowledged by philosophers and which corresponds neither to a relation of inherence or of immanence, nor to a relation of exteriority. It will be of the very essence—and here I must use the Latin word—of a genuine *coesse*, that is to say, a real intimacy susceptible to the kind of decomposition that a critical reflection subjects it to, but we know already that there exists another kind of reflection that reflects on this former one and takes as its reference point an underlying intuition, blind but efficacious, whose hidden magnetism guides this second reflection. (53ph,t)

It must be noted—and with this we are preparing to move into another realm—that the value of such an intimacy, especially in what affects the interactions between the living and the dead, will be that much greater and incontestable as the relationship situates itself more clearly in a world of complete spiritual availability, that is to say of pure charity, and I observe in passing that the ascending dialectic of creative fidelity corresponds to the ascending dialectic of hope to which I have alluded earlier. (54ph,d)

The notion of availability is no less important for our subject than is the notion of presence, and I add that there is an obvious connection that binds one to the other.

It's an undeniable fact of experience, but one that is difficult to translate intelligibly, that there are certain beings who reveal themselves to us as present, that is to say, who are available when we are suffering, when we need someone in whom to confide, and there are others who don't give us that feeling, despite whatever might be their good will. We must note right away that the distinction between presence and non-presence cannot in any way be reduced to the opposition between the fact of being attentive and that of being distracted. The most conscientious attentive listener can give me the impression of being unavailable; he or she brings me nothing; he or she cannot really create a space for me in his or her life, no matter what material services he or she may lavish on me. In reality, there is a way of listening that is a giving of oneself; there is another way of listening that is a refusal, *a refusal to give of oneself*: a material gift or a visible action is not necessarily a sign of presence. Let us not speak of proof. In this context the word would clash cacaphonously. Presence is something that reveals itself immediately and unmistakably in a look, a smile, a tone, a handshake.

I would say, to clarify all this, that the being who is available is the one who is capable of being totally with me when I need him or her; the being who is unavailable is the one who seems to extend a temporary loan from among the considerable resources that are at his or her disposal. For the first I am a presence, for the second I am an object. Presence includes a reciprocity that is doubtless excluded from any relation between a subject and an object or between a subject and a subject-object. (55ph) And here a concrete analysis of unavailability is no less necessary than was that of betrayal, denial, or despair.

Actually, at the heart of unavailability we find there is always a certain alienation. Others invite my sympathy for a certain misfortune they tell me about. I understand what they describe; I recognize in the abstract that the people they're talking about deserve my compassion; I know that it would be logical and just to respond to this case with sympathy, which sympathy I confer, if you will, but only in thought, because finally I have to admit that I am not moved. Besides, I regret this contradiction between what I am, in fact, experiencing—that is to say my indifference—and what I recognize that I should be experiencing. It is painful and it irritates me, it diminishes me in my own eyes, but all this is to no avail. What remains with me is the inadmissable feeling that, after all, these are people I don't know, and that if one had to be touched by every human misfortune, life would no longer be possible—and what's more, one's life would be inadequate to respond to all the needs. From the moment that I think, "After all this is only a case, # 75-627," it's all over; I can no longer feel anything. (56d)

But what characterizes the present or available soul is precisely to not think in terms of *cases*; there are no *cases* for the present or available soul. (57i,d,ph)

It is, however, clear that the normal growth of a being implies an increasingly precise and almost automatic sorting out of what is one's concern and what is not, what one is responsible for and what one is not. It's as if each one of us thus becomes the center of a kind of mental space that is arranged in concentric zones of decreasing interest and involvement. Basically it's as if each one of us secreted a shell that becomes increasingly hard and that imprisons us, and that sclerosis is linked to the hardening of the categories according to which we represent the world to ourselves and then evaluate it. (58d)

Fortunately, any one of us can experience an encounter that breaks down the categories of this egocentric topography. I can understand from personal experience that an unknown individual encountered by chance can suddenly give rise to an appeal so irresistible as to reverse all the usual perspectives, just as a sudden wind would blow over the panels of a stage set—what seemed close becomes infinitely far away, and vice versa; most often these are breaches that close up almost immediately. Such experiences often leave us with a bitter taste, an impression of sadness, almost anguish. I believe, however, that they are beneficial, for they show us, in a flash, what is after all quite contingent, yes, even accidental in the mental crystallizing that forms the basis of our personal systems.

But it is, above all, the sanctity realized in certain beings that reveals to us that what we call the normal order is, after all, from a higher point of view, that standpoint of a being rooted in the ontological mystery, merely the subversion of an order which is its opposite. In this respect, reflection on sanctity with all its concrete attributes seems to me to present immense speculative value; one would not have to push me too far to make me say that sanctity is the true introduction to ontology.

Here once again the comparison with the unavailable soul casts decisive light on our subject.

To be unavailable is to be not only preoccupied with oneself but also in some way encumbered with oneself. The immediate object can vary in an indefinite number of ways; to be preoccupied with oneself can mean to be caught up in one's health, one's wealth, one's romantic life, and *even with one's interior perfection.* One may conclude from this that to be absorbed in oneself is much less to be concerned with a given *object*, which can hardly be specified here, than to be preoccupied *in a certain manner* that remains to be defined. What must be recognized is that the opposite of the being preoccupied with himself or herself is not the being who is empty or indifferent. The opposition here is between the being who is transparent and the one who is opaque. But we must strive to conceive this inward opaqueness accurately. It's a question, I believe, of a sort of block or fixation, and I wonder if, generalizing considerably and adjusting certain psychoanalytic data, it wouldn't be found that this fixation in a particular area or zone is of a peculiar uneasiness which in itself is something quite different. Only what is remarkable is that this anxiety persists at the center of that fixation and gives it the constricted character that I spoke of in connection with the degradation of the will. (59t) All this leads us to think that this undefined anxiety in reality mingles with the anguish of temporality, with an aspiration not *toward* death but *for* death, which is at the heart of pessimism.

The roots of pessimism are the same as those of unavailability. If this latter increases in us as we age, that is because all too often anguish grows in us to the point of suffocation. As we approach what we consider to be an end, this anguish, in order to be protected from itself, has to put in place an increasingly heavy defense system, one more and more detailed, and also, I will add, more and more vulnerable. (60d) The inability to hope becomes proportionally more and more complete as a being becomes increasingly captive to his or her own experience and the prisoner of the categories in which that experience encloses him or her, that is as he or she gives him or herself over more totally and more desperately to the world of the problematic. (61d)

Here at last can be brought together the various motifs and thematic elements that we have been forced to present successively one after another.

In contrast to the captive soul we have described, the soul that is most at the disposal of others is the one who is the most consecrated, the most inwardly dedicated. This soul is protected against despair and against suicide, which resemble one another and are interrelated, because this soul knows that it does not belong to itself, and that the only legitimate use that it can make of its freedom consists precisely in recognizing that fact. It is starting with this recognition that one can act, that one can create… (62d,ph)

We cannot pretend for an instant that difficulties of every sort will not attack a philosophy of this type. It will inevitably be confronted with faulty alternatives. Either this philosophy will try to resolve those difficulties raised, to provide solutions to them, thus falling into the excesses of a dogmatism or, I will add, of a sacrilegious theodicy that misunderstand their vital principles; or, this philosophy will simply let these difficulties remain, labeling them as mysteries.

Between these two pitfalls I believe there exists a *via media*, a narrow road, difficult and perilous; it is this way that I have forced myself not so much to trace as to point out. But like Karl Jaspers (63i) in his *Philosophy of Existence*, I can only proceed in this territory by calling out to other travelers. If, as occasionally happens, certain minds respond—not the generality, but this or that person—then there really is a path. But—as I think Plato saw with incomparable clarity—this path is discoverable only through love, to which alone it is visible. This shows what is perhaps the deepest, most profound characteristic of the meta-problematical of which I have tried to explore certain facets.

Another very serious objection has to be mentioned. One may say: In reality, everything you say implies an unacknowledged and unformulated reference to Christian data, and is understandable only in this light. Thus we can understand what you mean by presence when we think of Eucharist, what you mean by creative fidelity when we think of Church. But what then will be the value of such a philosophy for a-Christian thinkers, that is to say, those who don't know Christianity or in any event declare that it is impossible for them to accept it?

My reply will be the following: It may be that the existence of certain fundamental Christian realities was requisite *in fact* to enable some minds to conceive certain notions for which I attempted to sketch an analysis, but one certainly cannot say that these notions depend on Christian revelation, *they do not suppose it.*

Besides, if some want to maintain that reason must abstract completely from what is not given universally to every thinking person, I will say that this is an abusive pretention and one that is in the last analysis an illusion. The philosopher today, as in any other time, finds himself or herself placed in a definite historical situation from which it is hardly likely that he or she would be able to realistically abstract; it is only in being duped by a fiction that one imagines oneself capable of starting from a void within and around oneself. Now, our situation involves as one of its essential givens the existence of the Christian reality with all that implies—and this is the case whether or not one adheres to a Christian religion, whether one considers the central Christian affirmations true or false. What is clear to my eyes is that we cannot think as if there had not been centuries of Christianity before our time, just as in the domain of the theory of knowledge we cannot pretend there had not been centuries of positive science. But in this context neither the existence of Christianity nor that of positive science plays more than the role of a fertilizing principle, one that favors in us the burgeoning of certain thoughts that might not have developed without it. Such fertilization can occur in what I would call a Christian environment, and I personally find evidence of this in the fact that experiences of this sort happened to me a good twenty years before I had the slightest notion of converting to Catholicism. (64i,d,ph)

Speaking more particularly to Catholics, I want to note that from my point of view the distinction between the natural and the supernatural should be rigorously maintained. Will some say that the use of the word *mystery* risks creating an equivocation and fostering the confusion I refuse? I will answer that there is no question of confusing those mysteries enveloped in human experience as such—knowledge, love, for example—and revealed mysteries, such as the Incarnation and the Redemption; no effort of reason alone reflecting on experience can enable us to attain to these latter mysteries.

One will then say: In that case, why use the same word for two distinct referents with very different meanings? But I will point out that any revelation whatsoever can only be thought insofar as it addresses itself to a being who is *involved*, in the sense I have attempted to define—that is to say, who participates in a reality that is non-problematizable and which grounds the subject as subject. After all, supernatural life has to find some connections and points of insertion in natural life—which in no way means to imply that supernatural life is merely the flowering of natural life—quite the contrary. It seems to me that if one penetrates deeply enough the notion of *created nature*, which is fundamental for a Christian, one is led to recognize at the heart of nature and of reason as geared to that nature, a sense of radical inadequacy to itself that is like an anxious anticipation of a different order.

To summarize my position on this difficult and particularly important point, I will say that a recognition of the ontological mystery, where I discover, as it were, the central core of metaphysics, is only possible in fact through a sort of fructifying radiance emanating from revelation itself, which can very well happen in the depth of souls unfamiliar with any form of positive religion. That this recognition can be effectuated through certain higher modes of human experience does not in any way imply any adherence to a definite religion, but it does enable those who have risen to this level of recognition to glimpse the possibility of revelation in an entirely different manner than could someone who, never having gone beyond the limits of the problematizable, remains on the hither side of the threshold where the mystery of being can be perceived and proclaimed. Such a philosophy moves toward an irresistible encounter with a light that it perceives from afar and of which it feels a burning predisposition and whose secret attraction touches a deep passionate longing. (65d,ph)

ENDNOTE REFERENCES

Abbreviations listed in [SQUARE BRACKETS] indicate the dictionaries and encyclopedia of philosophy cited in endnotes. On occasion the abbreviation of the book is followed by the name of the author of a particular article. [Translator's Note]

[ANGELES] *Dictionary of Philosophy*, Peter A. Angeles, New York, NY, Barnes & Noble Books, Harper & Row Publishers, 1981.

[CAMBRIDGE] *Cambridge Dictionary of Philosophy*, Robert Audi, Editor, New York, NY, Cambridge University Press, 1995.

[ENCYCLOPEDIA] *The Encyclopedia of Philosophy*, Paul Edwards, Editor-in-Chief, New York, NY, Macmillan Publishing Co. & The Free Press, 1967, Reprint Edition, 1972.

[FLEW] *A Dictionary of Philosophy*, Anthony Flew, Editorial Consultant, New York, NY, St. Martin's Press, 1979.

[OXFORD] *The Oxford Companion to Philosophy*, Ted Honderich, Editor, New York, NY, Oxford University Press, 1995.

[ROBERT] *Le Petit Robert Dictionnaire Universel des Noms Propres*, sous la direction de Paul Robert, Paris, Dictionnaires Le Robert, 1994.

[RUNES] *Dictionary of Philosophy*, Dagobert Runes, New York, NY, Philosophical Library, 1960.

[VOCAB.G.M.] *Vocabulaire Philosophique de Gabriel Marcel*, Simonne Plourde, René Davignon, Jeanne Parain-Vial, Marcel Belay, (Recherches, Nouvelle Série 6) Paris, Editions du Cerf; Montréal, PQ, Bellarmin, 1985.

Translator's Notes

1.i Maurice Maeterlinck (b. Ghent, Belgium 1862; d. Nice, France 1949), a symbolist poet, published two collections of poems expressing poignant melancholy, *Serres chaudes*, 1889, and *Quinze chansons*, 1896. He wrote several plays, which revived the fatality of Greek drama in an atmosphere of strange mysteriousness (*La Princesse Maleine*, 1889; *Pelléas et Mélisande*, 1892; *Monna Vanna*, 1902; and a story of fairies full of grace and freshness, *L'Oiseau bleu*, 1908). He developed a strange philosophy curious about all forms of life and their metamorphoses. First touched by the tragedy of the human condition, he sought silence and solitude and suffered great anguish before his thought moved toward serene certitudes that enabled him to overcome despair. A metaphysical meditation that is a sort of quest for happiness gradually developed throughout numerous collections of his works published over a period of 40 years. *Le Trésor des humbles*, 1896; *La Sagesse et la Destinée*, 1898; *La Vie des abeilles*, 1901; *L'Intelligence des fleurs*, 1907; *La Mort*, 1913; *Les Sentiers dans la montagne*, 1919; *Le Grand Secret*, 1921; *La Grande Féerie*, 1929; *La Vie des fourmis*, 1930; *La Grande Loi*, 1933; *Avant le grand silence*, 1934; *Le Sablier*, 1936. Negating time and death, Maeterlinck's thought affirms forcefully his acceptance of the world's order and his desire to overcome its apparent absurdity. [ROBERT, p. 1281]

2.i, ph *Ontological* refers to the study of the act-being of something, particularly human being wherein we can question, experience, and discover the immanent-transcendent act whereby beings are, rather than nothing. Ontology inquires about the nature of the immanent-transcendent act-being, and the meaning and value it can give to human existence and the totality of being. Cf. one descriptive usage of the term on p. 175; compare with Christiane's evocation in *The Broken World*, pp. 46-47; cf. also on p. 175 what withstands attempts to render it devoid of any intrinsic significance or secure lasting value in itself; cf. also p. 178.

3.ph Reference may be to convictions of modern idealists Kant, Fichte, Schelling, and even Hegel, or personalities like Leon Brunschvicg who dominated the official philosophic establishment. This reference also alerts us to a characteristic of Marcel's manner of philosophizing, which is always to proceed in a dialogue with real or imagined interlocutors, in this way considering objections to or varying interpretations of a point he is striving to clarify. Marcel's analyses look to clarify the essential traits of a phenomenon as this reality presents itself within one's experience. The investigations move through critical questioning and entertainment of alternative interpretations in order to explain in a cogent and rigorously reasoned way what he also evokes and describes as a positive interpretation of the nature of a particular phenomenon. These characteristics proper to Marcel's own way of thinking are such that Herbert Spiegelberg sees them as sufficient to designate Gabriel Marcel as a French representative of the Phenomenological Movement. Cf. Herbert Spiegelberg, *The Phenomenological Movement, A Historical Introduction*, 2 vols., The Hague, Martinus Nijhoff, 1965, vol. 2, pp. 421-44.

Certainly when Gabriel Marcel wrote that he was well aware of the resistances he would meet he realized that his philosophy stood in opposition both to the positivism or contemporary scientism and the neo-Kantian idealism that was taught at the Sorbonne by Brunschvicg and also by Dominique Parodi, and also at the University of Lyon by Lachièze-Rey. Kantian idealism had great influence in French universities from the time of Hamelin (1856-1907). Marcel's reference probably aims more at the French neo-Kantians than the Germans, although Marcel admits that during his student days he had been greatly influenced by Fichte. But the talk was addressed to French philosophers and envisaged the philosophic climate in which they lived. [Personal communication from Mme. Jeanne Parain-Vial. Dec. 4, 1996.]

4.i,ph *Metaphysical Journal*, Marcel's first major philosophic work, written in journal form, was begun in 1914 and published in 1927. Appended to it was a most important essay, "Existence and Objectivity." For a fine, clear commentary see Seymour Cain, *Gabriel Marcel's Theory of Religious Experience*, NY, Peter Lang, 1995.

5.i, ph A movement of existential analysis joining philosophic and psychological perspectives did emerge with Gordon Alport, Carl Rogers, Rollo May, Victor Frankl, Adrian Van Kaam, and F.J.J. Buijtendijk among its representatives. Cf. *Review of Existential Psychology and Psychiatry*, K. Hoeller, Editor, Seattle, WA.

6.i Auguste Comte (b. Montpellier, France 1798; d. Paris, France 1857), a graduate of the Polytechnic School, proposed "positivism" as a way to reorganize society. He wanted politics to be a physical and positive science: *Opuscules de philosophie sociale*, 1819-29. Such was the aim of his *Course of Positive Philosophy*, offered by him in 1828 but interrupted in 1829 by a severe psychological disorder that required his confinement. Comte affirms that humanity as a whole and individuals in particular pass through successive stages: the theological and military, characterized by an imaginative and supernatural explanation of phenomena — fetishism, polytheism, then monotheism; the metaphysical and legalistic, similar to the first but wherein supernatural agents are replaced with abstract forces; and finally the industrial stage, where people renounce trying to find the essence and profound causes of things and concentrate on finding the laws that govern facts as studied through observation and reason. Comte proposed a complete program of education through a linear classification proceeding from the broadest of sciences to the more complex:

mathematics (basis of all philosophy), astronomy, physics, chemistry, physiology, and social physics (sociology), a word created by Comte which he divided into dynamic and static sociology. Comte rejected the psychology of his time, involving introspection. In part under the influence of his platonic love for Clotilde de Vaux, whom he met 1844 and who died in 1846, he developed a veritable positivist religion. (*Système de politique positive*, 1851-54; *Catéchisme positiviste*, 1852; *Synthèse subjective ou Système universel des conceptions propres à l'état normal de l'humanité*, 1856.) Positivist society and state would have their religion, a cult of the Great Being of Humanity, and their morality whose motto is: "Love as its principle, Order as its basis and Progress as its goal." [ROBERT, p. 493.]

7.d Recall the apparently aimless and unimportant life of Augsburger, Christiane's retired and widowed father in *The Broken World*. He doesn't really count. In what ways does this character reflect such a function-centered view of life; in what ways does he not?

8.d Does not Marcel Belay's essay suggest this significance in considering why Denise commits suicide and Christiane does not? These lines move us to reconsider Marcel Belay's question and insightful reflection, pp. 159-64.

9.ph,t Cf. pp. 178-81.

10.d,ph Do you find any connection between Christiane's expression of her impression of a "broken world," Act I, p. 46, and this moment of reflective analysis in the philosophic essay? How do the two modes of expression and evocation differ; in what way might they be said to be similar?

11.d,ph Could this conception be taken as a more general statement of what Denise was living when she blamed Christiane for troubling Bertrand with her talk about a "broken world," Act II, p. 88, and even more so later when Denise breaks in on Lawrence and Christiane to say goodbye to them, Act III, pp. 112-14? Cf. also Act IV, pp. 129-30.

12.i Sigmund Freud (b. Pribor, Moravia 1856; d. London, UK 1939), an Austrian doctor and psychiatrist who founded psychoanalysis. His ingenious discoveries revolutionized the understanding of the structure and workings of the human psyche. His theories evolved first as discoveries of a way to treat mental illnesses. Later they were accepted as identifying the structure and functioning of the human psyche. Especially in popularized interpretations, Freudian categories seemed to diminish human dignity and autonomy by reductionist interpretations of love, freedom, conscience, and sexuality. Hence the sense of Marcel's comments.

13.i *La Ville*, an early drama by Paul Claudel, first version 1893, second version 1897, published 1904.

14.ph This is a seminal announcement of an insight central to identifying the nature of a mystery and its mode of presence to us. Like Max Scheler, Marcel offers a burst of new insight, ripe with meaning. The insight needs to be spelled out, but its mention evokes a fresh experience that gives rise to an new conceptual understanding. (Cf. pp. 178-81)

Max Scheler (b. Munich, Germany 1874; d. Frankfurt, Germany 1928) was a phenomenologist of the German Movement. His areas of central concern were ethics and social philosophy, fields wherein his works, especially his analyses of cultural relativity and realistic basis of value theory, his effort to establish an *a priori* hierarchy of values, and his identification of different forms of sociality are of great significance. (*The Nature and Forms of Sympathy*, 1923; *Ressentiment*, 1912; *Formalism in Ethics and Non-Formal Ethics of Value*, 1913; *On the Eternal in Man*, 1921; *Essays in Sociology and Philosophical World Views*, 1923-24; *Forms of Knowledge and Society*, 1926; *Man's Place in Nature*, 1928; and *Philosophical Perspectives*, 1929, containing "Philosopher's Outlook," and "Man and History." [ROBERT, p. 1883; Cf. H. Spiegelberg, Vol. I, pp. 228-70.]

15.i,ph René Descartes (b. The Hague, Holland 1596; d. Stockholm, Sweden 1650), one of the founders of modern thought. He wanted to found philosophy, giving it the reliable method modeled on mathematical sciences and an irrefutable foundation in a clear and distinct idea that resists all doubt. His writings progressively attempt to achieve the goal. *Regulae ad Directionem Ingenii* ("Rules for the Direction of the Mind") was written in 1628 or 1629 and published in 1701; in 1634 he published *Le Monde* (The World); and in 1637 he published a book containing three treatises on mathematical and physical subjects: the *Geometry*, the *Dioptrics*, and the *Meteors*, prefaced by *Discours de la méthode* (Discourse on Method). In 1641 *Meditationes de Prima Philosophia* (Meditations on First Philosophy) was published together with seven sets of *Objections* and Descartes' *Replies to the Objections*. *Principia Philosophiae* (Principles of Philosophy) followed in 1644. In 1649 Descartes published *Les Passions de l'âme* (The Passions of the Soul). [ROBERT, p.585; RUNES, pp.45-46, 57; ANGELES, pp. 29, 39.]

Cogito, ergo sum was offered as the indubitable first principle of knowledge, which could ground, i.e. give valid justification and foundation to, a theory of knowledge. In contrast to this Marcel offers a different kind of experience, one's lived experience of his or her awareness of "being" — as something that I am before it is an affirmation I utter, as something of which I am the stage rather than the spectator—that can proffer a realistic and adequate starting point for investigating the mystery of being.

These last three words, "mystery of being," a paraphrase of "the ontological mystery," became the title of Marcel's Gifford Lectures offered at the University of Aberdeen, Scotland, and published in 1950, *The Mystery of Being*, 2 vols.,London, Harvill Press, 1950-51; Chicago, Regnery/Gateway, 1960; Lanham, MD, University Press of America, 1984.

16.ph Marcel conveys, through evocative description and reasoned analysis, the sense of a global awareness that elsewhere he calls a blind intuition, which characterizes one's apprehension of being — as one's own and yet other and more than one's own. Cf. "Intuition aveuglée," pp. 323-26 in [VOCAB.G.M.]

17.ph In the context of phenomenology, a limit idea refers to an ideal the full realization of which exceeds human potential, but which nonetheless can authentically focus one's aim and striving.

To the metaphysical theory of participation as conceived and explained in the writings of Plato, e.g., *The Parmenides*, Marcel invites us to add an existential awareness of a participation in being that is personal and conscious. Cf. *Presence and Immortality*, "My Fundamental Purpose," p. 18.

18.i Paul Claudel (b. Aisne, France 1869; d. Paris, France 1955), poet and dramatist as well as a diplomat whose career led him to China, South America, and finally to serve as France's ambassador to Tokyo and then to the United States. During 14 years in China he wrote *Connaissance de l'Est*, 1907; *Art Poétique*, 1907; *Partage de midi*, 1906; and *Cinq Grandes Odes*, 1910. [ROBERT, pp. 470-71.]

19.ph This is the classic definition of the distinction Marcel conceives between problem and mystery. For interesting commentary on this notion, cf. *A Prelude to Metaphysics, Being Interrogated Through Reflection and History*, K. R. Hanley and J. D. Monan, S.J., Englewood Cliffs, NJ, Prentice-Hall, 1967. Ch.III, Being, Reflection and History, esp. Marcelian Distinction of Problem and Mystery, pp. 79-91. Marcel's approach begins with a preliminary sketch of a notion that concrete examples enable us to perceive imaginatively and verify experientially as these are clarified through critically reasoned analysis.

20.ph For a more thorough analysis of "the body subject," cf. Marcel's *Creative Fidelity*, Ch. I, Incarnate Being as the Central Datum of Metaphysical Reflection, pp. 11-37, originally published in French as *Du Refus à l'Invocation* (From Refusal to Invocation).

21.t, ph "placed before," i.e., viewed as a distinct, almost separate, object of distant perception and disengaged speculation.

22.ph For further exposition of Marcel's thought about evil, cf. René Davignon, *Le Mal chez Gabriel Marcel, Comment affronter la souffrance et la mort?*, (Recherches, Nouvelle Serie 4.) Paris, Ed. Cerf; Montréal, Bellarmin, 1985.

23.ph For Marcel's positive notion of God as "Ultimate Recourse," cf. *Creative Fidelity*, Ch. IX, Meditations on the Idea of a Proof for the Existence of God, pp. 175-83; cf. also Ch. VI, From Opinion to Faith, pp. 133-36.

24.ph For commentary on Marcel's distinction between first- and second-level reflection, cf. [VOCAB.G.M.], pp. 436-39.

25.ph For a fuller analysis of the notion of fidelity, cf. "Obedience and Fidelity," pp. 125-34 in *Homo Viator, a Phenomenological Approach to a Metaphysics of Hope*, and "Being as the Ground of Fidelity," mentioned in

Being and Having, pp. 45-46, pp. 55-56 in *Etre et Avoir*.

26.t,ph "Bring us close" — italics added. For a more extensive analysis of the notion of presence, cf. Marcel's essay "Presence and Immortality" (1951) originally entitled "The Existential Premises of Immortality," pp. 227-44, and author's preface, pp. 7-8 in *Presence and Immortality*, Pittsburgh, PA, Duquesne University Press; and Louvain, Nauwelaerts, 1967. Cf. also Ch. III, *The Unfathomable*: A Search for Presence, in Katharine Rose Hanley's *Dramatic Approaches to Creative Fidelity: A Study in the Theater and Philosophy of Gabriel Marcel (1889-1973)*, Lanham, MD, University Press of America, 1987, pp. 55-75.

27.ph The objection here can be summarized "what assures us of the existence of this content of thought that is metaproblematic?" It seems that this objection can come from common sense, from positivist philosophers and even idealist philosophers if like the positivists these latter distinguish between the representation of something outside the mind and the reality itself. Our representation may perhaps be erroneous or illusory. Much more so can the metaproblematic be illusory, pure invention, since it is a reality internal to consciousness. Marcel proceeds to reply to this objection by showing that the metaproblematic is not a "content of thought," not a representation, for it cannot be separated from the act that thinks it as one can dissociate the sun from the vision I have of it, or even the image I create of it when I'm not viewing it.

The objection may also have been occasioned by the mindset of the idealism represented by Leon Brunschvicg *et al.*, whose stances are so criticized by post-modernists today. Cf. *Bulletin de la Société Américaine de Philosophes de Langue Française*, Vol. VII, No. 1-2, Spring 1995, "Gabriel Marcel and Postmodernism," Dept. of Foreign Languages and Literatures, Northern Illinois University, DeKalb, IL 60115-2854, Prof. Colette Michael, Editor.

28.d,ph It is noteworthy in this connection that Christiane was the reflective person, capable of recollection even though at first some of its dimensions were cut off by the trauma of love believed lost. Cf. Belay, pp. 160-64. Cf. Gabriel Marcel, *Le Monde Cassé*, "Un Chef D'Oeuvre méconnu de Gabriel Marcel," *Ecclesia*, No.4, juillet 1949, pp. 83-92, esp. p. 86.

29.i *Für-sich-sein*. To be for oneself. A dialectical movement of turning back on oneself that is at the center of German Idealism. Immanuel Kant (1724-1804), Johann Gottlieb Fichte (1726-1814), and Friedrich Wilhelm Joseph von Schelling (1775-1854) represent this position in different ways. The aim of idealism is to achieve an intelligible unity of subject and object and thus establish a critical foundation for knowledge, especially as modeled on the sciences of mathematics and physics.

30.i I Corinthians 6:19.

31.i *Erlebnis* (Ger. *erleben*, to experience or live through). The mind's identification with its own emotions and feelings when it consciously "lives through" an experience contrasts with cognition, with its characteristic duality between subject and object. [RUNES, Ledger Wood, p. 97.] German term for experience used in late nineteenth- and early twentieth-century German philosophy. *Erlebnis* denotes experience in all its direct immediacy and lived fullness. It contrasts with the more typical German word *Erfahrung*, denoting ordinary experience as mediated through intellectual and constructive elements. As immediate, *Erlebnis* eludes conceptualization, in both the lived present and the interiority of experience. As direct, *Erlebnis* is also disclosive and extraordinary: it reveals something real that otherwise escapes thinking. Typical examples include art, religion, and love, all of which also show the anti-rationalist and polemical uses of the concept. It is especially popular among the Romantic mystics like Novalis and the anti-rationalists Nietzsche and Bergson, as well in phenomenology, *Lebensphilosophie*, and existentialism. [CAMBRIDGE, James Bohman, p. 240.]

32.i Intuition: (Lat. *intuere*, to look at) The direct and immediate apprehension by a knowing subject of itself, of its conscious states, of other minds, of an external world, of universals, of values or of rational truths. [RUNES, Ledger Wood, p. 149.]

33.ph On first- and second-level reflections cf. above on p. 179, also note 24. Likewise cf. Robert Rosthal's particularly clear and enlightening translator's introduction to the English edition of *Creative Fidelity*, pp. ix-xxvi.

34.t, ph, d Cf. earlier references to suicide, betrayal, denial, pp. 174-76. Consider also Denise's fate and Christiane's musings about suicide in *BW*, IV, p. 130. Cf. also Marcel Belay, pp.160-64.

35.i Jacques Maritain (b. Paris, France 1882; d. Toulouse, France 1973), a French Catholic philosopher whose innovative interpretation of Aquinas's philosphy made him a central figure in Neo-Thomism. Bergson's teaching saved him from metaphysical despair and a suicide pact with his fiancée. His major works are *Distinguish in Order to Unite or The Degrees of Knowledge*, (1932); *Art and Scholasticism*, 1920; *Man and the State*, 1961; and *Integral Humanism*, 1936. He is also known for his *Reflections on America*, 1975. His wife, Raissa Maritain, published several books, including *We Were Friends Together*, *Adventures in Grace*, *St. Thomas Aquinas: Angel of the Schools*, and *Pilgrim of the Absolute*. [CAMBRIDGE, Deal W. Hudson, p. 464.]

36.i The Catholic University of Louvain, Louvain, Belgium, founded 1425, has a Higher Institute of Philosophy founded by Désiré Cardinal Mercier in 1890. In the time of Etienne Gilson, Ferdinand van Steenbergen, Jacques Maritain, and others, the issue of the possibility and nature of Christian Philosophy was much debated. The Higher Institute of Philosophy was founded with the approval of Leo XIII to encourage a renewal of historic, textual, and scholarly study of the works of St. Thomas Aquinas; since its foundation and still today Louvain has kept alive this tradition of dialogue between principles of perennial philosophy and developments of contemporary thought.

37.i Martin Heidegger (b. Messkirch, Bade 1889; d. Messkirch, Bade 1976). Heidegger's project was to renew fundamental ontology. The path he took was to survey the distinctive traits of human existence; this led to the recognition of human existence as "Da-Sein"—"There-Being"—one whose very existence carries the questioning of Being—the why of one's being situated in the immanent-Transcendent Act (of) Being. The vocation of human existence is to dare the anguish of questioning not merely the essence of beings (individual entities) but also the question: Why there are beings at all, rather than nothing?, which opens the way to question Being, the Ground as immanent-Transcendent Act whereby beings are. A human's ultimate vocation is to be "Questioner of Being," "Shepherd of Being," "Hearer of the Word," and "Poet." As the classic text by William J. Richardson, S.J., *Martin Heidegger: Through Phenomenology to Thought*, Preface by Martin Heidegger, The Hague, Martinus Nijhoff, 1967, suggests, there is a development in Heidegger's thought. The first moment was to be an analysis of fundamental human existential traits: thrownness, being in the world, project, authenticity versus inauthenticity, temporality, being toward death etc.; the second moment was a poetic listening to the disclosure of Being, "Aletheia." Marcel's remark in passing no doubt refers to the early Heidegger's phenomenological analyses and the popular attention that was given to such "existential" themes as "Sein zum Tode" — "being toward death." Cf. *Presence de Gabriel Marcel Cahier 1*, "Gabriel Marcel et la pensée allemande, Nietzsche, Heidegger, Ernst Bloch," Paris, Aubier, Trois Inédits: "Ma relation avec Heidegger," pp. 26-38.

38.i Leon Brunschvicg (b. Paris, France 1869; d. Aix-les-Bains, France 1944) is a striking example of the critical idealist who studied the conditions of scientific spirit and its development. Considering reason as a legislative activity that presents and perfects its laws of demonstration, he saw mathematics as their most perfection expression. (*Les Etapes de la philosophie mathémathique*, 1912; *Les Ages de l'intelligence*, 1922; *L'Expérience humaine et la causalité physique*, 1922; *Le Progrès de la conscience dans la philosophie occidentale*, 1927.) [ROBERT, p. 328.]

39.ph For more extensive treatment of despair and faith, cf. *Creative Fidelity*, Ch. VI, From Opinion to Faith, pp. 120-39; Ch. VII, The Transcendent as Metaproblematic, pp. 140-46; Ch. VIII, Creative Fidelity, pp. 147-74; Ch. IX, Meditations on the Idea of a Proof for the Existence of God, pp. 174-83.

40.i Baruch Spinoza (b. Amsterdam, Holland 1632; d. The Hague, Holland 1677), a rationalist influenced by Descartes, wrote *Tractatus theologico-*

politicus 1670 (unfinished), and *Tractatus de intellectus emendationne*, an unfinished preamble to *L'Ethique* exposing Spinoza's self-made philosophy following the geometric method. [ROBERT, pp. 1963-64.]

41.ph For a more extensive treatment of hope, cf. "A Sketch of a Phenomenology and a Metaphysic of Hope," in *Homo Viator*, pp. 29-67. Cf. also a summary of this essay's highlights in Hanley and Monan, *A Prelude to Metaphysics*, Ch. III, pp. 91-100.

42.i Frederich Nietzsche (b. Rocken, Thuringe, Germany 1844; d. Weimar, Germany 1900). Cf. "Man Before the Alleged Death of God," an address given in the United States and other countries during the 1960s; this address was published for the first time as "L'Homme devant la Mort de Dieu," in *Présence Gabriel Marcel*, Cahier 1, Paris, Aubier, pp. 9-24; cf. also references to this in "Gabriel Marcel and Postmodernism: Perspectives on *The Broken World*," in *Bulletin de la Société Américaine de Philosophes de Langue Française*, Vol. VII, No. 1-2, 1995, pp. 144-46.

43.i Charles Péguy (b. Orleans, France 1873; d. Villeroy, France 1914), a writer who in polemic works addressed social and political issues of his day to inspire humanly wise and responsible forms of action. He also wrote lyric works charged with spirituality, yet revealing his own interior dramas. He wrote a free verse, three-part drama devoted to St. Joan of Arc in 1897. *Le Mystère de la charité de Jeanne d'Arc*, 1910, a meditation on love; *Le Porche du Mystère de la deuxième vertu*, 1911, which celebrates hope; and *Le Mystère des saints Innocents*, 1912; (The Mystery of the Charity of Joan of Arc; The Porch of the Mystery of the Second Virtue; and The Mystery of the Holy Innocents). In everyday language and in terms of solemn simplicity, these works underline the need to root the spiritual in the carnal (the Mystery of the Incarnation) and the amazing ways of Grace (the Mystery of the Redemption.) [ROBERT, p.1595.] The Porch of the Mystery of the Second Virtue is cited in Marcel's talk on "Man Before the Alleged Death of God," in *Presence de Gabriel Marcel*, Cahier 1, "Gabriel Marcel et la pensée allemande, Nietzsche, Heidegger, Ernst Bloch," Paris, Aubier, pp. 20-22.

44.i,t "Paralogism," the term Marcel uses, denotes an error due to faulty reasoning done in good faith.

45.ph Cf. p. 183 and earlier notes 24 and 33 on second reflection and also "My Fundamental Purpose," (1938), pp. 21-27.

46.t The original text included a reference to 1933, which invites us to recognize the penetrating foresight of Marcel's perception of trends in our Western culture.

47.ph Marcel's approaches, like the steps of Edmund Husserl's phenomenological method, speak of viewing a reality from different perspectives so as to bring to light its many different facets. This method also includes analysis, which by dialectical argumentation and reflection critically clarifies the essence of this same reality. Cf. Herbert Spiegelberg, *The Phenom-

enological Movement, vols. 1 and 2, The Hague, Martinus Nijhoff, 1965, especially Vol. I, Ch. 1: "Edmund Husserl 1859-1938," pp. 72-167.
48.i Baruch Spinoza, Dutch philosopher 1632-1677, cf. note 40.i.
49.t, ph, d Cross reference to misconceptions of recollection, e.g. rigidity, fixation, cf. pp. 181-83; 186-88. Consider Christiane's musings about her being mistaken in having married Lawrence. Even Lawrence criticizes these ruminations of the past as an accountant's review of a ledger, a mere reckoning of credits and debits, so far removed from any true recollection of deep personal feelings or of genuine human relationships. Cf. *BW,* II, pp. 96-97.
50.i Henri Bergson (b. Paris, France 1859; d. Paris, France 1941), Professor at the College de France 1900-14, was one of the rare university figures of his time whom Marcel found original, positive, and inspiring philosohically. Bergson was hostile to formalist intellectualism, especially that of Kant and neo-Kantianism, as well as scientific positivism and materialism. He elaborated his thought by developing a critical analysis of the scientific methods and findings of his day (particularly in biology and psychology). He wanted his philosophy to be a conscious and reflective return to what is immediately given in intuition. His major works include: *Les Donnés immédiates de conscience,* 1889; *Matière et Mémoire,* 1896; *Le Rire,* 1900; *L'Evolution créatrice,* 1907; *L'Energie spirituelle,* 1919; *Durée et Simultanéité,* 1922; *Les Deux Sources de la morale et de la religion,* 1932; *La Pensée et le mouvement,* 1934. [ROBERT, p. 237.]
51.i One of the main theses of *Deux Sources de la Morale et de la Religion,* 1932 (*The Two Sources of Morality and Religion,* Notre Dame, IN, University of Notre Dame Press, 1977.)
52.d,ph Do the last two scenes of Act IV of *The Broken World,* pp. 140-52, enflesh a situation that this philosophic description and interpretation seems to clarify? How so?
53.ph,t On first- and second-level reflection cf. above, notes 24, 33, 45. Cf. also the translator's introduction by Robert Rosthal to the English translation of *Creative Fidelity,* which is particularly clear and enlightening. Also cf. "Reflection seconde" in *Vocabulaire philosophique de Gabriel Marcel,* Simonne Plourde *et al.,* Montréal, Bellarmin, 1985, pp. 436-39. Consider the last ten pages defining second reflection and then exercising it as the data resourcing a critical clarification of hope. Cf. Hanley and Monan, *A Prelude to Metaphysics,* Ch. III.
54.ph,d Marcel traces an ascending dialectic passing from desire to hope, from covetous to generous, from egocentric to oblative love in his essay "Presence and Immortality," originally entitled "The Existential Premises of Immortality," published in *Presence and Immortality.* This book includes the first act of an unfinished play, *The Unfathomable,* and excerpts from Marcel's *Journal* 1938-44. Marcel also speaks of an ascending dialectic as characterizing the dramatic development of his plays. Cf. Intro-

duction to *Existentialist Drama of Gabriel Marcel,* West Hartford, CT, McAuley Press, 1974, p. 10.

Can such an ascending dialectic be sensed and traced in Christiane's development and spiritual journey through and beyond *The Broken World?* Has Christiane's notion and understanding of love developed and moved more into spiritual availability from her first shattered dream of life with Jacques Descroy, her notion of love in a marriage of convenience with Lawrence Chesnay, her notion of adulation within her circle of friends, manipulation of Lawrence for attention, carnal love with Gilbert, to a light of love that breaks through the breach in what would otherwise be a wall of despair, and an assurance of being loved that enables her to reach out for the first time for an authentic relation in a light of truth and therefore, also for a first time, a genuine love relationship with her husband?

55.ph A subject-object would be a human person treated like a thing. For clarification of this notion, cf. Marcel's first- and second-level reflections spelled out in Ch. II, Belonging and Disposability, in *Creative Fidelity,* pp. 38-57.

56.d Concrete portrayal of this attitude occurs in *Thirst* (*La Soif*) and in *The Votive Candle* (*La Chapelle Ardente*), where *charity cases* are considered in just this impersonal, disengaged way. Consider also Henry's and Gilbert's attitudes toward Christiane's volunteer work at hospitals, Act II, *The Broken World,* p. 91.

57.i,d,ph It is well known that Marcel's work with the Red Cross, notifying next of kin of soldiers killed or missing in action, occasioned his keen awareness of what became a central idea in his life and thought. Cf. "An Essay in Autobiography," in *The Philosophy of Existentialism,* pp. 104-28, esp. 121; and "An Autobiographical Essay," in *Gabriel Marcel* (Library of Living Philosophers,) Vol. XVII, La Salle, IL, Open Court, Paul A. Schilpp and Lewis E. Hahn, editors, 1984, pp. 3-68. This experience helped move Marcel beyond the abstract categories of idealism into the more concrete and existential categories of "I and Thou."

58.d How might we describe some of the categories according to which Christiane, Henry, Lawrence, and others represent and evaluate people with whom they deal and for whom they are to some extent responsible? Which people are "real" for them?

59.t Cf. reference to the constricted character of degraded wills, pp.187-88.

60.d Does Augsburger's behavior in Act III or IV manifest any of these characteristics? Could they plausibly be a reflection of the unconscious attitude Marcel identifies in his philosophic reflection?

61.d Can Denise's conversation and behavior in Act II, pp. 87-89, and Act III, pp. 113-14, be reflective of this attitude but in a more desperate situation lived by a far more lucid person?

62.d,ph Can this description or can it not apply to Christiane to clarify what she undergoes in the last two scenes of *The Broken World*, pp. 140-52? An interesting and more extensive analysis of the act and the person occurs in *Creative Fidelity*, Ch. V, Observations on the Notion of the Act and the Person, pp. 104-19.

63.i Karl Jaspers (b. Oldenberg, Germany 1883; d. Basel, Switzerland 1969) was a German psychologist and philosopher. His works in psychiatry and psychology introduced the comprehensive method of Dilthey and the phenomenology of Husserl. Spiritually akin to Nietzsche, and especially to Kierkegaard, for Jaspers to philosphize is for a person to become aware of his or her situation in relation to a world wherein he or she must engage his or her liberty, and in relation to others with whom he or she tries to communicate. Limit situations, (suffering, failure, death) reveal human finitude and the need for a Transcendence whose signs humans must decipher to discover the sense or the non-sense of existence and human history. Beyond any dogma or authority, the philosophic faith that Jaspers affirms is an exigency for clarity, rationality, and the foundation of a new ethics. This sheds light on his moral and political stands: his opposition to National Socialism, his analysis of *La Culpabilité allemande* (German Culpability) immediately after the war (1946), and his work on *La Bombe atomique et l'avenir de l'humanité* (The Atomic Bomb and the Future of Humanity.) [ROBERT, p. 1066.]

64.i,d,ph After years of philosophic searchings, Marcel had a religious experience and was subsequently baptized in 1929 at the age of 39 with François Mauriac as his sponsor. Marcel noted in his introduction to *The Existentialist Drama of Gabriel Marcel*, pp. 9-10, that without such an experience he could not have written *The Broken World*.

65.d,ph Note the similarities and differences of the metaphor as spoken by Christiane to Henry, Act IV, pp. 133-34, then Christiane and Genevieve, pp. 143-45, and then Christiane and Lawrence pp. 149-52, in *The Broken World* and its significance and referent in the final paragraph of the essay "Concrete Approaches to Investigating the Ontological Mystery."

Appendices I - VIII

For readers desiring more information about Gabriel Marcel's life and work we have appended biblio-biographies and several lists of his works.

Appendix I is a biblio-biography, following a French convention of chronologically listing the major events and publications of an author's life.

Appendix II is a biblio-biography of Gabriel Marcel's entrance into the English-speaking world. This appendix lists chronologically the publication of English translations of Marcel's writing. Such a listing enables readers to perceive how Gabriel Marcel was introduced to and encountered by an English-speaking audience.

Appendix III is a presentation of Gabriel Marcel's plays. The French titles are listed chronologically on the left-hand page, and equivalent English titles are listed on corresponding lines on the right-hand page.

Appendix IV is a presentation of Gabriel Marcel's philosophic books. Again the French titles are listed chronologically on the left-hand page, and equivalent English titles are listed on corresponding lines on the right-hand page.

Appendix V lists (in English) titles of Marcel's plays on the left-hand page and titles of his philosophic books on the right-hand page. A chronological and parallel listing of Marcel's plays and philosophic writings enables readers to note important aspects of his work. First, dramatic inquiry always precedes philosophic investigation. This is necessary to provide a concrete approach which alone allows for an encounter with mystery. Second, parallel chronological listing of dramatic and philosophic works demonstrates the important fact that Marcel's theater is a prospective theater of inquiry, not a theater contrived to illustrate philosophic theses or preconceived ideas. *The Broken World* and the philosophic meditation **"Concrete Approaches to Investigating the Ontological Mystery"** are printed in bold face type to accent visually the central and capital position these works hold in the development of Marcel's thought.

Appendix VI lists Gabriel Marcel's books of drama criticism and cites Roger Troisfontaines's bibliography where interested readers can find exact references to Marcel's many articles of drama criticism in diverse periodicals.

Appendix VII lists some of Gabriel Marcel's piano compositions, gives reference to the publication of some of his writings about music, and announces the availability of a compact disk featuring music by G. Marcel, G. Fauré, C. Debussy, and D. Saroglou.

Appendix VIII lists Resource Centers for Research in France and in the United States of America.

In all appendices the following conventions are observed:

—Titles for works that have not been published are not italicized. This applies in rare instances to French titles, for example, unpublished plays. It is more frequently the case that plays have not yet been published in English translation, and in these instances we have given an equivalent English title but left it in Roman type to signal that an English translation has not yet been published.

—In Appendix VII the titles of Gabriel Marcel's musical compositions are in italics because these have been published as poems even though Marcel's piano compositions have not yet been published.

—Works are listed chronologically, not only for historic and bibliographic accuracy, but also because this convention allows readers to perceive at a glance and, if they so choose, to examine more closely the progressive development that is characteristic of Marcel's thought.

In appendices III, IV, and V, dates of composition are listed in parentheses. In instances where the specific dates of composition are unavailable, date of publication is offered without parentheses.

Appendix I
Gabriel Marcel Biblio-Biography

1889   Born December 7 in Paris.

1893   November 15, death of his mother, born Laure Meyer, July 30, 1866.

1898   His father, Henry Marcel, married Marguerite Meyer, sister of the first wife, before going to Stockholm as ambassador. They stayed in Sweden 1898-99 until Henry Marcel returned to Paris to fill the post of Minister of Fine Arts.

1904   Submitted to Fernand Gregh a play in the style of Ibsen that was a childish presentiment of *A Man of God.*

1909   Friends at the Sorbonne with Jacques Rivière, Henri Franck, and Jean Wahl. Degree conferred with the submission of "The Metaphysical Ideas of Coleridge and Their Connection with the Philosophy of Schelling." Followed the lectures of Henri Bergson,who taught at the Collège de France.

1910   Agrégation de philosophie.

1911   Taught at Lycée de Vendôme.

1912-13   Taught in a small private school above Lake Geneva.

1914   Began writing his *Metaphysical Journal.* Published his first plays: Paris, Ed. Grasset, *Le Seuil Invisible*: Preface, *La Grâce, Le Palais de Sable* (The Invisible Threshold: Preface, Grace, The Sand Castle). During the war, he directed a Red Cross Center in Paris and an information service on those missing in action.

1915-18   Taught at Lycée Condorcêt in Paris.

1916-17   Metapsychical experiences.

1919   Married Jacqueline Boegner.

1919-23   Professor at Sens.

1921   *Le Coeur des Autres* (*Rebellious Heart*) published (Théâtre: Ed. Grasset).

1922   Encounter with Charles Du Bos, whom he succeeded as editor of Plon's Collection "Feux Croisés."

1923   Settled in Paris, 21 rue de Tournon. Worked with *Nouvelle Revue Française*, and became dramatic and then literary critic for *L'Europe Nouvelle*. *L'Iconoclaste* (The Iconoclast) published (Théâtre: Ed. Stock).

1925   *Le Quatuor en fa dièse* (Quartet in F#) published (Théâtre: Ed. Stock). *Un Homme de Dieu* (*A Man of God*) published.

1926   March 6. Death of his father, Henry Marcel, who was born November 1854.

1927   Publication of *Journal Métaphysique* (*Metaphysical Journal*) (Ed. Gallimard).

1929   Religious experience and conversion. Baptized March 23 with François Mauriac as sponsor.

1931   *Trois pièces: Le Regard neuf, Le Mort de demain, La Chapelle ardente*, (Three plays: The New Look, Tomorrow's Dead, *The Votive Candle*), published (Plon).

1933   *Le Monde cassé* (*The Broken World*) published (Théâtre: Ed. Desclée de Brouwer), followed by the essay "Position et approches concrètes du mystère ontologique" ("Concrete Approaches to Investigating the Ontological Mystery").

1935   *Etre et avoir* (*Being and Having*) published (Aubier).

1936   *Le Chemin de crête, (Ariadne)* published (Théâtre: Ed. Grasset). *Le Dard* (The Sting) published (Théâtre: Ed. Plon).

1938   *La Soif* (Thirst) (Théâtre: Ed. Desclée de Brouwer) reprinted under the title *Les Coeurs avides* (Eager Hearts) (La Table Ronde, 1952).

1939-40   Taught at Lycée Louis-le-Grand.

1940   Death of Henry Marcel's second wife, Marguerite, who raised

Gabriel Marcel. Published *Du Refus à l'invocation (Creative Fidelity)* (Gallimard). Acquired the Chateau de Peuch in Corrèze, where the family lived from 1941-43.

1941   Taught several months at Lycée de Montpellier.

1944   Became drama critic for *Nouvelles Littéraires*. Before the war he worked for several reviews, *L'Europe Nouvelle, La Nouvelle Revue Française, Sept, Temps présent, La Vie intellectuelle*, etc.

1945   *L'Horizon* (The Horizon) published (Théâtre: Edition des Etudiants de France). *Homo Viator (Homo Viator)* published (Ed. Aubier). *La Métaphysique de Royce (Royce's Metaphysics)* published (Ed. Aubier). For the years 1945 through 1947 music was at the center of creative activities.

1947   Death of his wife. *Aperçus phénoménologiques sur l'être en situation* (Phenomenological Notes on Being in a Situation) (Ed. Boivin). *Théâtre Comique: Colombyre, ou le Brasier de la Paix; La Double Expertise; Les Points sur les I; Le Divertissement posthume* (Comic Theater: *Colombyre, or the Torch of Peace, The Double Expertise, Dot the I,* The Posthumous Joke) (Ed. Albin Michel). *Existentialisme Chrétien* (Christian Existentialism) (Ed. Plon, collection "Présences" in collaboration with Étienne Gilson, Jeanne Delhomme, Roger Troisfontaines, Pierre Colin, J.-P. Dubois-Dumée).

1948   Directed a UNESCO conference at Beyrouth.

1949   Received the Grand Prize for Literature from the French Academy. Published *Vers un autre Royaume: L'Emissaire; Le Signe de la croix* (Toward Another World: The Emissary, The Sign of the Cross) (Théâtre: Ed. Plon). Delivered the Gifford Lectures at University of Aberdeen, Scotland, *The Mystery of Being*, I. *Reflection and Mystery*, II. *Faith and Reality.*

1950   *La Fin des temps* (The End of Time) Théâtre: *Réalités.*

1951   *Le Mystère de l'être (The Mystery of Being)* 2 vols. (Aubier). *Rome n'est plus dans Rome* (Rome Is No Longer in Rome) (Théâtre: Ed. de la Table Ronde). *Les Hommes contre l'humain* (*Man Against Mass Society*) (Ed. La Colombe).

Travel in North Africa, then in South America.

1952   Elected a Member of the Institute of France, Academy of Political and Moral Sciences.

1953   *Le Declin de la sagesse (The Decline of Wisdom)* (Ed. Plon).

1954   *L'Homme problématique (Problematic Man)* (Ed. Aubier).

1955   *Mon temps n'est pas le vôtre* (My Time Is Not Your Time) (Théâtre: Ed. Plon). *Croissez et multipliez* (Increase and Multiply) (Théâtre: Ed. Plon).

1956   Received the Goethe Prize from the city of Hamburg, conferred in Germany to one who fosters a supranational spirit and work in favor of humanity.

1956-66   Numerous trips to the United States and Canada and to Japan, where he was received by the emperor.

1958   Received the National Grand Prize for Literature. *La Dimension Florestan*, "Le Crepuscule du sens commun" (The Florestan Dimension, "The Twilight of Common Sense") (Ed. Plon).

1959   *Présence et immortalité (Presence and Immortality)* (Ed. Flammarion). *L'Heure Théâtrale* (The Theater Hour) (Ed. Plon).

1960   *La Prune et la prunelle* (The Plum and the Apple of My Eye) (L'Avant scene).

1961   Delivered the William James Lectures at Harvard University: *The Existential Background of Human Dignity.*

1963   Received the Osiris Prize. *The Existential Background of Human Dignity*, Harvard University Press.

1964   Received the Frankfurt Peace Prize, conferred by German editors, publishers, and book dealers. *Auf der Suche nach Wahrheit und Gerechtigkeit*, (Searchings) ed. Wolfgang Ruf, Freiburg im Bresgau, Verlag Knecht. *Regards sur le theatre de Claudel* (Reviews of Paul Claudel's Theater) (Ed. Beauchesne).

1965   Delivered the opening discourse at the Salzburg Music Festival. *Paix sur la terre* (Peace on Earth) (Ed. Aubier). Lectures in the United States.

1967   *Le Secret est dans les îles* (The Secret Is in the Isles) (Ed. Plon).

1968   *Entretiens Paul Ricoeur, Gabriel Marcel (Conversations between Paul Ricoeur and Gabriel Marcel)* (Ed. Aubier).

1969   Received the Erasmus Prize. "An Autobiographical Essay" in *The Philosophy of Gabriel Marcel*, La Salle, Open Court, 1984. Visited Dresden and Prague.

1971   *Le Siècle à venir* (The Century to Come) Fondation Roland de Jouvenel. *Pour une sagesse tragique et son au-delà (Tragic Wisdom and Beyond)* (Ed. Plon). *En chemin, vers quel eveil?* (En Route Toward What an Awakening?) (Ed. Gallimard). *Coleridge et Schelling* (Coleridge and Schelling) (Ed. Aubier).

1972   Received the Dignity of the Grand Cross of the National Order of Merit of the Legion of Honor, of which he was already an Officer and a Commander.

1973   *Percées vers un ailleurs* (Breakthrough Toward a Beyond) (Ed. Fayard). *Cinq Pièces Majeures* (Five Major Plays) (Ed. Plon). Colloquium at Cerisy la Salle, International Cultural Center, Aug. 24-31, 1973, discussing his theater and philosophy.

1973   October 8. Died in Paris.

1975   Foundation of an international association, Présence de Gabriel Marcel, which includes his family, friends, and associates and continues the study of his work. Address: 21 rue de Tournon, 75006 Paris, France.

1976   *Entretiens autour de Gabriel Marcel* (Conversations Around Gabriel Marcel) (Neuchâtel, à la Baconnière). Proceedings of 1973 international colloquium on the Theater and Philosophy of Gabriel Marcel, published with the sponsorship of the European Cultural Foundation.

1978   *Gabriel Marcel interrogé par Pierre Boutang* (Gabriel Marcel Interviewed by Pierre Boutang) (Archives du XXe Siècle). Paris, Editions J.-M. Place, 1978. Followed by a reprinting of "Position et approches concrètès du mystère ontologique" ("Concrete Approaches to Investigating the Ontological Mystery").

1981   *L'Existence et La Liberté Humaine chez Jean-Paul Sartre*, (Exist-
        ence and Human Liberty according to Jean-Paul Sartre) [origi-
        nally published in *Les Grands Appels de l'Homme Contemporain*
        (Great Challenges for Contemporary Man), Editions du
        Temps Présent, 1946] *Précédé d'une présentation de Denis
        Huisman, Gabriel Marcel Lecteur et Juge de Jean-Paul Sartre*
        (Preceded by Denis Huisman's Presentation, Gabriel Marcel
        Reader and Judge of Jean-Paul Sartre. Paris, Librarie Philoso-
        phique J. Vrin, 1981.

Sources for Biographic and Biblio-Biographic Information:

Louis Chaigne, *Vie et oeuvres d'écrivains* (Life and Works of Writers),
Vol. 4, F. Lanore, 1954, pp. 183-201.

Jeanne Parain-Vial, *Gabriel Marcel et les niveaux de l'expérience* (Gabriel
Marcel and the Levels of Experience) (Seghers, 1966), Biblio-biographie,
pp. 99-107.

Gabriel Marcel interrogé par Pierre Boutang (Gabriel Marcel Interviewed
by Pierre Boutang) (J.-M. Place Ed., 1978), p. 116.

Troisfontaines, Roger, S.J., *De L'Existence à L'Etre, La Philosphie de
Gabriel Marcel.* Paris: Béatrice Nauwelaerts-Vrin, 2 vols., 1953, 2e éd.
1968.

Katharine Rose Hanley, *Dramatic Approaches to Creative Fidelity: A Study
in the Theater and Philosophy of Gabriel Marcel* (1889-1973), Lanham,
MD: University Press of America, 1987, pp. 173-83, Cf. also pp. 184-
201, 211-18.

Appendix II
Biblio-Biography of Gabriel Marcel's Entrance into the English-Speaking World

1949   *The Philosophy of Existence.* London, Harvill Press, 1949; New York, The Philosophical Library, 1949; Freeport, NY, Books for Libraries Press, 1969 reprint of 1949 edition. Includes: Introduction by Gabriel Marcel, "On the Ontological Mystery," "Existence and Human Freedom," "Testimony and Existentialism," and "An Essay in Autobiography."

   Being and Having. Westminister, Dacre Press, 1949; New York, Harper and Row, 1965.

1949-50 Gifford Lectures at Aberdeen University, Scotland.

1950   *The Mystery of Being.* Vol. I. *Reflection and Mystery.* Vol. II. *Faith and Reality.* London, Harvill Press, 1950-51; Chicago, Regnery/Gateway, 1960; Lanham, MD, University Press of America, 1984.

1951   *Homo Viator.* London, V. Gollanoz, 1951; Chicago, H. Regnery Co., 1951; New York, Harper and Row, 1962; Magnolia, MA, Peter Smith, 1978.

1952   *Three Plays by Gabriel Marcel, A Man of God, Ariadne, and The Votive Candle (The Funeral Pyre).* London, Secker and Warburg, 1952; New York, Hill and Wang, 1965. Includes preface "The Drama of the Soul in Exile" (a lecture given in July 1950 by Gabriel Marcel at L'Institut Français in London).

   Metaphysical Journal. Chicago, H. Regnery Co., 1952; London, Rockliff Press, 1952, with essay "Existence and Objectivity" in appendix.

   Man Against Mass Society. London, Harvill Press, 1952; Chicago, H. Regnery, 1952; Gateway edition, 1962; Lanham, MD: University of America Press, 1985.

Marcel wanted "Humanity Against Mass Society" as the title of this work but publishers overrode his preference.

1954   *The Decline of Wisdom.* London, Harvill Press, 1954; New York, The Philosophical Library, 1955; Chicago, H. Regnery, 1955.

1956   *The Philosophy of Existentialism.* New York, The Philosophical Library, The Citadel Press Inc., 1956.

       Royce's Metaphysics. Chicago, H. Regnery Co., 1956, 1975.

1958   *The Lantern* in *Cross Currents.* West Nyack, New York, 1958.

1961   The William James Lectures delivered at Harvard University.

1963   *The Existential Background of Human Dignity.* Cambridge, MA, Harvard University Press, 1963.

1964   *Creative Fidelity.* New York, Farrar, Straus, and Co., 1964, reprinted New York, Crossroads Press, 1982.

1964-65 Lectures and travel throughout the United States and Canada.

1965   *Philosophical Fragments (1904-1914) and The Philosopher and Peace.* Notre Dame, IN, Notre Dame University Press, 1965.

1967   *Problematic Man.* New York, Herder and Herder, 1967.

       Presence and Immortality. Pittsburgh, PA, Duquesne University Press, 1967. Includes *The Unfathomable,* the first act of an unfinished play (1919).

       Searchings. New York, Paulist-Newman Press, 1967. Includes "My Dramatic Works as Viewed by the Philosopher" (1959).

1973   *Conversations Between Paul Ricoeur and Gabriel Marcel,* included in *Tragic Wisdom and Beyond.* Evanston, Illinois, Northwestern University Press, 1973.

1974   *The Existentialist Drama of Gabriel Marcel: The Broken World, The Rebellious Heart* and an Introduction by Gabriel Marcel. ed. F.J. Lescoe, West Hartford, CT, McAuley Institute, St. Joseph's College, 1974.

1984   "An Autobiographical Essay" in *The Philosophy of Gabriel Marcel* (The Library of Living Philosophers, Vol. XVII). ed. P.A. Schilpp and L. E. Hahn, LaSalle, IL, Open Court, 1984.

1986   *Two One Act Plays by Gabriel Marcel: Dot the I and The Double Expertise.* Translated by Katharine Rose Hanley. Introduction by Jean-Marie and Anne Marcel, Lanham, MD, University Press of America, 1986.

1988   *Two Plays by Gabriel Marcel: The Lantern and The Torch of Peace plus a previously unpublished essay "From Comic Theater to Mu sical Creation" by Gabriel Marcel.* Lanham, MD, University Press of America, 1988.

1998   *Gabriel Marcel's Perspectives on The Broken World.* Milwaukee: Marquette University Press, 1998.

Appendix III
List of Plays by Gabriel Marcel (1889-1973)

French

La Lumière sur la montagne (1905) inédit
Le Seuil invisible (1914)
   La Grâce (1911)
   Le Palais de sable (1913)
Le Quatuor en fa dièse (1916-17)
Un Juste (1918)
L'Insondable (1919)
Le Petit Garçon (1919) inédit
Trois Pièces (1931)
   Le Regard neuf (1919)
   La Mort de demain (1919)
   La Chapelle ardente (1925) (plusieurs versions 1920-25)
L'Iconoclaste (1920)
Le Coeur des autres (1920)
Un Homme de Dieu (1922)
L'Attelage ou le Noeud coulant (1926) inédit
L'Horizon (1928)
Le Monde cassé (1932)
Le Fanal (1935)
Le Chemin de Crête (1935)
Le Dard (1936)
Théâtre comique (1947)
   Les Points sur les I (1936)
   Le Divertissement posthume (1923)
   Colombyre ou le Brasier de la Paix (1937)
   La Double Expertise (1937)
La Soif (1937) reimprimée avec le titre *Les Coeurs Avides* (1952)
Vers un autre Royaume (1949)
   L'Emissaire (1945)
   Le Signe de la Croix (1938-48) Epilogue (1953)
La Fin des Temps (1948)
Rome n'est plus dans Rome (1951)
Mon Temps n'est plus le votre (1955)
Croissiez et multipliez (1955)
La Dimension Florestan (1958)
La Prune et la prunelle (1960)

English

The Light on the Mountain (1905) unpublished manuscript
The Invisible Threshold (1914)
  Grace (1911)
  The Sand Castle (1913)
Quartet in F# (1916-17)
A Just One (1918)
The Unfathomable (1919)
The Little Boy(1919) unpublished manuscript
Three Plays (1931)
  The New Look (1919)
  Tomorrow's Dead (1919)
  The Votive Candle (1925) (several versions 1920-25)
The Iconoclast (1920)
The Rebellious Heart (1920)
A Man of God (1922)
The Yoke or the Noose (1926) unpublished manuscript
The Horizon (1928)
The Broken World (1932)
The Lantern (1935)
Ariadne (1935)
The Sting (1936)
Comic Theater (1947)
  Dot the I (1936)
  Posthumous Joke (1923)
  Colombyre or the Torch of Peace (1937)
  The Double Expertise (1937)
Thirst(1937) reprinted as Eager Hearts (1952)
Toward Another World (1949)
  The Emissary (1945)
  The Sign of the Cross (1938-48) Epilogue (1953)
Out of Time (1948)
Rome Is No Longer in Rome (1951)
My Time Is Not Your Time (1955)
Increase and Multiply (1955)
The Florestan Dimension (1958)
The Plum and the Apple of My Eye (1960)

Appendix IV
List of Philosophy Books by Gabriel Marcel
French

Coleridge et Schelling (1909), (Preface 1967), Aubier, 1971.

Fragments philosophiques (1909-14), Nauwelaerts, 1961.

La Métaphysique de Royce (1917-18), Aubier, 1945.

Journal métaphysique (1914-23), Gallimard, 1927.

"Position et approches concrètes du mystère ontologique"(1932) Desclée
de Brouwer, 1933.

Etre et avoir (1928-33), Aubier, 1935.

Du Refus à l'invocation, Gallimard, 1940.

Homo Viator (1941-43), Aubier, 1945.

Le Mystère de l'être, 2 vols, (1949-50), Aubier, 1951.

Les Hommes contre l'humain, La Colombe, 1951.

Le Declin de la sagesse, Plon, 1954.

L'Homme problématique, Aubier, 1955.

Présence et immortalité (1919-51), Flammarion, 1959.

Auf der Suche nach Wahrheit und Gerechtigkeit (1959-63), Verlag Knecht, 1964.

La dignité humaine et ses assises existentielles (1961), Aubier, 1965.

Paix sur la terre (1964), Aubier, 1965.

Entretiens Paul Ricoeur-Gabriel Marcel, Aubier, 1968.

Pour une sagesse tragique et son au-delà, Plon, 1969.

En chemin, vers quel éveil?, Gallimard, 1971.

Entretiens autour de Gabriel Marcel (1973), Baconnière, 1976.

English

Coleridge and Schelling (1909) (Preface 1967), Aubier, 1971.

Philosophical Fragments (1909-14), Notre Dame, 1965.

Royce's Metaphysics (1917-18), Regnery, 1956.

Metaphysical Journal (1914-23), H. Regnery, 1952.

"Concrete Approaches to Investigating the Ontological Mystery," in this volume, pp. 172-96.

Being and Having (1928-33), Harper and Row, 1965.

Creative Fidelity, Farrar, Straus and Co., 1964.

Homo Viator (1941-43), Harper and Bros., 1962.

The Mystery of Being, 2 vols. (1949-50), H. Regnery, 1962.

Man Against Mass Society, H. Regnery, 1962.

The Decline of Wisdom, Harvill, 1954.

Problematic Man, Herder and Herder, 1967.

Presence and Immortality (1919-51), Duquesne, 1967.

Searchings (1959-63), Paulist Newman Press, 1967.

Existential Background of Human Dignity (1961), Harvard, 1963.

"The Philosopher and Peace" (1964), in *Philosophical Fragments and the Philosopher and Peace,* Notre Dame, 1965.

Conversations Between Paul Ricoeur and Gabriel Marcel, included in *Tragic Wisdom and Beyond,* Northwestern, 1973.

"An Autobiographical Essay" (Spring 1969), in *The Philosophy of Gabriel Marcel,* Open Court, 1984.

En Route, Toward What an Awakening?

Conversations Around Gabriel Marcel, (1973), Baconniere, 1976.

Appendix V
Dramatic Inquiry Precedes...

The Light on the Mountain (1905) unpublished manuscript
The Invisible Threshold (1914)
   Grace (1911)
   The Sand Castle (1913)
Quartet in F# (1916-17)
A Just One (1918)
The Unfathomable (1919)
The Little Boy(1919) unpublished manuscript
Three Plays (1931)
   The New Look (1919)
   Tomorrow's Dead (1919)
   The Votive Candle (1925) (several versions 1920-25)
The Iconoclast (1920)
The Rebellious Heart (1920)
A Man of God (1922)
The Yoke or the Noose (1926) unpublished manuscript
The Horizon (1928)
The Broken World (1932)
The Lantern (1935)
Ariadne (1935)
The Sting (1936)
Comic Theater (1947)
   Dot the I (1936)
   Posthumous Joke (1923)
   Colombyre or the Torch of Peace (1937)
   The Double Expertise (1937)
Thirst(1937) reprinted as Eager Hearts (1952)
Toward Another World (1949)
   The Emissary (1945)
   The Sign of the Cross (1938-48) Epilogue (1953)
Out of Time (1948)
Rome Is No Longer in Rome (1951)
My Time Is Not Your Time (1955)
Increase and Multiply (1955)
The Florestan Dimension (1958)
The Plum and the Apple of My Eye (1960)

...Philosophic Investigations

Coleridge and Schelling (1909), (Preface 1967),
Philosophical Fragments (1909-14).
Royce's Metaphysics (1917-18).
Metaphysical Journal (1914-23).

"Concrete Approaches to Investigating the Ontological Mystery" (1932).
Being and Having (1928-35).
Creative Fidelity, 1940.
Homo Viator (1941-43).
The Mystery of Being, 2 vols. (1949-50).
Man Against Mass Society, 1951.
The Decline of Wisdom, 1954.
Problematic Man, 1955.
Presence and Immortality (1919-51).
Searchings (1959-63).

The Existential Background of Human Dignity, (1961).
"The Philosopher and Peace" (1964).
Conversations between Paul Ricoeur and Gabriel Marcel, in *Tragic Wisdom and Beyond,* 1969.
"An Autobiographical Essay" (Spring 1969).
En Route, Toward What an Awakening?, 1971.
Conversations around Gabriel Marcel (1973).

Appendix VI
Drama Criticism

Théâtre et Religion (*Theater and Religion*), Lyon, Emmanuel Vitte Editeur, 1958.

L'Heure Théâtrale de Giraudoux à Jean-Paul Sartre (*The Theater Hour from Giraudoux to Jean-Paul Sartre*), Paris, Editions Plon, 1959.

Regard sur le théâtre de Claudel (*A Look at the Theater of Claudel*), Paris, Editions Beauchesne, 1964.

Roger Troisfontaines, S.J. *De L'Existence à L'Etre: La Philosophie de Gabriel Marcel* (*From Existence to Being: The Philosophy of Gabriel Marcel*), 2 vols., Paris, Béatrice Nauwelaerts, Louvain, Nauwelaerts, 1968. Vol. 2, pp. 385-422 and pp. 427-50 provide lists of articles published, many of which are drama reviews published in the following: *Convegno* (*Il*), *Courrier Royal, Europe Nouvelle, Hommes et Monde, Horizon, Ici-France, J'ai Lu, Jour, Métier de Chef, Nef, Nouvelle Revue Française, Nouvelles Littéraires, Sept,* and *Temps Présent.*

Appendix VII
Music

Gabriel Marcel created musical compositions as piano improvisations that were notated by his wife, Mme. Jacqueline Boegner Marcel. Marcel's improvisations sought to bring some of his favorite poems to full expression as song. These piano compositions are preserved in the National Library of France in Paris.

The Collection of Gabriel Marcel Piano Compositions includes:

Mélodies I Sur les poèmes de Baudelaire, Lamartine, Chénier, Ch. Guérin

Baudelaire	*Noesta et Errabunda* 12sept'45	pp. 1-6
	Brumes et Pluies	pp. 7-10
	La Cloche fêlée	pp. 11-13
Lamartine	*Le Lac*	pp. 14-23
A. Chénier	*Mes Mânes à Clytie*	pp. 24-26
Ch. Guérin	*L'Abeille*	pp. 27-29

Mélodies II Sur des poèmes de Paul Valery et de Jules Supervielle

Paul Valéry	*Le Cimetière Marin*	pp. 1-24
	L'Insinuant	pp. 1b, 2b, 3b
	Un feu distinct m'habite	pp. 4-6
	Le Vin perdu	pp. 7-9
Jules Supervielle	*Ce peu...*	pp. 10-12
	L'Enfant	pp. 13-15
	Le petit bois	pp. 16-18
	La Nuit	pp. 19-21
	Le Relais	pp. 22-25

Mélodies III

Madeleine Sabine	*La Solitude*	pp. 1-3
Rodenbach	(*Le règne du Silence*)	
	Il flotte une musique....	pp. 4-8
J. de la Ville de Mirmont	*Si j'étais Gabarre ou chaland*	pp. 9-10
Jean Cocteau	*Je n'aime pas dormir*	pp. 11-14
Catherine Pozzi	*Ave*	pp. 15-18
	Nyx 05/11/34	pp. 19-21

Gérard d'Houville	*Les Eaux douces du Songe*	pp. 22-27
R.M. Rilke	*Das Land ist weit...*	pp. 28-32
	Stunden-Buch p.66	
Hölderlin	*Hyperion Schicksalslied* dec'45	pp. 33-36
R.M.Rilke	*Sonnet à OrphéeII.no. XV* jan'46	pp. 36-39
R.M.Rilke	*Lösch mir die Augen aus*	pp. 39-40
	Stundenbuch.p.58	
R.M.Rilke	*Lösch mir die Augen aus*	pp. 41-42
	Stundenbuch p.58, version définitive	
Odilon Jean Périer	*Sonnet* jan'46	pp. 43-46
	(*Que m'importe de vivre...*)	
Odilon Jean Périer	*Sonnet* fev'46	pp. 46-51
	(*Amour, je ne viens pas....*)	
Odilon Jean Périer	*Je t'offre un verre d'eau glacée* fev.6'46	
		pp. 52-54

Mélodies IV

Hofmannsthal	*Ballade des Aüsseren Lebens* avril-mai'46	pp. 1-5
Laotse	*Wahre Grösse* Le Peuch août'46	pp. 6-9
Louis Emié	*Perséphone* juillet-août'46	pp. 10-13
Laotse	*Dauer im Wechsel* 13-19 août'46	pp. 14-16
Patrice de la Tour du Pin	*Il n'est pas de chambre en mon coeur...*	
	(*Concerts sur la Terre*) 17 avril'46	pp. 17-18
	Qu'y a-t-il de mort...	
	(*Concerts sur la Terre*) Le Peuch 9 août'46	pp. 19-22
	Laurence endormie	
	(*La Quête de joie*) terminé 17août'46	pp. 23-28
Laotse	*Milde* 25 août'46	pp. 29-30
J. Supervielle	*Hommage à la Vie* Le Peuch terminé 2 sept'46	
		pp. 31-35
	Le Double terminé 18 sept'46	pp. 36-39
	Tuerie Le Peuch fin août'46	pp. 40-44
	O Calme terminé 17 août'46	pp. 45-47
Paul Valéry	*La Fausse Morte* Le Peuch 22 sept'46	pp. 48-51
Joachim du Bellay	*La Complainte du Désespéré*	4 pp. unnumbered
	Kyrie eleison 1 line of melody,	p. unnumbered

Mélodies V

| Emily Bronté | *No Coward Soul Is Mine* | pp. 1-5 |
| Gérard de Nerval | *Vers Dorés* | pp. 6-10 |

Présence de Gabriel Marcel Cahier 2-3, L'Esthétique musicale de Gabriel Marcel, Paris, Aubier, 1980, contains a keynote essay by Mme. Jeanne Parain-Vial, ("Gabriel Marcel's Musical Aesthetics"), and numerous important articles and essays by Gabriel Marcel about music. A brief introduction to the general articles cites the places where Marcel's writings on music originally appeared and announces the structure of the present volume. General articles include "Réflexions sur la nature des idées musicales. L'idée chez César Franck" (Reflections on the nature of musical ideas. An idea in César Franck's work), pp. 21-31; "Bergsonisme et musique" (Bergsonism and Music), pp. 33-41; "Musique comprise et musique vécue" (Music Understood and Music Lived), pp 43-47; "Musique et le regne de l'esprit" (Music and the reign of the spirit), pp. 49-59; "La Musique selon saint Augustin" (Music according to Saint Augustine), pp. 61-67; "Réponse à l'enquête de 'Images musicales'" (Replies to the survey on "Musical Images"), pp. 69-70; "L'Irruption de la mélodie" (The Dawning of a Melody) pp. 71-73; "La musique et le merveilleux" (Music and the Marvelous), pp. 75-76; "Méditation sur la musique" (Meditation on Music), pp. 77-83; "Humanisme et musique" (Humanism and Music), pp. 85-87; "La musique dans ma vie et mon oeuvre" (Music in My Life and Work), pp. 89-115.

In a second section entitled "Gabriel Marcel et l'Autriche" (Gabriel Marcel and Austria) there appears a study "Les mélodies espagnoles et italiennes d'Hugo Wolf" (The Spanish and Italian Melodies of Hugo Wolf), pp. 119-30; and "Discours d'ouverture du festival de Salzburg" (Gabriel Marcel's Opening Discourse for the Salzburg Music Festival), pp. 131-38.

A third section includes articles on the French School: "Un intimiste-Ernest Chausson" (Ernest Chausson-an intimist), p. 141; "Le lyrisme Debussiste" (Debussy's lyricism), p. 145; "Paul Dukas," p. 151; "Henri Duparc," p. 163; "Gabriel Fauré," p. 173; "César Franck," p. 187; "Vincent d'Indy," p. 189; "Albéric Magnard," p. 197; "Maurice Ravel," p. 201; "Albert Roussel," p. 211.

In a fourth section "Divers" (Variety) there follow brief comments by G. Marcel on the music of various other composers, pp. 223-83.

"Reference aux exemples et métaphores musicales dans l'oeuvre de Gabriel Marcel" (References to musical examples and metaphors in Gabriel Marcel's work), an item of particular interest to philosophers appears pp. 287-90. "Témoignage: Gabriel Marcel et le disque" (A Testimonial: Gabriel Marcel and Musical Records) by Jean Marcovits, pp.291-93 and then an Index of Composers cited, pp. 295-97, completes this volume.

A compact disk with melodies for voice and piano composed by G. Marcel, C. Debussy, G. Fauré, and D. Saroglou has been made available by the Association "les Compagnons d'Orphée," 8 rue Delambre, 75014 Paris, France. Performing artists are Dimitris Saroglou and Dominique Parain, pianists, Lisa Levy, soprano, and Henri Bougerolle, baritone.

Appendix VIII
Resource Centers for Research

Présence de Gabriel Marcel
21 rue de Tournon
75006 Paris, France
  http : //www.edirom.fr/~gabriel.marcel/
  e-mail : gabriel.marcel@edirom.fr

Bibliothèque Nationale
58 rue Richelieu
75054 Paris, France
  http: //www.bnf.fr
  fax: 011 (33) 47 03 76 65
  (include sender's address via e-mail)

Mme. Michèle Sacquin
  Conservateur en chef au département des manuscrits
  Responsable des Fonds Gabriel Marcel
  (Curator of Gabriel Marcel Collection)

Harry Ransom Humanities Research Center
The University of Texas at Austin
Austin, TX 78713
  http : //www.utexas.edu
or
  http : //mahogany.lib.utexas.edu:1000/libs/hrc/hrhrc

Ms. Linda Ashton, Assistant Curator of the French Collection
  e-mail: l.ashton@mail.utexas.edu

Gabriel Marcel Society
  http : //web.lemoyne.edu/~hanleykr/gmshp.htm
  e-mail: hanleykr@aol.com

Prof. Patrick Bourgeois
Loyola University, New Orleans, LA 70118
  e-mail: pbb31740@aol.com

Prof. Thomas Michaud
Wheeling Jesuit University, Wheeling, WV 26003
  e-mail: tmichaud@xavier.wju.edu

Prof. Robert Lechner
Carthegena Station, Celina, OH 45822

Bibliography of Major Works on Gabriel Marcel

Works in English

Applebaum, David. *Contact and Alienation, The Anatomy of Gabriel Marcel's Metaphysical Method.* (Current Continental Research 214) Washington, D.C.: Center for Advanced Research in Phenomenology & University Press of America, 1986.

Bourgeois, Patrick and Hanley, Katharine Rose. "Gabriel Marcel" in *Routledge Encyclopedia of Postmodernism,* General Editors: Charles E. Winquist and Victor E. Taylor. London, New York: Routledge Press, 1997.

Busch, Thomas. *The Participant Perspective: A Gabriel Marcel Reader.* Lanham, MD: University Press of America, 1987.

Cain, Seymour. *Gabriel Marcel.* New York: Hillary House; London: Bouer and Bouer, 1963; South Bend, IN: Regnery/Gateway Inc., 1979.

Cain, Seymour. *Gabriel Marcel's Theory of Religious Experience.* New York: Peter Lang Inc., 1995.

Cooney, William, ed. *Gabriel Marcel's Contributions to Philosophy: A Collection of Essays.* (Problems in Philosophy, Volume 18) Lewiston, NY: Edwin Mellen Press, 1989.

Gallagher, Kenneth T. *The Philosophy of Gabriel Marcel.* New York: Fordham University Press, 1963, 1975.

Hanley, Katharine Rose. *Dramatic Approaches to Creative Fidelity: A Study in the Theatre and Philosophy of Gabriel Marcel (1889-1973).* Lanham, MD: University Press of America, 1987.

Hanley, Katharine Rose. *Two One Act Plays: Dot the I and The Double Expertise.* Lanham, MD: University Press of America, 1986.

Hanley, Katharine Rose. *Two Plays by Gabriel Marcel: The Lantern and The Torch of Peace plus "From Comic Theater to Musical Creation" a previously unpublished essay by Gabriel Marcel.* Lanham, MD: University Press of America, 1988.

Hanley, Katharine Rose. "Gabriel Marcel" in *The Cambridge Dictionary of Philosophy,* General Editor: Robert Audi. Cambridge, New York, Melbourne: Cambridge University Press, 1995.

Keene, Sam. *Gabriel Marcel.* Richmond, VA: John Knox Press, 1967.

Lapointe, Francis H. and Lapointe, Claire C. *Gabriel Marcel and His Critics: An International Bibliography (1928-1976),* New York: Garland Publishing Co., 1977.

Lazaron, Hilda. *Gabriel Marcel The Dramatist.* London: Colin Smythe Ltd., Gerrards Cross, Bucks, 1978; distributed in North America by Humanities Press, Inc., Atlantic Highlands, NJ.

Lescoe, Francis J. *Existentialism with or without God.* New York: Alba House, 1974.

Miceli, Vincent P. *Ascent to Being: Gabriel Marcel's Philosophy of Communion.* Foreword by Gabriel Marcel. Paris: Desclée de Brouwer, 1965.

Michaud, Thomas, special ed. "Gabriel Marcel and the Postmodern World." *Bulletin de la Société Américaine de Philosophie de Langue Française,* Vol. VII, No. 1-2, Spring 1995, Dept. of Foreign Languages and Literatures, Northern Illinois University, De Kalb, IL 60115-2854.

Moran, Denis P., S.J. *Gabriel Marcel: Existentialist Philosopher, Dramatist, Educator.* Lanham, MD: University Press of America, 1992.

Pax, Clyde. *An Existentialist Approach to God: A Study of Gabriel Marcel.* The Hague: Martinus Nijhoff, 1972.

Pax, Clyde. "Marcel's Way of Creative Fidelity" in *Philosophy Today,* Vol. 19 (Spring 1975), pp. 12-25.

Peccorini, Francisco L. *Selfhood as Thinking Thought in the Work of Gabriel Marcel: A New Interpretation,* (Problems in Contemporary Philosophy, Volume 3), Lewiston, NY: The Edwin Mellen Press, 1987.

Randall, Albert B. *The Mystery of Hope in the Philosophy of Gabriel Marcel (1889-1973), Hope and Homo Viator.* (Problems in Contemporary Philosophy Vol. 33). Lewiston,NY: The Edwin Mellen Press, 1992.

Schilpp, Paul A. and Hahn, Lewis E. *The Philosophy of Gabriel Marcel:* (Library of Living Philosophers Vol. XVII), La Salle, IL: Open Court, 1984.

Traub, Donald F. *Toward a Fraternal Society: A Study of Gabriel Marcel's Approach to Being, Technology and Intersubjectivity,* New York, NY: Peter Lang, 1988.

Works in French

Association Présence de Gabriel Marcel. *Cahiers: Présence de Gabriel Marcel.* Paris: Aubier, 1975-83.

    1: *Gabriel Marcel et la pensée allemande,* Paris: Aubier, 1979.

    2/3: *L'Esthétique Musicale chez Gabriel Marcel,* Paris: Aubier, 1980.

    4: *Gabriel Marcel et les injustices de ce temps: La responsabilité du philosophe.* Paris: Aubier, 1983.

Association Présence de Gabriel Marcel. *Entretiens autour de Gabriel Marcel.* Neuchâtel: à la Baconnière, 1976.

Belay, Marcel. *La Mort dans le theatre de Gabriel Marcel,* Paris: Vrin, 1980.

Boutang, Pierre. *Gabriel Marcel interrogé par Pierre Boutang,* Paris: J.-M. La Place, 1977.

Chenu, Joseph. *Le Théâtre de Gabriel Marcel et sa signification métaphysique.* Paris: Aubier, 1948.

Davignon, René. *Le Mal chez Gabriel Marcel: Comment affronter la souffrance et la mort?* (Recherches, Nouvelle Serie-4) Montreal: Bellarmin; Paris: Cerf, 1985.

Davy, Marie Madeleine. *Un philosophe itinérant Gabriel Marcel.* Paris: Flammarion, 1959.

De Corte, Marcel. *Gabriel Marcel.* Paris: Tequi, 1938.

De Corte, Marcel. Preface, *Approches concrètes du mystère ontologique.* Paris: Vrin; Louvain: Nauwelaerts, 1949.

Fessard, Gaston. *Théâtre et mystère. Introduction à Gabriel Marcel.* Paris: Tequi, 1938.

Morel-Flont, Teresa. *La Solitude dans le Theatre de Gabriel Marcel,* Paris: Sorbonne, 1987.

Nseka, Ngimbi. *Tragique et intersubjectivité dans la philosophie de Gabriel Marcel.* Inkisi, Zaire: Mayidi, 1981.

Parain-Vial, Jeanne. *Gabriel Marcel et les niveaux de l'expérience.* Paris: Seghers, 1996.

Parain-Vial, Jeanne. *Gabriel Marcel Un Veilleur et un eveilleur,* Lausanne: Editions L'Age d'Homme, 1989.

Plourde, Simone. *Gabriel Marcel, Philosophe et témoin de l'espérance.* Montréal: Les Presses de l'Université de Québec, 1975.

Plourde, Simone; Parain-Vial, Jeanne; Davignon, René; Belay, Marcel. *Vocabulaire Philosophique de Gabriel Marcel.* (Recherches, Nouvelle Serie-6) Montreal: Bellarmin; Paris: Cerf, 1985.

Prini, Pietro. *Gabriel Marcel et la méthodologie de l'invérifiable.* Paris: Desclée de Brouwer, 1953.

Prini, Pietro. *Gabriel Marcel.* Paris: Economica, 1984.

Ricoeur, Paul. *Gabriel Marcel et Karl Jaspers.* Paris: Ed. Temps Présent, 1948.

Sacquin, Michèle. *Gabriel Marcel: Colloque organisée par la Bibliothèque Nationale et la "Présence de Gabriel Marcel,"* Paris: Bibliothèque Nationale, 1989.

Société française de Philosophie. *Bulletin de la Société française de Philosophie.* Séance du 28 janvier 1984: La Pensée de Gabriel Marcel. Paris: Société française de Philosophie, 1984.

Sottiaux, Edgar. *Gabriel Marcel: philosophe et dramaturge.* Louvain, Paris: B. Nauwelaerts, 1956.

Troisfontaines, Roger, S.J., *De L'Existence à L'Etre. La Philosophie de Gabriel Marcel.* Paris: Béatrice Nauwelaerts–Vrin, 2 vols., 1953, 2e éd. 1968.

Wahl, Jean. *Vers le concret.* Paris: Vrin, 1932.

More complete bibliographies of Gabriel Marcel's extensive writings and many significant secondary sources are given in:

Hanley, Katharine Rose. *Dramatic Approaches to Creative Fidelity: A Study in the Theater and Philosophy of Gabriel Marcel (1889-1973)*, after Chapter I, pp. 27-49. Works by and about Gabriel Marcel. Lanham, MD: University Press of America, 1987.

Lapointe, Francis H. and Lapointe, Claire C. *Gabriel Marcel and His Critics*. Works by and about Gabriel Marcel, pp. 9-273. New York: Garland Publishing Co., 1977.

Troisfontaine, Roger, S.J. *De L'Existence à L'Etre. La Philosophie de Gabriel Marcel.* Vol. 2, pp. 381-464. Works by Gabriel Marcel. Paris: Béatrice Nauwelaerts–Vrin, 2 vols., 1953, 2e éd. 1968.

Autobiographical information may be found in:

"An Essay in Autobiography," in *The Philosophy of Existentialism*. Secaucus, NJ: Citadel Press, 1956, pp. 104-28.

"An Autobiographical Essay," (Spring 1969) in *The Philosophy of Gabriel Marcel*. (The Library of Living Philosophers Vol. XVII), ed. Paul A. Schilpp and Lewis E. Hahn, La Salle, IL: Open Court, 1984, pp. 3-68.

Marcel, Gabriel. *En Chemin vers Quel Eveil?*. Paris: Gallimard, 1971.

Geographic Glossary
of Places Mentioned in *The Broken World*

Annecy- Picturesque town on the northern shore of Lake Annecy in the foothills of the French Alps; capital of High Savoy.

Berlin- Capital of Germany, situated on the Spree River having canal connections with the Oder, Elbe, Weser, and Rhine Rivers.

Biarritz- Fashionable resort on the southwestern Atlantic coast of France near its border with Spain; mineral baths and sea bathing on the Gulf of Gascogne.

Brussels- Commercial and political center; capital of Belgium; on the Senne River in Brabant province.

Cannes- Fashionable resort town on the French Riviera, situated on the Gulf of Napoule, a Mediterranean bay.

Cantabre- An autonomous region of northern Spain; its capital, Santander, is one of the leading ports of northern Spain.

Cap Martin- One of the beautiful capes on the French Riviera.

Capri- Island in the Bay of Naples, Italy; four square miles; cliffs on eastern side rise 900 ft., on western side 1,923 ft. On its north shore is the famous Blue Grotto.

Cimiez- A fashionable section of Nice on the Côte d'Azur (azure coast) of the French Riviera; ancient Gallo-Roman provincial capital ruins remain there.

Geneva- Scenic town situated at southern tip of Lake Geneva, in the Swiss Alps, southwestern Switzerland.

La Clusaz- Traditional style mountain ski resort in the High Savoy region of the French Alps near the Swiss border, between Annecy and Mont Blanc. Home of Edgar Grospiron, gold medalist for mogul skiing at the Albertville Olympics.

London- City located on either side of the Thames River. Capital of the United Kingdom.

Megève- Fashionable ski resort in the French Alps southeast of Mont Blanc.

Morocco- A North African kingdom bordered by the Sahara, Algiers, the Mediterranean, and the Atlantic.

Napoli- Seaport and capital city of Naples province in southwestern Italy.

Nice- Fashionable resort with a warm sunny climate situated on the Mediterranean Rivera coast and sheltered by the Alpes-Maritime.

Paris- Capital of France bridging the Seine River.

Perm- Mineral and industrial center stretching 60 miles along the Kama River; the western foothills of the Ural Mountains form its eastern border. The city dates from 1723 when a copper foundry was built there.

Porquerolles- Quiet island off the coast of the French Riviera; one of the Hyères Islands, or Les Isles d'Or (Golden Islands).

Rio de Janeiro- Largest city of Brazil, chief port situated on a magnificent land-locked harbor between Sugar Loaf Mountain and Corcovado.

Solesmes- Benedictine abbey 125 miles southwest of Paris, still famous for its Gregorian Chant liturgies and recordings.

St. Lunaire- Beach resort near Saint Malo on the northwestern Atlantic coast of France.

St. Moritz- World-famous winter sports resort in Switzerland's Alps with fashionable shops and palatial hotels.

Tunis- Seaport capital of Tunisia in North Africa, bordered by Algiers, Libya, and the Mediterranean.

Valparaiso- Port and capital city of Valparaiso province, situated between the Pacific and the Andes in central Chile; one of the main commercial centers on the western coast of South America.

Venice- Seaport in northeastern Italy on the Gulf of Venice at the head of the Adriatic Sea; is built on 118 small islands and traversed by many canals.

Vienna- Capital of the Austro-Hungarian Empire and of today's Austria, located on the Wien River that flows into the Danube River at the Vienna Woods foothills of the Alps.

Villiers- The neighborhood of a fashionable high school situated on Avenue de Villiers in the rich bourgeois VIIth district of Paris.

Index

Index of Proper Names